THE BIOGRAPHY OF

F. AUGUSTUS HEINZE

COPPER KING AT WAR

A REMARKABLE STORY TOLD
BY THE WATCHMAN'S DAUGHTER

SARAH McNELIS

———

AFTERWORD BY
ZENA BETH McGLASHAN

RIVERBEND
PUBLISHING

The Biography of F. Augustus Heinze: Copper King at War
All elements of this edition copyright © 2018 by Friends of the Butte Archives
Published by Riverbend Publishing, Helena, Montana

ISBN 13: 978-1-60639-110-5

Permission to reprint *Copper King at War* granted by
the University of Montana Press.

Printed in the United States of America.

1 2 3 4 5 6 7 8 9 0 VP 25 24 23 22 21 20 19

Front cover illustration: Studio photograph of F. Augustus Heinze in 1900.
Montana Memory Project, Butte-Silver Bow Public Library.

Cover design by Sarah Cauble, www.sarahcauble.com

Riverbend Publishing
P.O. Box 5833
Helena, MT 59604
1-866-787-2363
www.riverbendpublishing.com

INTRODUCTION TO THIS EDITION

In 1947, in the final lines of the introduction to her master's thesis, Sarah McNelis described telegrams, business and personal letters all jumbled together with other papers in a room at a mine watchman's house where she was living. Because some of the trash belonged to F. Augustus Heinze, it was worth saving. She ended the introduction by writing, "At that time I was unaware this biography would ever engage my attention."

Sarah hoped her carefully documented study of Heinze, the youngest of the Copper Kings, would become a book. Many factors obscured that dream.

In 1968, Sarah received a letter from K. Ross Toole, still considered by many to be the best Montana historian his native state has ever produced. Toole said the University of Montana history department, of which he was chairman, had "a modest grant from the UM Foundation to publish valuable unpublished works in Montana and regional history." Toole asked if Sarah would consider having the University of Montana publish her "Biography of F. Augustus Heinze because "it is an outstanding manuscript."

Sarah had waited 21 years for her dream of Heinze's story becoming a book to come true.

The Afterword, The Watchmen's Daughter, starts on page 233.

COPPER KING AT WAR

THE BIOGRAPHY OF

F. AUGUSTUS HEINZE

By
Sarah McNelis

UNIVERSITY OF MONTANA PRESS

1968

TABLE OF CONTENTS

LIST OF ILLUSTRATIONS

INTRODUCTION

Eclipsed by the more celebrated William Andrews Clark and Marcus Daly, Frederick Augustus Heinze is to many critics almost a fictional personality. Relatively little authentic information is available concerning him and no comprehensive biography of his life exists. The impression held of him generally is that presented in the propaganda disseminated by his enemies. Heinze, however, was a central figure in the second phase (1896-1906) of the nation-rocking Copper War. This period of litigious activity which promulgated the name of Montana throughout the press of the United States and the metal markets of Europe is largely responsible to F. Augustus Heinze.

The robber barons—the "malefactors of great wealth," as Theodore Roosevelt dubbed the manipulators of the stock market in those greedy days of plunder that precipitated the trust-busting period in American history—designated Heinze as their quarry and found him no easy mark. In fact, Heinze's adamant assertion that he would fight rather than concede his holdings, his perception in designating his enemies' objective to be an international copper trust, and his refusal to do business according to the program mapped by Standard Oil, Henry H. Rogers and his associates incalculably spoiled the original plans for that trust.

Rogers's plan necessarily began with the holdings of two copper companies, the Boston and Montana, and the Butte and Boston. Two actions effected by Heinze prevented the consummation of this scheme. First, he chose to fight the Michael Davitt apex case to a conclusion, rather than to sell to the Boston and Montana company. Secondly, when the Boston and Montana illegally transferred all of its assets overnight to another company, Heinze, through two loyal followers, forced the company into the hands of a receiver. As it would require months to solve this situation, Rogers and his associates were forced to search elsewhere for a cornerstone to the proposed copper trust. It was this situation which developed Rogers's negotiations with Marcus Daly and the former's purchase of the Anaconda Copper Company's properties at a figure much higher than might otherwise have been paid. As a result of these transactions, the Anaconda became the nuclear stone of the projected copper trust, Amalgamated.

The involuted relationship between the Copper War and the Panic of 1907 has never been sufficiently and specifically demonstrated. Without doubt that national economic illness can be traced to the fact that the men whom Heinze had beaten in the mine fields effected their vengeance in an attempt to ruin him in his later financial endeavors. The chaotic handiwork of F. Augustus's enemies exceeded their control and settled smotheringly about them; this result, however, does not refute their vindictive guilt. Equally pertinent is the fact that Heinze's genius in prospecting and developing ore veins in Butte did not extend to enlightening him to the more devious ways of banking and financial manipulation when he ventured into those fields after selling his Butte properties.

This essay also attempts to present the complete account of the extensive credit that was available to Heinze and of the unsuccessful attacks made on it by his rivals. Critics tend to minimize the depth of F. Augustus's credit, simply because he consciously projected a "poor boy" front and his opponents continually predicted his imminent bankruptcy. In fact, the most paralyzing threat to F. A.'s credit originated within the family organization—through a trusted partner's injudicious speculation, rather than from those sources which would deliberately have ruined Heinze.

F. A. Heinze, furthermore, pioneered scientific processes and new machinery in his properties. Systematic improvement of his holdings attests a thorough absorption in his enterprises. Heinze's prime interest was expanding the scope of the mining and smelting industry, rather than acquiring personal wealth.

This essay utilizes, in addition to newspapers, pamphlets and court records of the Copper War period, the manuscript notes, the reminiscences of Otto Charles Heinze, only surviving brother of F. Augustus Heinze. In 1947 Otto Heinze is in his eightieth year. From 1943 through 1947, Otto most kindly and painstakingly answered many inquiries concerning his brother. Several letters from F. Augustus's associates, both at the Columbia School of Mines and in his early mining career in Canada, have also been helpful. Interviews with persons who either knew or knew of Heinze, or of some phase of his career, have been integrated in this biography. The author's personal background of a life spent in Butte, Montana, the scene of Heinze's greatest successes, has enabled her to understand and visualize much that is herein related.

A number of authentic telegrams, pertinent to the affairs of the Montana Ore Purchasing Company, which were transmitted between the New York and Montana offices of that corporation have also been employed. The original wires were always in code, but the translation was fastened to each. Particularly valuable among these telegrams are the messages that are relevant to the early offers to buy Heinze's Butte mines. The use of these original sources, particularly the telegrams and Otto Heinze's manuscript notes, should aid the author in presenting a picture of F. Augustus Heinze and his activities which is more correct than that generally accepted by critics of the Copper War.

Missoula, Montana
August, 1947

Sarah McNelis

COPPER KING AT WAR

Chapter I

THE HEINZE FAMILY AND FRITZ

The square-rigged sailing vessel, *Elizabeth*, left Bremen, Germany, during April, 1850. She was bound for New York City and carried in her first cabin a youth of nineteen. He was Otto Heinze, son of a Lutheran minister who preferred to have this son enter the ministry of that church. Fate, however, decreed otherwise. The freedom and opportunity of the United States beckoned this young man from his native Germany which then suffered the growing pains of political revolution. In his pocket was one hundred dollars to finance him until he secured a foundation in America. The thirty-day voyage was a genuine adventure to Otto and that which lay beyond was a constant wonder. Perhaps the spell would have been broken if he had perceived the subsequent comfort and success which he would achieve as an able businessman in a land of commerce.

Several letters of introduction helped Otto Heinze on his arrival in New York City; they secured for him a position in the large importation firm of Unkert and Company. Otto lived initially in a clean, third-floor, front room on Chambers Street. For his residence and his board, which he later described as "plain but good food," he paid $2.50 a week. Diligence and genuine interest in the company which employed him no doubt explains the fact that in eight years he was a partner in the business. Within the first six years of his residence in the United States, Otto also became a citizen.

On February 12, 1862, Otto Heinze married Eliza Marsh Lacey, his junior of twelve years. She was born in Middletown, Connecticut, in 1842 and was baptized in Christ Church (Episcopal) on November 17, 1842. The families of her mother and father came to America about 1776. The Lacey family was of Irish extraction, and the Marsh

2

family of English lineage.[1] The DeLacy family was famous in Irish history and could trace its ancestry to 1150.[2]

The Heinze family was also distinguished. Its members were lineal descendants of Caspar Aquila, Protestant Bishop of Saalfield, Thuringia, Germany, who died there in 1560. From this bishop a Bible has remained in the family through eight generations of Heinzes who were Lutheran clergy. Nowhere is there any Semitic strain in the family, although later the rumor was circulated that F. Augustus Heinze was a Jew. The family possesses copies of all public records and birth certificates, certified in Germany, that prove there is no Jewish blood in the Heinze line.[3]

Otto Heinze and Eliza Lacey were a most devoted couple; their marriage was blessed by the advent of six children, five of whom survived to maturity. As a successful and ambitious importer, Otto provided well for his family. Upon his death, Otto left his family a fortune of somewhat over half a million dollars.

A son, Fritz Augustus, was born on December 5, 1869—the fifth child in the family and the third boy. Five months later he was baptized in the Grace Church (Episcopal) in Brooklyn, New York, and given the name, Fritz Augustus, which he seldom used in its entirety. Within the family circle he was called "Fritz." After he attended college, he was referred to as "F. Augustus"; during the Copper War,

---

[1] Otto C. Heinze's letters to Sarah McNelis, pp. 1-4. The author has assembled these letters, written between 1943 and 1947, into a cohesive body as, in effect, they are manuscript notes. These letters are subsequently cited as: O. C. Heinze MS., with page number. The assembled manuscript is in the possession of the author.

[2] "The Story of Heinze, A Tale of Copper—and Brass," *Current Literature*, XLIV (February, 1908), pp. 34-36. "DeLacy" was the original family surname; it was altered by the family's American descendants sometime during the late eighteenth century to "Lacey."

[3] O. C. Heinze MS., p. 5. An erratum was written by Otto C. Heinze, Jr., to correct a misstatement in the *Dictionary of American Biography* regarding F. Augustus's Semitic lineage, and was published in that periodical (VIII, p. 507). A letter written by O. C. Heinze to *Fortune* magazine and published in March, 1937, corrected similar statements made in an article (December, 1936) earlier published in that magazine.

In September, 1902, Heinze's Butte newspaper, the *Reveille*, refuted an allegation made in the Amalgamated's press that he was "a Judas and a Jew." The *Reveille* stated, "It is well known that Heinze is of Dutch and Irish blood and the appellation 'Jew' does not fit him."

however, he was called "F. A." or "Frederick Augustus."[4] Fritz's mother once explained his adoption of the name "F. Augustus."

"He came to me one day when he was a very little fellow going to school in Brooklyn and said, 'Mother, when I am a man, I am going to be called by my middle name, Augustus, and not Fritz any longer. The boys call me German Fritz and I don't like it.' "[5]

Fritz's formal education was most thorough. He early was sent to kindergarten and then attended the Juvenile High School in Brooklyn, New York, until he was about nine years of age. As a boy Fritz was a good student.

"His teachers spoke well of his ability and industry, but were not so well pleased with his conduct; his marks were high, except in conduct."[6]

As a child he was difficult to discipline and somewhat intractable; he would question the authority of his teachers and confute them. Completely without fear of anything or anyone, he sometimes had to be disciplined severely. In those days of "spare the rod and spoil the child," his father did what was necessary to control his sons.

An incident of Fritz's early childhood illustrates this rebellion. When he was "just a little shaver," his mother interrupted his play one day by asking him to go upstairs to get something for his grandmother. He immediately responded, before the maternal glance quelled him, "Haven't she got legs?" This remark prompted paternal discipline.[7]

One May day in 1876, patrons of the Black Friars Hotel in London, England, witnessed an unusual sight—the arrival, bag and baggage, of an American family composed of the father, mother, four

[4] O. C. Heinze MS., p. 6. Please see Appendix One.

[5] William R. Stewart, "Captains of Industry—Part XXI: F. Augustus Heinze," *Cosmopolitan*, XXXVI (January, 1904), p. 290.

[6] O. C. Heinze MS., p. 4.

[7] O. C. Heinze MS., p. 5.

children (the youngest a tiny babe of five months), a governess and a nurse. This family was traveling to Leipzig, Germany, where the children would be enrolled in different schools and where the entire family intended to remain for two years. The trip was only the first of many crossings of the Atlantic for all of the Otto Heinze family. In this instance the Heinzes followed the oldest son, Arthur, who had traveled to Germany two years earlier and was living with his father's brother in Leipzig.[8]

When the family arrived in Leipzig, they visited the two brothers of Otto who were professors respectively at Leipzig and Heidelberg Universities; several years later each was elected to the presidency of his institution. F. Augustus's oldest brother, Arthur, was already familiar with the German school system, for he was enrolled in the Nicolaey Gymnasium, a Latin high school. Completion of the Gymnasium's nine-year course qualified one to attend any university in Europe. Fritz was enrolled immediately in the first year of the Gymnasium's program.

Fritz's experience at this school was to have international implications, for here his interest in rock formations was aroused. This intense curiosity concerning the earth's structure and the kinds of ore it held grew into a vast fund of information and applicable knowledge. One quarter century later, this knowledge baffled the best engineering and legal minds of the United States and repeatedly outwitted them. F. Augustus's quality of thoroughness is also based in the years he spent at Leipzig. The school's program was not committed to freedom of expression but to high standards of scholarship. The routine was so rigorous that,

"Some boys broke down under this regime; some even at the age of fourteen or fifteen years committed suicide by shooting themselves, if they failed to pass their examinations; and a considerable number dropped out after four or five years of such schooling."[9]

---

[8]O. C. Heinze MS., p. 6.

[9]O. C. Heinze MS., p. 6.

Although the boys did not enjoy the method of education, they conformed to the routine by which classes began in the summer at seven in the morning, in the winter at eight in the morning, and comprised thirty-six hours of recitation each week. Neither could they anticipate a weekend recess: classes on Saturday and Wednesday consumed five hours, those on Tuesday and Friday, seven hours, and on Monday and Thursday, eight hours. Each night, following the evening meal, the boys devoted two hours to the preparation of lessons for the next day.

Classical studies began immediately, Latin being a first-year subject; Greek was introduced in the second year. Mathematics and French appeared before third-year classes; English and other languages were studied by the more advanced pupils. Approximately once a month the students were taken on excursions to the country where they camped overnight and spent their days hunting fossils, flowers, fishes, and rocks which they later studied and classified in the schoolroom. On such weekends F. Augustus learned the fascination of the earth and its treasures.[10]

Fritz's two years at the gymnasium at Leipzig were followed by another two years in a similar school in Hildesheim, an ancient city near Hanover. The reason for the transfer was Otto's desire that his sons acquire a perfect mastery of German. F. Augustus and Otto Heinze, Jr., were placed in the home of a professor in Hildesheim. They were otherwise entirely independent in a city of strangers. Youth being resilient and adaptable, however, in a short time both boys made friends among their schoolmates and were rarely homesick. Family ties were maintained by the required weekly letters—in English to their mother and in German to their father. The boys, however, retained always the promise of their return to New York.

As a student in Germany, Fritz was different neither in temperament nor character from what he had been as a Brooklyn schoolboy. His obstinacy in supporting his own opinions made him a problem to his teachers, who found him difficult to control and sufficiently

---

[10]O. C. Heinze MS., p. 6.

bold to retort if he felt he was correct. He considered it his personal obligation to avenge any derogatory remark regarding America; his method of effecting this mission was battle on the schoolground. Doubt did not deter him from tackling boys larger than he, nor did defeat subdue him, for he would risk another thrashing rather than concede that his opponent was right.

Each of the Heinze boys received weekly a mark as personal allowance.[11] Fritz rarely spent any of his money on himself, but saved it to buy Christmas and birthday presents for his family.

Otto Heinze, Sr., considered four years in Germany sufficient education in a foreign country. In 1882, therefore, the boys were reunited with the family at Hildesheim. The family continued to Paris and Switzerland and it was agreed that Fritz and Otto should join them when the school term ended. The summer of 1882 was an enjoyable one for the boys; they climbed mountains, hiked, and visited the ancient cathedrals and museums of Switzerland and northern Italy.[12]

Most American and British schoolboys recognize Joseph Addison as an eminent author; few of them, however, remember him as well as did Otto and Fritz. Addison's *Letters to his Son* became their textbook for the only exercises required of them during this pleasant summer. Their father insisted that, on their return to the United States, they must again be able to speak fluent English. Four years of German conversation and school experience had given them a thorough grounding in the Teutonic tongue. Their assignment was to take Addison's letters, translate them from English to German and, on the following day, retranslate them to English. The brothers initially found the difference between Addison's version and theirs revolutionary; after three months of this practice, however, their translations closely approximated that of their model.

Regaining English fluency was also accelerated by the family practice of speaking only English during that summer. In later years Otto

---

[11] A mark is a monetary unit of the old German Empire, valued at 23.8 cents; the mark was superceded in 1924 by the reichsmark.

[12] O. C. Heinze MS., p. 8.

Heinze, Sr., prevented the loss of the boys' familiarity with foreign languages by initiating the conversation at the dinner table on succeeding days in German and French. It was also a custom in the Heinze home that a question be answered in whatever language it had been asked. These practices maintained the trilingual skill of all the children.[13]

In September, 1882, the entire Heinze family again occupied the old house in Brooklyn. The occasion was happy for each of the Heinzes. For Arthur, Fritz's oldest brother, the move signified the end of six years' absence from the United States.

A meal with the Otto Heinze family during the 1880's was an unforgettable experience for a visitor. Punctuality was demanded. Supper was at seven; if one were late, his setting was removed and nothing was kept warm for him. He would eat later and in the butler's pantry. Each diner was presentable—brushed and combed. No dressing gowns, negligees or boudoir slippers were permitted. If all were present, they numbered nine—six children, their parents and their maternal grandmother. Supper was a time for family discussion and argument. Each member presented his view and frequently the differences became so heated that *Webster's Dictionary* or the *Encyclopedia Britannica* was obtained to verify a fact and to close the controversy. The parents rarely included themselves in the discussion, except to provide information which none of the children knew. If the conversation became so spirited that acrimony and personality became involved, the father intervened to introduce a new subject.

Breakfast was always at eight and similar punctuality was demanded. As age determined one's status at the Heinze table, F. Augustus was served penultimately at all meals. The baby, Paul, was the last to receive his portion. At the meal the family was not permitted to remark derogatorily regarding the food. None was allowed to ask for any special dish or anything additional, but was expected to eat whatever was on his plate. The meals included soup, meat, vegetables, dessert, and wine, either red or white.

---

[13]O. C. Heinze MS., p. 8.

Strict discipline was maintained in the Heinze home regarding late hours. Unless they were attending a party or other special event, the boys were required to be home by eleven o'clock. Fritz found this regulation difficult to observe and violated it once or twice. His father warned him and, when he next returned about 11:15 one cold winter night, he found the door bolted. Otto Heinze, Sr., informed him from an upstairs window, "This boarding house has been closed for the night."[14] There was no recourse for F. Augustus but to take a room at the Pierrepont House, a nearby hotel.

"It cost him three dollars for the night which was rather painful for his allowance at this time was only about $300 a year for clothes and amusements. He was much more careful after that. When we three boys were home and one or another was not in and we heard my father go down to bolt the door, we would sneak down a little later and unbolt it. I think my father knew this and winked at it, but said nothing."[15]

Even during Fritz's college years this custom was observed. That it was an unusual practice in the homes of the brothers' contemporaries is evident from the remark of F. G. Zinsser, a fraternity brother of F. Augustus at Columbia.

"He [Fritz] was a member of a family ruled by a stubborn German father, with strict rules for the family, one of which was that no member was allowed out of the home after 11 P.M. As it happened Heinze had a job with the *American Mining Journal* [i.e. *Engineering and Mining Journal*] and was detained one night to rewrite an editorial for an edition that had to go to press that evening. As a result he was late and when he rang the bell at his home in Brooklyn at about 11:30 he was denied admission."[16]

---

[14]O. C. Heinze MS., p. 11.

[15]O. C. Heinze MS., p. 11.

[16]Letter to the author from F. G. Zinsser of Hastings-on-Hudson, New York, July 18, 1947.

In September, 1882, F. Augustus was enrolled in the Polytechnic Institute of Brooklyn. When he graduated (June, 1885), he took and passed the entrance examinations to the Columbia School of Mines. He designated his age as sixteen, since that was the minimum age for admittance according to the college's rules.[17]

Records at Columbia University show that Frederick Augustus Heinze was enrolled in the School of Mines from June, 1885, to June, 1889, as a candidate for the degree of Engineer of Mines. This degree was conferred on June 6, 1889. His average was approximately a "C" and is entered in the college records as 7.8. His birthdate is not provided by the data available, but it is recorded that he was in good standing.[18]

A natural interest in geology and in mining motivated his entrance into the School of Mines, but understandably equally strong was the factor of material ambition. F. A. noticed that there was a dearth of mining engineers in comparison with other professional men; he was aware that, whereas the life was hard and often unpleasant, the possibilities for advancement and the rewards were great. The fact that a career in mining could include international travel also intrigued him. Always an avid reader of travel books in college, Heinze was captivated by the developments in South Africa and China. "It fascinated him to imagine himself roaming around all over the world."[19]

At both Polytechnic and Columbia, F. Augustus was a good, but not a brilliant, student. He usually ranked among the first ten or twelve in his classes; he was never the highest ranked. He, however, did not study diligently. About four or five weeks before the final examinations he would "buffalo." This term was his description of the practice of appropriating the family library, sweeping everyone from it, locking the door, and confining himself with his books and a pitcher of water. He would then study all evening and sometimes as late as three in the morning. F. Augustus's vitality pervaded: after

---

[17]O. C. Heinze MS., p. 9. Please see Appendix One.

[18]Information in a letter to the author from Thomas T. Read, Executive Officer, School of Mines, Columbia University, New York City, New York, June 21, 1943.

[19]O. C. Heinze MS., p. 10.

such long and concentrated study periods, he would rise at the usual time and show no sign of his night's industry. He never failed to pass any subject and earned the respect of fellow students for his determination.

The culmination of a school year did not signal the beginning of recreation for Fritz. He instead made the summer vacations a practical laboratory period. In the summer of 1886, when the other members of the family were in Europe, he went to Michigan where he familiarized himself with the great copper mines of Calumet and Hecla. He passed another vacation in the coal mining region of Pennsylvania and a third in the gold and silver mines of Colorado.

At Columbia, Heinze had half a dozen intimate friends. One classmate wrote that he did not know Heinze personally, but that he believed their classmates called him either "Heinze" or "Fritz."[20] A more relevant description of the man is provided by Herbert P. Whitlock, a member of Heinze's class at the Columbia School of Mines.

"I was a classmate of Augustus Heinze at Columbia School of Mines. My recollection is that he was of medium height, light in coloring.

"He thought a great deal of himself. I recall an anecdote that gives point to this: At the height of the Clark-Heinze controversy, Richard Wainright, another member of the class of 1889 at Columbia, met Heinze on the street; he said, 'Hello, Gus, what are you doing now?' Heinze replied, 'Why, Dick, don't you read the papers? I'm the Heinze of the headlines.' "[21]

As a young college man, Fritz Augustus was selective in the choice of his friends, no great mixer and not known generally among the students. As his family was included in the social set of Brooklyn, Fritz had an opportunity to attend social affairs; he did so, particularly

---

[20]Information in a letter to the author from Thomas Harrington, Scarsdale, New York, July 17, 1943.

[21]Letter to the author from Herbert P. Whitlock, Curator Emeritus of the American Museum of Natural History, New York City, New York, July 15, 1943.

in his senior year.[22] As a socialite later in Butte, F. A. was remembered as a most magnetic and charming gentleman. This ability to socialize with and to win friends did not develop until he was older; adult contacts and independence revealed this quality. Fritz seems to have been uninterested in all but his special friends during his years at Columbia—he was only nineteen when he came to Montana. Heinze's remark to Wainright reveals an arrogant self-confidence which has its own appeal. He did join a circle at Columbia with which he played poker and billiards. He was initiated into Columbia's Delta Chapter of Phi Delta Theta fraternity on March 11, 1887.[23] The stakes in these college games were small, but F. Augustus was regarded as a good poker player. He retained this social skill in his mining days. Old timers in British Columbia tell a story concerning his relation to poker.

"There was a celebrated Episcopal parson in the territory known as Father Pat. Beloved by all, he went wherever his duties called him. Heinze used to tease him and badger him to get into a poker game in one of the hotels. Father Pat ignored him until there was a big jackpot on the table; then he made occasion to walk past and as usual Heinze asked him to get into the game. Father Pat looked at him, took off his hat and said, 'All right.' Sweeping the pot into the hat, he said, 'This is the church's pot.' "Heinze backed him up and Father Pat's mission was that much better off."[24]

---

[22]O. C. Heinze MS., p. 13.

[23]Otto Heinze stated that his brother gave a chapter house to this fraternity in later years, but he seems to be in error. F. G. Zinsser, F. Augustus's fraternity brother and contemporary at Columbia, is definite in his comment: "He certainly never donated anything to either the chapter or the university as far as I know." (Letter to the author, July 18, 1947.)

A letter to Professor E. E. Bennett, Montana State University, Missoula, Montana, from Paul Beam, Executive Secretary of Phi Delta Theta, July 2, 1947, is the source of the date of Heinze's initiation into the Columbia chapter. Beam says also that, in the ten years which he has occupied his present position, no one has ever mentioned a chapter house donated by F. Augustus.

[24]Letter to the author from S. G. Blaylock, Consolidated Mining and Smelting Company of Canada, Ltd., July 6, 1943.

A very retentive memory, a genuine interest in mining, and the intensive "buffalo" sessions before examinations guaranteed that Fritz succeed at Columbia. Although he was not a great favorite with his classmates, he seems to have been respected by his professors. The basis of this respect was the meticulous neatness of his notebooks and the mastery of subject to which his subsequent career testifies.

In addition to his studies at Columbia, F. Augustus had other diverse interests. Shortly after his return from Germany, he was confirmed in Grace Church (Episcopal) in Brooklyn and for a time was assistant librarian at its Sunday school. He even attempted to teach a class of small boys; his severity as instructor, however, was such that within a few Sundays he was a teacher without pupils. Marching in Sunday school, however, gave him an opportunity to sing. F. Augustus was vain concerning his vocal ability and thoroughly enjoyed the weekly hymns. His most beloved hymns had the battle tone and the urge to action typified by one of his favorites, "Onward, Christian Soldiers."

Chapter II

F. AUGUSTUS'S EARLY DAYS IN BUTTE

Graduation from Columbia School of Mines in June, 1889, immediately opened to F. Augustus Heinze those vistas of opportunity and travel of which he dreamed. His father offered to finance a two-year mining course at the celebrated University of Freiburg, but F. Augustus was already impatient to prove himself in the American West. The discussion of advanced study in Germany precipitated a heated argument between father and son. It terminated in the proposition that, if Fritz would go to Freiburg, his father would provide all necessary funds; if, however, he persisted in going west, his father would give him only one hundred dollars and subsequently F. A. would be independent.

Determined that he had studied sufficiently, F. Augustus, at nineteen, left New York for Pittsburgh where he stopped only briefly before continuing to visit various mining towns in Colorado. Then, by way of Salt Lake City, he moved to Butte in early September, 1889. His first letters home from the bustling Montana mining camp narrate his success in securing a position as mining engineer with the Boston and Montana Company at $250 per month. His letters mention applying for no other position and it is probable that he did not. F. Augustus's success delighted his father, but did not convince him that the young man had selected the wiser course.

"Every now and then he would shake his head and say, 'Fritz is too young; he should have gone to Freiburg.' And after these many years, considering all that took place, I must agree that my father was right: Fritz should have gone immediately to Freiburg."[1]

---

[1] O. C. Heinze MS., p. 12.

Heinze entered a city sharply factionalized by the first two Copper Kings, W. A. Clark and Marcus Daly. F. Augustus was almost six feet tall, broad and sturdy; he possessed an aura of strength. He stood erect and walked with an elastic, quick stride. His brown eyes were accentuated by hair of deeper brown; he had a good voice and a pleasant smile. Not the least of his assets was his ability, when engaged in conversation, to give full attention to the other person. This air of complete absorption in what another was telling him established his reputation of being a very pleasant person. "When he entered a room full of people, you could very near feel it."[2] One of F. A.'s contemporaries described him as:

". . . the spoiled product of a wealthy home in which he had had everything he wanted. He never, however, traded on the fact he came from wealth. He did resent somewhat that Butte did not at once pay much attention to him. There were too many rich men here then."[3]

A writer who regarded Montana as a great feudal stronghold, contested by the rival barons, Clark and Daly, saw Heinze as a "new faction for feudal conflict."

"Heinze came to town as a young man, fresh from college, and found employment in a subordinate position in the engineering force of the Boston and Montana Copper Mining Company, then an independent organization and the most formidable rival of the Anaconda Company in the camp. Heinze's position enabled him to acquire a thorough knowledge of underground conditions in Butte as well as practical experience in the most successful and extensive copper mining field in the country. He possessed brains in abundance, a fine address, a strong physique, tireless

[2]O. C. Heinze MS., p. 15.

[3]Interview by the author with Mrs. T. J. Murray of Butte, Montana, July 21, 1943. Mrs. Murray knew the Heinze brothers in Butte and her sister became Mrs. Arthur Heinze.

energy, boundless egotism, was a 'good mixer' and had no moral restrictions. He made both friends and money rapidly, and spared neither in the promotion and accomplishment of his purposes."[4]

To be near his work, F. A. rented a small shack in Meaderville, just north of Butte, where he lived more than a year. He worked long days performing the tasks assigned to him by the Boston and Montana engineers. His best friends during this period were a Mr. and Mrs. Johnson who lived nearby and whom he mentioned in his letters to his family. He was particularly grateful to them because they cared for him during an attack of mountain fever to which he fell victim. He visited them often and enjoyed having them as neighbors. After each day's work, F. Augustus studied the vein system of the Butte Hill and of the mines he had surveyed. He thereby acquired a sound mental picture of this cavernous copper chest and realized its potential wealth.

The nucleus of social and business contact in Butte at that time was the Silver Bow Club, then located in an office building on West Granite Street. Heinze joined the club and subsequently took an apartment in town. At the Silver Bow Club he associated with many old timers. He listened to them carefully and obtained much information concerning mining and smelting, the costs of both operations, the possibilities of buying mines in Butte and other places, and the facets and progress of the Clark-Daly feud.

This conversation was not lost on the young Heinze. Complementing his knowledge of the vein system of the Hill, this incidental data convinced him, by the fall of 1890, that opportunity existed in Butte for an independent smelter. This conviction developed from his belief that the smelting charges paid by the smaller, independent mines were exorbitant and that an independent smelter could make considerable profit, if it reduced charges only slightly. The profit to

---

[4]Jerre C. Murphy, *The Comical History of Montana* (San Diego: Scofield; 1912), p. 24

the new smelter owner could be increased and assured if he also had his own mine. As early as 1890, F. Augustus had "his eyes focused on the Rarus."[5] Heinze began immediately to effect his plan. He carefully calculated the cost of erecting such a smelter and issued a detailed prospectus which projected the capacity of the smelter. He resigned his position with the Boston and Montana Company in the autumn of 1890 and returned to New York City to raise funds for the project. His father, a cautious and shrewd businessman, refused to invest the necessary $100,000 in a business with which he was not personally familiar. Otto advised his son to form a stock company and to discover what funds he could secure on the market from friends and others. The elder Heinze consented to aid the venture with an investment of one-tenth of the required capital. A depressed financial market made the time inauspicious for F. A. to attempt to raise the necessary capital. Until the market became more promising, Heinze worked as a reporter on the *Engineering and Mining Journal* and remained in New York during the winter of 1890-1891. Fritz's relationship with the *Journal* was particularly helpful because he could remain informed of matters pertaining to the sale of mining products and in contact with men interested in mines and mining throughout the nation.

Early in 1891 F. Augustus met the leaders of the firm, Lewisohn Brothers, then powerful in metals business and controller of the Boston and Montana and the Butte and Boston companies. Jesse Lewisohn, son of one of the founders of the firm, subsequently came to Butte to engage in Heinze's schemes. Although the Lewisohns briefly were sales agents for Heinze, F. A. did not want them "on the inside." This desire engendered bitterness; Otto Heinze believes the Lewisohns prodded Albert S. Bigelow, president of the Boston and Montana Company, to initiate the second phase of the Copper

---

[5]O. C. Heinze MS., p. 17. F. Augustus subsequently leased the Rarus property (1893) and purchased it (1895); it became the foundation of his mining complex in Butte.

War (1896-1906) against Heinze.[6] As the financial market remained in a slump, F. Augustus left his work in New York and returned to Butte in the spring of 1891. His experience on the *Journal* indicated that there was more to be gained by actual copper buying and selling than by remaining divorced from the production scene. He resumed his position with the Boston and Montana Company upon returning to Butte.

F. Augustus found, however, that he could not effect the smelter project from Butte. Early in 1892 he again resigned his engineering position in Butte to travel east to discuss the proposition with his family. Fritz's father had died the preceding November and the family firm was reorganized with F. A.'s brother, Otto Charles, designated as representative of the deceased's estate.

After the three brothers discussed the smelter project thoroughly, they determined to proceed. This decision initiated the Montana Ore Purchasing Company. Arthur Heinze, the oldest brother, assumed twenty-five percent of the capital stock; Otto Heinze took fifteen percent; F. Augustus held the controlling interest with fifty-one percent. Of the remaining nine percent, five was taken by Stanley Gifford, a college friend of F. Augustus, and two percent was given to John MacGinniss who was, throughout the Copper War, one of Heinze's staunchest associates. The Heinze family retained the last two percent for future use.

F. Augustus Heinze voyaged immediately to Europe to secure strong lines of foreign credit for the infant company. Although European finances were depressed throughout 1892, he was able to align some support in London and on the Continent by the middle of the summer. F. A. then took advantage of his presence in Europe to

---

[6]O. C. Heinze MS., pp. 17-18. Leonard Lewisohn, one of the brothers who founded the firm, was a director of the Butte and Boston Company, as well as the Boston and Montana Company—*Engineering and Mining Jounal*, LXIII, p. 115, as quoted in R. G. Raymer, *Montana, The Land and Its People*, I, p. 463.

The War of the Copper Kings can justifiably be divided into two phases or battles. The initial phase pitted Marcus Daly and his Anaconda holdings against William A. Clark and his properties. In effect this battle began in 1888 in the political arena; after 1890, however, the warfare was extensive and bitter—economically and politi-

fulfill his late father's wish; he enrolled in an intensive course of mining and geology at the University of Freiburg. Heinze remained at the University for several months; Otto Heinze credits this concentrated study with much of F. A.'s subsequent success in discovering profitable veins in mines of the Butte Hill which other companies had abandoned as barren and valueless.[7]

Early in 1893 F. Augustus returned to New York City from Germany. During the first half of the year, he commuted between New York and Butte to co-ordinate the erection of the Montana Ore Purchasing Company's smelter; he spent most of the second half of the year in Butte, directing the construction of the smelter.

The Montana Ore Purchasing Company began the smelting of ore in Butte on leased ground because the stockholders of the new organization did not possess the capital to purchase the site. They leased it for many years, with the option to buy for $35,000. Heinze's enemies utilized this apparently insignificant item during the Copper War. They persuaded the owners of the ground to refuse to sell it to the M. O. P. C. Court action was necessitated before Heinze secured the site at the price cited in the original contract.[8] A contemporary account summarized the formation of the smelter.

"The Montana Ore Purchasing Company was organized under the laws of the state of Montana, March 1, 1893, as a mining, ore purchasing, and smelting concern. The company had existed for some two years previous to its formal incorporation as a co-partnership of F. Augustus Heinze, Stanley Gifford, and others.

---

cally, it involved virtually every Montana citizen. This opposition extended until Daly's death in 1900, but dissipated somewhat after 1898.

Heinze entered the Butte scene with relative force in 1896 and squared off with A. S. Bigelow of the Boston and Montana Company—thereby initiating the second major battle of the Copper War. W. A. Clark joined Heinze for a short time (1898-1901) in opposition to Bigelow but, after Amalgamated (Standard Oil) assumed control of Daly's Anaconda properties (1899), Clark slowly defected to Amalgamated. Amalgamated gained effective control of the Boston companies in 1900 and subsequently the battle pitted Heinze, virtually alone, against H. H. Rogers and the Standard Oil trust. Heinze lost the battle and, by selling his properties to the Amalgamated in 1906, culminated the second phase of the Copper War.

[7]O. C. Heinze MS., p. 12.

[8]O. C. Heinze MS., p. 18.

The operations of the co-partnership had been mainly in leasing mines, concentrating the product obtained at the old Liquidator concentrator in Meaderville, near Butte, and either selling the concentrates to the local smelters or shipping them to outside works. A large quantity was shipped to New York City. "The copper produced thus in [the] last six months of 1891 and in the year 1892 amounted to six million pounds, obtained mostly from leasing operations on the Ramsdell, Parrot, and Estella mines. There was a large amount of silver obtained in the copper. When the company was incorporated the Liquidator concentrator was purchased and its daily capacity increased to 600 tons from 100. Great economies were effected in cost of concentration by the installation of improved machinery for automatic treatment.

"In the fall of 1893 the erection of the smelter was begun. First copper matte from it was produced January 3, 1894. It assayed fifty-five per cent copper and was produced until 1895 when a converting plant was installed. Since then production has been pig copper assaying ninety-nine per cent and carrying large quantities of silver and gold."[9]

Heinze's next venture, the purchase of the Rarus mine (1895), commenced the prelude of the second half of the Copper War. This act released, into the courts of Montana and the nation, the greatest flood of litigation concerning one subject that any decade ever witnessed. Critics have related various situations and prices regarding the terms by which the Heinze brothers acquired the Rarus; Otto Heinze's account is possibly most correct.[10]

Following the successes and the profits which accrued to the Heinzes from the Montana Ore Purchasing Company's smelting program, F. Augustus traveled to the East to discuss the mine scheme

[9]"The Montana Ore Purchasing Company," *Copper Manual*, (New York: Houston; 1899), II, pp. 93-94. Please see Appendix One.

[10]O. C. Heinze MS., p. 18. The subsequent paragraph is paraphrased from Otto Heinze's letters to the author.

with his brothers. They had in the bank, applicable to such a purchase, thirty thousand dollars; the price in the option was ten times that amount. F. Augustus was convinced that it would be wise for them to secure the mine. His ultimatum, that if they did not join him, he alone would obtain the mine, was all the incentive necessary. To their inquiries regarding how the money was to be delivered, F. Augustus had the answer. The $30,000 would suffice as down payment and, within the allotted twelve-month period, profits from the mine itself would cover the remaining $270,000. F. A. was prophetic: the Rarus became a mammoth producer of rich ores. The brothers Heinze accurately regarded it as the nucleus of their properties.[11]

The general concept of the Heinze acquisition of the Rarus cites a figure higher by $100,000; $400,000 is the amount F. Augustus Heinze quoted in his speeches when referring to the Rarus. This quotation, however, includes the purchase of other properties, for example the Johnstown, covered by the Rarus title. A contemporary article in the *Copper Manual* explained the combined transaction.

"The Montana Ore Purchasing Company purchased the Glengarry No. 2 mine in 1893. It was located in an hitherto unproductive section of Butte. Exceedingly large bodies of ore were developed in it. They also leased the Rarus and Johnstown mines which had been valueless although the Rarus had a shaft of 650 feet. Very large ore bodies were developed. These were later purchased by the M. O. P. Company for $400,000. The original Rarus shaft was sunk to 800 feet and made a double compartment throughout. Second shaft was sunk to 1,000 feet with both equipped with adequate hoisting works. The Rarus and the Johnstown properties . . . are considered among the most valuable mines in the Butte district."[12]

As a result of F. Augustus's scientific and engineering training, especially that obtained in Germany, he pioneered advanced methods

[11]O. C. Heinze MS., p. 18.
[12]"Montana Ore Purchasing Company," *Copper Manual*, II, p. 93.

of mining and smelting in Butte. He was repeatedly among the first to introduce newer, proven methods in every operation and to eliminate the old. Historians have underemphasized this facet of Heinze's career in Butte. By making his properties a testing ground for revolutionary methods, F. A. performed a valuable service for the industry. His initiative was later recognized by the copper critics and emulated by mining and smelting concerns.

". . . Another company has recently grown into prominence, the offspring of an ore purchasing company established by the Messrs. Heinze. Though it operates a well-equipped furnace plant supplied largely from its own mines, it retains the original designation of Montana Ore Purchasing Company. Heinze, the Butte and Boston, and the Boston and Montana [with which F. Augustus had been associated] use the cupola rather than the reverberatory method. Butte has been the arena in which great revolution in copper metallurgy has been worked out, which has made it possible to treat in limited space the enormous output of the mines. The works today are the largest in the world and would have been unmanageable under the old Vermont or English roasting and reverberating furnace lines. The stagnation which for years characterized the metallurgy of copper has been replaced by intense activity. Old prejudices and fallacies that copper depended upon secrets passed down from generation to generation together with highly technical inherited skills have vanished and a new era of scientific investigation and rational practice has dawned."[13]

These newer methods were quite profitable for the Heinzes.

"Advanced and progressive methods reduced costs and increased profits of the owners of the Montana Ore Purchasing Company. Ore produced is delivered to works of the company by rail and is treated there more economically than in any smelting plant in Montana. Present smelting works treat between 500 and 600

---

[13]"Copper Smelting in the United States," *Mineral Industry*, (1895), IV, p. 275.

tons of concentrates and first class ores daily. The introduction of additional machinery within the last six months has doubled the capacity of the smelter. . . . The Montana Ore Purchasing Company since its inception has produced over 100 million pounds of copper, 2½ million ounces of silver and 125,000 ounces of gold; now it is producing at the rate of 24,000,000 pounds copper annually. Total dividends paid by the company since January 1, 1895, to November 1, 1899, amount to $1,356,000 of which $560,000 has been paid this year."[14]

In addition, F. Augustus Heinze was credited with being a pioneer of depth mining.

"He was the first—the very first—to appreciate the value of Butte ores at a depth, and it was his foresight and faith in this direction which hastened development of deep mining in this region."[15]

---

[14]"Montana Ore Purchasing Company," *Copper Manual*, II, p. 94. The final reference is to the year 1898.

[15]Butte *Miner*, November 5, 1914. The pertinent article quotes a tribute paid to Heinze by Richard R. Kilroy, editor of the *Evening News* (Butte).

Chapter III

THE CANADIAN INTERLUDE

"British Columbia," "gold," "lack of smelting facilities"—these words and phrases were repeated in the smoke-filled lounges and bar of the Silver Bow Club during the early 1890's. In 1894 F. Augustus Heinze went to British Columbia to evaluate the talk personally. Heinze was invited to Canada by mining men of that province.[1] A survey of Rossland, B. C., and its mines was sufficient for him to send information immediately to his brothers. F. A. advised them that they could profit by helping him to build a smelter at Trail, on the Columbia River, which could handle the ores mined at Rossland. Arthur and Otto Heinze secured the required $300,000 for the venture. The investment proved profitable to the entire Heinze family.

"Lida and Willie [F. A.'s sister and her husband] should like to participate B. C. [British Columbia] proposition $25,000 to $30,000 same terms as George [Waetjen, the husband of the other Heinze sister]."[2]

F. Augustus's answer is typically efficient.

". . . Referring to Fleitman [Lida and Willie] use your own judgment as regards offer."[3]

---

[1] F. A. Heinze, "Standard Oil Methods," *The Political Situation in Montana 1900-1902* (Butte; 1902), p. 44. This pamphlet, published privately in Butte, is comprised of four of F. Augustus's speeches during this period.

[2] Telegram of February 28, 1896; wire from Arthur P. Heinze to F. Augustus. This message, as well as those subsequently cited, was coded and most commonly sent from one office of the Montana Ore Purchasing Company to another. These telegrams have been compiled in a file which is in the possession of the author. The subsequent reference will be: "M. O. P. C. Telegram File," with the relevant date. In cases in which other pertinent information is available, it will be included in the reference.

[3] M. O. P. C. Telegram File, March 23, 1896. Wire from F. Augustus to the New York office.

The richest property in the Rossland district was the Leroi mine and F. Augustus, with his sure instinct for ore, planned to acquire it. His original contract with the Leroi owners required that they furnish six hundred tons of ore daily to the Heinze smelter. To facilitate the handling of this product, Heinze built a twenty-mile, narrow-gauge railroad from Trail to Rossland; he later extended it to Robson, British Columbia.[4] In addition to being a freightway, this road carried passengers at two dollars a ticket. An abundance of rolling stock placed passenger comfort at a premium; the cars were crowded—particularly on holidays, when even the roofs were used for passengers.

Heinze entered negotiations to purchase the Leroi mine, but he and the owners were unable to establish a satisfactory price. While the meetings continued, the role of crusader developed for F. Augustus. With the caustic pen of P. A. O'Farrell—who, after these Canadian days, continued as Heinze's protagonist and editor in Butte—Heinze inaugurated an attack on the Canadian Pacific Railroad for its failure to build a line from Rossland to Victoria, B. C.[5] O'Farrell's explication of the situation in the columns of the Heinze-owned Rossland *Miner*, the only newspaper in the region, convinced the populace that the Canadian Pacific was a villainous exploiter and further that the resident savior was F. Augustus Heinze. The objective of the acrid articles was to mellow the legislature of British Columbia to the point at which it would grant land to Heinze for his own proposed railroad to the coast—the Columbia and Western.

F. Augustus watched carefully the activities of Parliament in Ottawa and the British Columbia legislature in Victoria. He supported legislation before both bodies by which he could secure government subsidies and land grants similar to those enticements that the United States made to railroad companies within its borders. A telegram which F. A. sent (April 11, 1896) from Victoria informed his brothers of his progress.

---

[4] Anaconda *Standard*, November 5, 1914.
[5] C. P. Connolly, "The Fight of the Copper Kings," *McClure's*, XXIX (May, 1907), p. 4.

". . . Government grant 10,000 acres per mile narrow gauge will pass today or tomorrow."[6]

This land quotation reduced by half his estimate of March 23.

"Think we are certain to get out at least 20,000 acres per mile of railway, possibly guaranteed interest on $12,000 per mile of bonds and 10,000 acres."[7]

On April 26, 1896, Heinze's Canadian representative, F. E. Ward, wired to him from Montreal, Quebec.

"Columbia Western 50 miles this year [at] $3,200 [per mile] passed Executive Council. This means on return of the conservatives to power the entire line will be subsidized."[8]

An aggregate of 600,000 acres was finally allotted to Heinze; his trackless railroad, the Columbia and Western, approached reality.[9]

"Heinze had obtained charters for a railway connection from Trail to Robson and from Robson to the boundary country. He also obtained a lot of land grants. The latter did not appear of much value owing to the fact that the country is very mountainous and rough. It so happened that the Canadian Pacific Railway was interested in their railway charters and the hauling of products from and to Rossland."[10]

In addition to securing subsidization, Heinze carefully followed all mining bills. Chester Glass, initially an associate of Heinze in the

---

[6]M. O. P. C. Telegram File, April 11, 1896. Wire from F. A. in Victoria to the New York office.

[7]M. O. P. C. Telegram File, March 23, 1896. Wire from F. Augustus in Butte to the New York office.

[8]M. O. P. C. Telegram File, April 26, 1896. Wire from F. E. Ward in Montreal to F. Augustus at the Butte office.

[9]Anaconda *Standard*, November 5, 1914.

[10]Letter to the author from S. G. Blaylock, July 6, 1943.

British Columbia railway enterprises, kept him informed of their status. Glass's telegram of February 27, 1896, is indicative of his service.

"Government have modified their views on bill taxing mining output; present intention to deduct freight and treatment and reasonable amount for production. Think three dollars then two percentage on balance. Telegraph me your opinion of bill with above modifications. Will wire you when action will be taken."[11]

Another telegram from Glass reveals one of the developments in the mining-railway dealings.

"Important letters from Dewdney. Canadian Pacific likely to get cash subsidy from Dominion government for Crows Nest railway. Think with the option got from Baker we could force the Canadian Pacific to terms, perhaps give them part of land grant and retain coal and oil land and get special freight agreement and other concessions. Speedy action required."[12]

Heinze's delay in negotiating an agreement with the Leroi owners was fateful; it prevented his entrenchment in the British Columbia mining region. By 1896 the first guerrilla attacks of the second phase of the Copper War (1896-1906) were being staged in Butte. F. A. decided to relinquish his Canadian holdings and to return to Montana to protect his established properties. The Canadian Pacific directors and the Leroi mine owners were convinced that F. Augustus was a

---

[11]M. O. P. C. Telegram File, February 27, 1896. Wire from Chester Glass in Canada to F. Augustus at the Butte office.

[12]M. O. P. C. Telegram File, April 23, 1896. Wire from Chester Glass in Spokane, Washington, to F. Augustus at the Butte office.

Little information exists regarding Chester Glass, although the author gathers from the tone of the telegrams over a period of time that Glass and F. A. severed relations over some unknown issue. The author's research has uncovered a legal indenture dated May 11, 1897, and notarized by E. T. White of Spokane, Washington. By this document Glass surrendered to F. A. Heinze, for the sum of $3,250, one-half of all his interests in "The British Columbia railway enterprises, or any other enterprises in the Province of B. C., of the party of the second part [Heinze] which the party of the first part [Glass] now has with the party of the second part in said province of B. C."

typical crusader—his purpose was to become King of Jerusalem, rather than to save the Holy Land; they would facilitate his withdrawal.

F. Augustus sold his smelter and railroad to the Canadian Pacific in 1898 for "a splendid profit," probably $900,000.[13] The negotiations were concluded by F. Augustus Heinze and two of the C. P. R.'s executives, Angus and Shaughnessy, in their private capacities. These men bought from Heinze all the stocks and bonds of the Columbia and Western Railway Company and the lands of the British Columbia Smelting and Refining Company.

Heinze subsequently brought action against Angus and Shaughnessy for the cost of certain oil and stores. The suit was settled in 1900 with the payment of $55,000 to Heinze.[14] This incident exemplifies a description of Heinze pertinent to his Canadian dealings.

"Heinze was shrewd and unscrupulous. He was considered to be pretty tough in the days when a man to be considered tough had to earn the reputation."[15]

In 1899, D. F. Fitzgerald, one of F. Augustus's most trusted associates in Canadian affairs and the agent who concluded his business there after F. A. returned to Butte, wired Heinze concerning a meeting with Race, an intermediary for the Canadian Pacific.

"Race has left for Butte. We are offered twenty-five thousand for Rossland *Miner* [Heinze's Canadian newspaper]. Shall leave on February 23 for Butte."[16]

The figure $3,250 seems very low in view of the $900,000 which Heinze eventually received from the Canadian Pacific (1898). Of course, the indenture does not stipulate exactly what Glass's holdings were or their real value.

[13]Some accounts—for example, "Heinze, The Copper King," *American Review of Reviews*, XXXIII (June, 1904)—set this figure closer to one million dollars. Otto Heinze, however, insists that the price was $900,000.

[14]Information in a letter to the author from J. M. Gibbon, General Publicity Agent, Canadian Pacific Railway Company, Montreal, Quebec, Canada, July 7, 1947.

[15]Letter to the author from S. G. Blaylock, July 6, 1943.

[16]M. O. P. C. Telegram File, February 17, 1899. Wire from Fitzgerald in Rossland, B. C., to F. Augustus at the Butte office.

Fitzgerald elaborated on this offer in a telegram sent the next day.

"Race will try to purchase Rossland *Miner* in the interest of C. P. R. I would advise you not to sell. Neither one nor the other can start another paper nor injure *Miner*."[17]

As the battle in Montana had become heated, however, and all weapons were recognized, perhaps F. A. felt he needed the vitriol that his editor, Pat O'Farrell, could inject into a newspaper article. In any event, Heinze's curt, immediate directive severed his last integral tie with Canada.

"Advise offering to sell the Rossland *Miner* at $25,000."[18]

Heinze retained the land grants and he, therefore, remained an annoyance to the Canadian Pacific directors. They pursued him in the courts until December 15, 1909, when the Supreme Court of British Columbia (Victoria) awarded F. A. title to 550,000 acres, valued at ten to one hundred dollars an acre. When Heinze was congratulated concerning this favorable outcome and asked whether it was final, he smilingly remarked, "Maybe they'll take it to the House of Lords."[19] They did not, but he subsequently sold some of the land, for at his death he retained only 300,000 acres of the original 550,000-acre settlement.[20] After relinquishing the railroad, the smelter and the newspaper, Heinze was no longer active in British Columbia mining circles. He was, however, aware of metallurgical development there and acquired other property in Canada years later.

---

[17]M. O. P. C. Telegram File, February 18, 1899. Wire from Fitzgerald in Rossland, B. C., to F. Augustus at the Butte office.

[18]M. O. P. C. Telegram File, February 18, 1899. Wire from F. Augustus in Butte to Fitzgerald in Rossland, B. C.

[19]The *Reveille*, December 15, 1909. One should not forget that the *Reveille* is F. Augustus Heinze's own Butte paper, by which he disseminated his opinions and desires. Pat O'Farrell was its editor after coming from the Rossland *Miner* in 1899; he remained with the paper through most of the second stage of the Copper War.

[20]The Anaconda *Standard*, November 5, 1914.

Chapter IV

HEINZE'S COPPER WAR BEGINS

The Boston and Montana Mining Company planned the earliest ambush of F. Augustus Heinze—the first of numerous attacks on him during the second phase of the Copper War (1896-1906).[1] The situation pertained to the application of the apex theory in mining.[2] Mining law and practice, apparently to encourage individual initiative among prospectors, decreed that whoever had claim to a vein of ore at its apex—that point at which the vein surfaces—may follow that vein underground and remove its ores, despite the fact that the vein runs beneath the surface holdings of another person or company.[3] To determine the course of any ore vein after it has crossed other veins underground is a problem for experts; cases involving the apex theory, therefore, continued for years in the nation's courts.

A mining engineer, C. H. Batterman, had been resident director of the Heinze properties in Montana during F. A.'s Canadian interlude. He proved a poor selection for the task. Heinze's associates, Stanley Gifford and John MacGinniss, informed him that Batterman had betrayed him by attempting to sell his holdings to the Boston and Montana Company and to the Lewisohn Brothers, the selling agents for the Boston organization. Heinze immediately left Rossland (1896) and returned to Butte. Investigation and talk with Batterman clearly revealed the situation. The Boston and Montana Company asserted that the ore being extracted from F. A.'s Rarus mine

---

[1] Please see the summary of the Boston and Montana Mining Company in Appendix Two of the essay. See also the explanation of the two phases of the Copper War, page 16, n. 6.

[2] Please see several statutes which establish the apex theory in Appendix Three of the essay.

[3] Please see Appendix Three.

actually belonged to it, under the apex theory. The B. and M. stated that this ore came from its Michael Davitt mine, the side walls of which adjoined the Rarus. Batterman, who apparently lacked character, advised Heinze to sell to the Boston and Montana, as he could see no recourse.

F. Augustus Heinze functioned quickly under pressure. He discharged Batterman. He then took the maps, papers, and notes of the geologic formation in that part of the Butte Hill which Batterman had not surrendered to the Boston firm and studied them carefully. He emerged from his intensive study convinced that the Michael Davitt, not the Rarus, was violating the apex theory.

It was also characteristic of Heinze to take the direct, rather than the circular course. He went immediately to Boston to learn if he could reach a satisfactory solution with A. S. Bigelow, president of the Boston and Montana. Bigelow, critics agree, was malevolent and vindictive because the B. and M. had not been treated kindly in Montana.[4] Heinze's arrival and situation suggested the young man as an admirable scapegoat by which to teach others proper respect for the Boston and Montana. Otto Heinze states that Bigelow was poorly informed regarding mining matters and very likely did not understand the maps and surveys which Heinze laid before him—as director of the Globe National Bank (Boston), he made loans and financed mining ventures, but possessed no practical knowledge of mining.[5] Bigelow apparently acted upon the advice of the engineers and managers who worked the company's property.

The conversation of Bigelow and Heinze addressed the ownership of the Rarus ores. The Boston and Montana claimed them as part of the apex of the Michael Davitt mine. This property had not returned substantial profits, but Bigelow's engineers valued it. Heinze realized that there were rich ore bodies in the Boston property, and this knowledge was as much reason for his monetary offer as the more altruistic claim that the beginning of legal action on the basis of the apex

[4] Connolly, "Fight," p. 5. Please see also Appendix One.

[5] O. C. Heinze MS., p. 20.

theory would be endless. Regarding this point, F. A. proved himself particularly prophetic. He offered $250,000 to the Bigelow group for the Davitt mine. They considered this figure a mere pittance and immediately ordered their lawyers to sue F. Augustus on the grounds of the apex theory. Their refusal of the offer precipitated Heinze's threat to Bigelow to the effect that, if the matter were forced to the courts, a fight would ensue that could be heard across the continent.

"Mr. Bigelow, you have a great deal of property in Montana which is subject to the same kind of litigation as that which you say you will thrust upon me. If your program is to fight, you will find I am prepared. Before you and I have finished, I will give you a fight that will be heard from one end of this continent to the other."[6]

Fate plays strange tricks. Bigelow, who arrogantly began the second campaign of the Copper War (1896-1906), became its first casualty and disappeared completely from the scene by 1900. "Within less than four years, the Copper War ruined him and helped bring about the failure of his Globe Bank."[7] At this point (1899) the ruin of the immediate opposition ironically was of no advantage to the Heinze interests, for,

". . . debris of this collapse was under the guidance of Thomas W. Lawson, a stock broker in Boston; he had been selected by Henry H. Rogers, who was associated with William Rockefeller of Standard Oil Company and James Stillman, president of the National City Bank. Thus, these men became the owners of the controlling stock interest in the Boston and Montana Consolidated Copper and Silver Mining Company, a splendid company, and of the Butte and Boston Mining Company which had never been successful at mining, but had been a football on the Boston Stock Exchange and was selling at a very low figure."[8]

---

[6]Connolly, "Fight," p. 5. See also, F. A. Heinze, "Standard Oil Methods," p. 44.

[7]O. C. Heinze MS., p. 20.

[8]O. C. Heinze MS., p. 20.

The encounter with Bigelow convinced Heinze that the Boston and Montana did not want justice, only his Rarus mine and the assets of the Montana Ore Purchasing Company. The initial advantage appeared to be on the side of the B. and M.

"They believed they had Judge Hiram Knowles in their pocket and with some justice. The litigation over the Michael Davitt was to be brought before him. He had been a former attorney for them, had received fees from them and had been an associate of their head counsel, John F. Forbis, who did file his suit before that judge."[9]

The case was tried in the federal court in Butte in March, 1898. Judge Knowles instructed the jurors to return a verdict favorable to the Boston concern, but they risked contempt of court charges and asserted a verdict for Heinze. This aberration necessitated a retrial.

During the complete Copper War (1888-1906), the high jinks of Montana politics peaked. These manipulations brought smiles to disinterested parties throughout the nation and prompted many ethical homilies in the country's newspapers. As a basis of Montana's political frolic after 1898, Henry H. Rogers, Thomas Lawson, William Rockefeller and James Stillman attempted to effect the formation of an international copper trust, Amalgamated, on the scale of their oil trust, Standard Oil—of which Rogers was a prime executive and the brain of its machinations.

The basic property of this industrial complex, as they envisioned it, was the Boston and Montana. To facilitate this acquisition, the corporation-controlled Montana legislature passed the Two-Thirds Act (1899). This act made it legal for a corporation to sell, lease, mortgage or exchange for the part, or whole, capital stock of any other corporation, its ground, smelter, and all assets, if two-thirds of

---

[9]O. C. Heinze MS., p. 21. It is possible that Otto Heinze's prejudice is present in this statement. Neither pertinent issues of *Who's Who* nor any Montana histories state that Knowles was a Boston and Montana lawyer. William Scallon of Helena, however, a lawyer for, and director of, Amalgamated, has stated informally that Knowles and Forbis "probably" were Boston and Montana Company lawyers. (Interview by the author with William Scallon, Helena, Montana, June 3, 1944.)

the stockholders favor the move.[10] The veto of Montana's Governor Robert Smith was only a minor obstacle to the venal legislature which repassed the measure. As Heinze and his legal staff realized, the purpose of the legislation was a retrial of the Davitt case in New York state. F. Augustus's footwork, however—underground, in the shafts and tunnels, and above ground, in the courts—was sufficient to keep Amalgamated from complete supremacy for several subsequent years.

---

[10]*Laws, Resolutions and Memorials of the State of Montana Passed at the Sixth Regular Session of the Legislative Assembly, 1899* (Helena: State Publishing Co., 1899), H. B. 132.

Chapter V

HEINZE CREDIT

In 1899 Henry H. Rogers and his tycoons forced A. S. Bigelow, president of the Boston and Montana Company, to the wall by engineering a drop in the price of the Boston stock, so that they could purchase it at their own price. They meant this action also to be a demonstration of their power to F. Augustus Heinze. When the B. and M. stock dropped twenty-eight points, Bigelow apparently was sufficiently naive never to suspect that he was battling financial experts; he thought that his only opposition was Heinze, relevant to a receivership of his company.

As Bigelow assessed the situation, if he could secure the discharge of Thomas Hinds, the Heinze orderly who had been designated the receiver by the courts, his troubles would cease.[1] He, therefore, brought countersuit to have the receivership terminated. His stock, however, failed to rally. In desperation he threw his personal fortune of ten million dollars—earned primarily as president of the Globe National Bank (Boston)—on the market in a final attempt to save the Boston and Montana values. At this expense Bigelow learned that, when the tyrants of the market determined to obtain something, they usually were successful.

Rogers and his cohorts prescribed a dose of the same medicine for Heinze. It was not equally lethal, however, because of the unlimited credit which F. Augustus commanded. Critics generally ignore the

---

[1]Historians have generally taken the position that Hinds functioned only in F. Augustus's name. Otto Heinze states, however, that Hinds was primarily a Daly man who also worked occasionally for W. A. Clark. For a more detailed discussion of the receivership of the Boston and Montana, please see Section VII-A.

degree of this support. It is a tribute to the clan spirit of the Heinze brothers that F. A.'s credit was not effectively weakened. Both Arthur and Otto risked their fortunes in the Copper War when their brother was attacked.

F. Augustus often joked regarding how close to poverty he was. He delighted in creating the impression that he had very little cash and no available reserve. This talk overcame the initial characterization which circulated early in his Butte career that he came from a wealthy Eastern family. His reputation for having rather precarious finances was strengthened further by his method of securing new holdings. The purchase of the Rarus mine, however, subsequently an excellent investment, assured his brothers that F. A.'s judgment could be trusted. He constantly bought additional properties. In making these deals,

"He did not take into consideration whether the money was on hand or not, but would simply issue a draft on the New York office and expect of them that they find the money. This policy made the company appear to be in a condition of being hard up and created the belief generally that with a good blow to the financial solar plexus, the whole structure would come crashing to the ground. That was the reason why the Boston crowd, as well as Rogers, thought that they could get our properties at their own price."[2]

As a result of F. Augustus's charade, the enemies of the Heinzes consistently underrated the finances which F. A. could secure.

"Both the Boston crowd and the Rogers crowd thought it was not necessary to pay us anything [for the Heinze holdings], as it would be a simple matter to bankrupt us and to take our properties and assets for nothing. We well knew Rogers' reputation and the terrible power he controlled as one of the leading men in the all-powerful Standard Oil Company. I confess we were much depressed at the great struggle we clearly foresaw would

---

[2]O. C. Heinze MS., p. 22.

have to be met, but we were young and hopeful and ready to fight anyone or anything for our rights."[3]

After 1850, when Otto Heinze, Sr., came to America, the family engaged in dry-goods importation, through the firm of Heinze, Lowy and Company. By 1894 Otto Heinze, Jr., succeeded his father and held the controlling interest in the firm of Otto Heinze, although the basic company was retained. The organizational structure was nearly fifty years old and had an international record of integrity; it maintained banking connections in New York, England, Germany, and France. Although the Heinze brothers could easily raise large sums of money through these contacts, the firm did not regularly utilize them.

Otto Heinze was also a fifteen-percent stockholder in the Montana Ore Purchasing Company. A shrewd businessman, he decided to increase the profits of the dry-goods firm by "joining up more closely with the Montana Ore Purchasing Company."[4] By this arrangement, Otto contracted to avail the Montana smelting business of a credit of $300,000 to $400,000 against copper ore extracted from the mines. The Otto Heinze firm received a lucrative commission for this accommodation. The alignment also benefited F. Augustus. He could purchase any property for cash on the spot or could issue a draft on a New York bank which would be processed promptly by the Otto Heinze Company. This firm would then either sell its letter of credit on some of its foreign bankers or, more frequently, effect a loan with a local bank on its open note.

Otto Heinze always maintained a credit reserve of twenty-five percent; regardless of the demand for other advances, this percentage remained intact. His conservative policy was rewarded when F. A.'s credit was attacked during the Copper War. As a result of the unfavorable reports which F. Augustus's enemies circulated regarding his credit, bankers occasionally became concerned and refused to renew the Heinze loans. Their fears dissipated when they were imme-

[3] O. C. Heinze MS., p. 24.
[4] O. C. Heinze MS., p. 24.

diately and fully paid; shortly they returned to do business with the brothers.[5]

The first advances obtained from the dry-goods firm were used by F. Augustus in his activities in British Columbia. After he sold these holdings, the funds were applied to his Copper War battles.

The family firm, however, did not provide the complete credit available to F. Augustus Heinze. His brother-in-law, George W. Waetjen, directed one of the oldest and wealthiest banking and shipping firms in Germany. Waetjen demonstrated his faith in the Heinze ventures by occasional advances of two or three hundred thousand dollars. The Montana Ore Purchasing Company could also borrow several hundred thousand dollars from the Nichols Chemical Company and from the American Metals Company, the refining and selling agents respectively of the M. O. P. C. In addition, F. Augustus periodically secured loans of $50,000 to $100,000 from the W. A. Clark and Brothers Bank and the State Savings Bank, both of Butte. The two banks also allowed Heinze the usual trade credits for the purchase of machinery and supplies. These long-term loans were generally for substantial amounts.[6]

While F. Augustus engaged in mining and smelting in British Columbia (1894-1898), those telegrams which kept the Canada, Butte, and New York offices informed of developments predominantly pertained to financial matters—the acquisition of credit, the security of collateral, and the liquidation of obligations. Although Otto Heinze was the brother who supervised credit and finances, Arthur's name appears on the messages from the New York office of the Montana Ore Purchasing Company. This procedure reflects the Heinze brothers' desire to restrict Otto's name from such transactions.

"I was always most anxious to keep out of the limelight on account of my banking business; credit is a very delicate thing and can be destroyed very quickly."[7]

---

[5]O. C. Heinze MS., p. 25.

[6]O. C. Heinze MS., p. 25.

[7]O. C. Heinze MS., p. 26.

Administrators of the Montana Ore Purchasing Company transmitted all telegrams in code; the messages, therefore, were intelligible only to the select circle concerned. A telegram regarding the Heinzes' credit manipulations illustrates the code.[8] On March 7, 1896, Arthur Heinze informed the Butte office of the Montana Ore Purchasing Company:

"Have Birthained Crape on soirees for timekeeper citatory. Pillowbear also bluntness trimmed for Tinglass. Tastefully dishielout Homeward same."[9]

The apparent jargon translates to a pertinent, intelligible text.

"Have cashed draft on F. Augustus Heinze for $8,000 six days sight also check No. 150 for $9,325. Must without fail meet same."[9]

This type of credit discussion was continuous.

"Today have paid $10,000 in cash 2 days sight draft on you for $10,000 and 20 days draft for $33,125. $10,000 early tomorrow and $10,000 Monday. Must reduce overdraft. Can we draw $30,000 more from H. L. and Co. [Heinze, Lowy and Company] against M. O. P. receipts?"[10]

A subsequent message from Arthur Heinze to the M. O. P. C. office in Butte reveals the asperity which permeates many of the communications to F. Augustus from his older brother. Arthur was often mildly exasperated with the apparent irresponsibility of his younger brother; he assuaged his vexation with sarcasm.

"Did not receive any cash. Your recent telegrams confused. To what amount have you drawn on H. L. and Co. and what sight

---

[8]All of the telegrams in the Montana Ore Purchasing Company Telegram File which the author has used have the translation attached to the original wire. Subsequently, only the deciphered text will be given.

[9]M. O. P. C. Telegram File, March 7, 1896. Wire from Arthur Heinze to the Butte office.

[10]M. O. P. C. Telegram File, March 10, 1896. Wire from F. Augustus to the New York office.

since March 5? Answer a few of the questions of our recent telegrams. Mail tonight 3 B/L [bills of lading] dated tomorrow. H. L. and Co. may help us next week but that will be the last. We shall then owe them $314,000."[11]

John MacGinniss, a vice-president of the Montana Ore Purchasing Company, most often was delegated to answer the specific questions from New York.

"Referring to your letter of March 7 after No. 217 have drawn on M. O. P. Co. for $121,000 and H. L. and Co. March 7th and 9th $10,000 each 3 days. March 10th $9,400 one day, March 11th $15,000 two days, W. A. Clark declined more time. B. C. S. and R. Co. [British Columbia Smelting and Refining Company] has drawn No. 19 and No. 20 for $5,000 each. Have mailed 3 bills of lading tonight. Cannot transfer Friday. $5,000 payable James Breen tomorrow. Unanswered questions referred to F. Augustus Heinze, Driard Hotel, Victoria. Have transferred through Hoge March 7th, March 9th and March 11th $10,000 each. Answer immediately if did not receive."[12]

Arthur also applied his castigating tone to others—for example, to W. A. Clark, who denied the extension of time on notes due him.

"Refuse absolutely to accept any sight drafts so you do not draw same. Inform W. A. Clark all drafts on us including No. 224 coming due next week amounting to $50,000 also all drafts on Heinze, Lowy and Co. already provided for. Will agree to reduce overdraft to $30,000 by March 25th. What is the matter with Clark anyway?"[13]

[11]M. O. P. C. Telegram File, March 11, 1896. Wire from Arthur Heinze to F. Augustus at the Butte office.

[12]M. O. P. C. Telegram File, March 11, 1896. Wire from MacGinniss in Butte to Arthur Heinze at the New York office.

[13]M. O. P. C. Telegram File, March 12, 1896. Wire from Arthur Heinze in New York to the Butte office.

Credit lines within the Heinze clan are exemplified by the telegram from Arthur to John MacGinniss concerning repayment of an advance from Alice Heinze's husband, George Waetjen.

"Mail today B. C. [British Columbia] ore receipts $15,000 to $20,000 for Waetjen, Toel and Company on old form. You may sign as assistant manager."[14]

Heinze's credit lines were equally strong in American business. Another wire from Arthur Heinze to MacGinniss reveals financial support from the American Metals Company and the Lewisohn Brothers.

"Transfer $10,000 or $15,000 tomorrow, $15,000 Monday, same Tuesday. Mail tonight 3 bills of lading American Metals Company dated Saturday. Mail Sunday or tomorrow 3 Lewisohn Brothers bills of lading and 3 American Metals Company bills of lading all dated Monday. Draw at 8 days sight only on us, but Tuesday you may draw for $17,000 on Lewisohn Bros. and $15,000 on American Metals Company both at 3 days sight. Telegraph if 4 bills of lading mailed M'   ˙9 and 19. Keep us exactly informed of what you do."[15]

The Heinzes, however, constantly sought additional sources of credit. On March 19, 1898, F. Augustus, in Victoria, B. C., was advised by the New York office of the Montana Ore Purchasing Company:

"If you are able to make any financial arrangements you had better do so quick."[16]

F. A. sent his reply four days later.

---

[14]M. O. P. C. Telegram File, March 14, 1898. Wire from Arthur Heinze in New York to MacGinniss at the Butte office.

[15]M. O. P. C. Telegram File, March 20, 1896. Wire from Arthur Heinze in New York to MacGinniss at the Butte office.

[16]M. O. P. C. Telegram File, March 19, 1898. Wire from Arthur Heinze in New York to F. Augustus in Victoria, B. C.

"Both Bank of Montreal and Bank of British America are anxiously looking forward to doing business, 6% per annum interest talked of by Bank of British America. They are W. A. Clark's correspondents."[17]

F. Augustus Heinze is often, and incorrectly, regarded as a lone wolf in his mining activities. For purposes of credit security, Otto C. Heinze restricted the use of his name in the brothers' Montana ventures. Arthur Heinze, however, the oldest of the three brothers and the only one trained in law, frequently joined F. Augustus in Butte after 1893. When the Montana Ore Purchasing Company began to return sound profits, he discontinued his New York law practice to manage the Eastern (New York City) office of that organization.

After 1893 Arthur visited Butte several months of each year, familiarizing himself with the mining properties and frequently going underground to study geological formations. He diligently studied mining and combined this knowledge with his understanding of law. His preparation in both fields proved valuable when the M. O. P. C. litigation of the Copper War began. Arthur assumed control of all matters pertaining to lawsuits and directed the actions of the Heinze lawyers. It was his advice that the Heinzes should buy shares in the companies of their opponents; this device made it possible for them, as minority stockholders, to force the Boston and Montana Company into the hand of receivers. Arthur also developed other schemes to confound the enemy: the Johnstown stock transfer, the Copper Trust, and the Delaware Surety Company.[18]

F. Augustus recognized the assistance that Arthur rendered to the family projects.

"Arthur has been of almost incalculable benefit to us. The combination of legal knowledge with what mining knowledge he has acquired here during his different sojourns has enabled him

---

[17]M. O. P. C. Telegram File, March 23, 1898. Wire from F. Augustus in Victoria to Arthur Heinze in New York.

[18]Please see Chapter VI for a more comprehensive discussion of the legal devices conceived by Arthur Heinze and applied by the large group of M. O. P. C. attorneys.

to see opportunities and to take advantage of them in ways which without him I alone or with all the legal advice in the state could never have been able to do. In the demands upon his abilities which he has had to face here this spring, he certainly found his work. I am sorry you have been forced to miss him in New York but it is at least a consolation to know that his services here to us have been so valuable."[19]

The tripartite association of Arthur, the legal expert, Otto Charles, the businessman and financier, and F. Augustus, the mining expert and politician, continued through the years of conflict in Montana, until F. A. settled with his enemies in 1906. They discussed all problems and were completely loyal to each other. They customarily followed F. Augustus's advice regarding mining or politics, acted upon Arthur's dicta pertaining to legal procedure, and assented to Otto's opinions concerning finance. The apparent rashness of F. Augustus's mining purchases occasionally perturbed the conservative brother, Otto. As the acquisitions were a uniform success and paid large dividends, however, Otto decided that "while it was not a good policy for New York, for the West and mining it worked well; after all, success is what counts."[20]

The powerful sense of family loyalty and fraternity which supported the business affiliation is exemplified by a financial crisis which occurred in 1896.[21] Otto Heinze spent much of that year in Europe trying to secure greater lines of credit. As a result of the agitation for silver in the United States in 1896, Otto encountered some difficulty in London and Berlin, but he was generally successful. Upon his return to New York in July, Otto found the stock market

---

[19]Letter to Mrs. Otto Heinze, Sr., from her son, F. Augustus, May 30, 1898. The author possesses a copy of this letter; the original, however, is in the possession of O. C. Heinze.

[20]O. C. Heinze MS., p. 26.

[21]O. C. Heinze MS., pp. 27-31. The subsequent story is a paraphrase of Otto Heinze's description of the events. In no instance does Otto Heinze provide a first name for Lowy; neither does it appear in the telegrams which refer to the initial firm of Heinze, Lowy and Company.

in a mild slump and business in a fluctuant condition. The news from Montana was also somewhat depressing.

The time seemed auspicious for Otto Heinze to review the firm's resources. He asked his partner, Lowy, to aid him in checking the content of the firm's safe deposit box. Lowy had been associated with the Otto Heinze firm for more than twenty years; he also had been a partner of Otto Heinze, Sr. In 1896 Lowy owned approximately $100,000 of the associated firms' capital stock. For two weeks he postponed joining Otto to ascertain the firm's resources; when he was not present for their third appointment, Heinze called his hotel. In a discreet conversation, the hotel manager informed him that Lowy was dead.

Heinze suspected trouble and he confirmed his suspicion with a letter addressed to him and discovered in Lowy's office desk. This note explained that Lowy had speculated with J. S. Bache and Company. He lost all of his own capital stock in these ventures. In a futile effort to recover his losses, Lowy gambled the Heinze firms' securities, the assets of a deceased partner's estate, and bonds left with him by several European friends. All these securities were lost. The elderly Lowy felt that he could not bear the obvious disgrace and was convinced that the Heinze firms could not survive his actions. He expressed his sorrow to Otto Heinze for creating such a precarious position and stated that he planned to take morphine that night to end his plight. Otto wrote of this calamitous experience over forty years later.

> "I was not only deeply shocked, but greatly frightened at what the consequences of his suicide might mean for us all if it became public property. All my credits would be cancelled and my firm bankrupted and God only could tell what effect that might have on our Western situation. The first and instant thing to do was to kill all publicity."[22]

Otto fortunately found the hotel eager to avoid notoriety and was

---

[22]O. C. Heinze MS., p. 28.

assured that the house physician had filed the cause of death as apoplexy. Heinze subsequently released the apoplexy story from his own office. His solitary analysis of the firms' safe deposit box that afternoon revealed that Lowy's speculations totaled approximately $500,-000. He confided the matter of Lowy's defection only to the trusted head of the parent firm's office—who was necessarily told, as other defaults might exist in the books. Investigation revealed that these accounts were correct. Another possibility existed: Lowy had issued notes on the firm. Six months of anticipation ensued before a complete inventory could be taken; Lowy had issued no such notes.

The final accounting established that the total losses were slightly less than half a million dollars, that the entire capital of the two Heinze firms was eliminated, and that Otto Heinze's sole remnant was the fifteen percent interest that he held in the Montana Ore Purchasing Company. Letters quickly dispatched to Arthur and to F. Augustus in Montana detailed the grim story of the losses and requested that they prepare to return shortly to Otto the bulk of his advances to them. They answered that within a few months they would, if necessary, return his full advances—about $400,000—but that he must endeavor to survive without such immediate reimbursement. Otto's conservatism was rewarded during these several months of tension. His twenty-five percent reserve, maintained as a matter of policy, covered the firms' notes and obligations which matured immediately following the defalcation.[23]

George Waetjen, the German husband of Alice Heinze, was also informed of the calamity. His offer of financial assistance never had to be accepted. Arthur Heinze returned to New York City in the fall of 1896 and reviewed the entire situation with Otto. They concluded that Otto's firm must be maintained. The greatest continuous asset of the family enterprise had been its excellent credit standing. As a firm with a single owner was considered a poor credit risk, Arthur Heinze became a partner in the Otto Heinze Company on January 1,

---

[23]O. C. Heinze MS., p. 29.

1897. Arthur placed his name and entire fortune at the firm's disposal with this act of "great generosity and brotherly love."[24] In November, 1897, Otto Heinze contacted his European credit sources and resumed business with them. It was both fortunate and wise that the firm was maintained; in the next few years it advanced large sums of money to the Montana Ore Purchasing Company. These amounts approached, and in several cases exceeded, two million dollars and were immeasurably valuable to F. Augustus in the Copper War. The brothers Heinze had collaborated to repel a serious threat to their financial base.[25]

Financial tycoons, like Henry Rogers and T. W. Lawson, employed a common weapon on a firm or person whose property they desired: attack the victim's credit standing. Especially the Rogers group tried this tactic, repeatedly and unsuccessfully, on F. Augustus, his brothers, his associates, the Montana Ore Purchasing Company and the Heinze family firms before realizing the strength of Heinze credit.

In one instance they designated the Otto Heinze Company to receive the effects of their well-placed rumors.[26] These enemies of the Heinzes were partially, temporarily successful: they rendered the firm's bills of exchange entirely unsaleable in New York City. Otto Heinze, however, foresaw this possibility and neutralized the attempt. He had previously arranged with some European bankers to accept bills of exchange directly from him, to discount them in Europe, and to honor his checks drawn upon them.

This instantaneous ability to become entirely independent of the New York financial scene was necessary because the Heinzes were constantly subjected to threats of blackmail. Although the brothers' opponents launched constant attacks on each of them, with periodic—but only temporary—success, the coalition of the three men was able to survive all attacks on its character and credit.

[24] O. C. Heinze MS., p. 30.
[25] O. C. Heinze MS., p. 31.
[26] Editorial: "Fighting the Rockefellers," New York *World*, Oct. 25, 1903; as fully quoted in the *Reveille* (Butte), November 3, 1903.

"Our enemies were well aware that my firm was making advances of considerable amounts to F. Augustus and whenever he had a setback in Montana, rumors were put out that he and everyone connected with him, especially our firm, would very shortly be destroyed. This would have its effect upon my credits but due to the fact that I always insisted on having my credit reserve and with these paid anyone who wanted his money immediately in full, these efforts would not have the desired result. . . . Without these financial resources F. Augustus could not have carried through his fight successfully; the constant effort of our enemies was to close down sufficient of his mines to reduce his production of copper so as to strangle him financially. Notwithstanding his extremely farsighted and constant purchases of new mining property they would at times be successful in this temporarily but then our firm would step in and fill the gap until his production could be increased again."[27]

A rumor that the Heinze properties in Montana were relatively worthless was disseminated during the spring of 1896. The Heinze brothers decided to refute the charge with the factual report of an impartial inspector. On March 10, F. Augustus wired his assistant, John MacGinniss, in Butte.

"Arthur wishes parties in Butte whose names he will wire to inspect ore reserves. Have parties to examine mining properties with Rowe, Rowe to quote value as per reports to Arthur."[28]

Arthur's subsequent telegram to the Butte office contained the name of the examiner.

"L. T. and Company, recommend Bouglise, connected with the Lexington Company now in Butte, to expert [inspect] our

---

[27]O. C. Heinze MS., pp. 31-32.

[28]M. O. P. C. Telegram File, March 10, 1896. Wire from F. Augustus in Victoria, B. C., to MacGinniss at the Butte office.

mines. He is unfavorably impressed. Advisable to win him. You must see him at once."[29]

MacGinniss executed his instructions and wired the results to F. A.

"Bouglise offers to begin examination of mines April 15. Charge will be $3,000. Would Mr. F. Augustus Heinze wish to be present?"[30]

These coded telegrams present no attempt to gull or delude; the Heinzes did not doubt the value of their holdings. Bouglise and his assistant were allowed to inspect the mines and made their report. F. Augustus Heinze concurrently secured credit with two Canadian banks. Both matters appear in a telegram from Arthur to F. A.

"We congratulate on banks' offer. L. T. and Company examination confidential and report belongs to us."[31]

After F. Augustus sold his Canadian properties (1898), the daily M. O. P. C. telegrams primarily address the strategy for lawsuits in which he was a party. Matters of credit and finance, however, continued to permeate the wires. Three telegrams from early 1899, when the Michael Davitt suit was in the courts, are typical. The first is from Stanley Gifford, an associate in the M. O. P. C.'s New York office, to F. Augustus in Butte.

"What ails your production? Congratulations on W. A. Clark loan. Think you should transfer $20,000 tomorrow. Same will assist our credit here more than at Butte, and besides will cover your bill of lading draft payable January 14 and required

[29]M. O. P. C. Telegram File, March 20, 1896. Wire from Arthur Heinze in New York to MacGinniss at the Butte office. Bouglise was "unfavorably impressed" because he had heard rumors that the Heinze mines were overrated.

[30]M. O. P. C. Telegram File, March 27, 1896. Wire from John MacGinniss in Butte to F. Augustus in Victoria, B. C.

[31]M. O. P. C. Telegram File, April 25, 1896. Wire from Arthur Heinze in New York to F. Augustus in Victoria, B. C.

through our financing plan. Sold 400,000 [pounds of copper ore] April delivery 13½ cents. Paid Bank of America $40,000 bills of lading loans yesterday."[32]

Gifford wired again to the Butte office shortly thereafter.

"A. P. Heinze draft December 23rd on Otto Heinze and Company for $20,000 was paid here December 28, 1898 and charged to Montana Ore Purchasing Co. in Butte. Do not send such item among your December receipts. Should this have been charged to A. P. Heinze personally?"[33]

Two days later Gifford informed F. A. in Butte,

"Sold 400,000 lbs. March delivery at 15½ cents. We have only 200 tons our April delivery sold. How much more can we sell for delivery subsequent to April 1st? We have noted your production for this month as most unsatisfactory."[34]

The last message reveals the effect that court injunctions had upon production. At this time (early 1899) Heinze was enjoined from removing the Rarus ores, pending the second hearing of the Michael Davitt suit.

One of the coded messages sent between the two offices of the Montana Ore Purchasing Company presents elements of the firm's asset and credit situation. At this time the Butte office attempted to have its properties rated for the monthly book published by Bradstreet.

"Bradstreet's representative here cannot rate large companies. Months ago state agent promised representative would call at our head office New York. Telephone head office to call upon

---

[32]M. O. P. C. Telegram File, January 9, 1899. Wire from Gifford in New York to F. Augustus at the Butte office.

[33]M. O. P. C. Telegram File, January 25, 1899. Wire from Gifford in New York to F. Augustus at the Butte office.

[34]M. O. P. C. Telegram File, January 27, 1899. Wire from Gifford in New York to F. Augustus at the Butte office.

you and state capital $2,500,000, in treasury $500,000, November and December earnings over $40,000 each, paid $800,000 in dividends, and will pay $78,500 in January; indebtedness aside from bonds and current month's bills entirely covered by good bills receivable; mention refused offer and demand highest rating and credit. They attach much more weight to statements of interested parties than to outsiders. Too late to get into January books from here. Handle in New York."[35]

F. Augustus Heinze's sources of income were extensive. F. A.'s enemies, primarily the Rogers coalition after 1898, worked diligently to close a sufficient number of his Butte mines, thereby effecting a slump in copper production which would strangle him financially. To cope with such attacks, Heinze subscribed to a policy of buying and owning many mining properties. When his enemies then secured injunctions against some of his holdings, he could extract ore from others.

"Aside from our litigious activity we have been more active than ever before in the acquisition of additional mining property, and in this, if I may judge from present indications, and I am not often misled in these matters, we have been marvelously lucky. I do not think it at all beyond the possibilities of the case if we should decide that it was advantageous for us to do so, to close down the Rarus mine and all the adjacent property we own and be able to run the smelter on ores from other properties since acquired and developed. This is, of course, not yet a certainty but indications point strongly in that direction."[36]

Otto Heinze corroborates F. A.'s account.

[35]M. O. P. C. Telegram File, December 28, 1898. Wire from F. Augustus in Butte to the New York office. The "refused offer" which is cited refers to Henry Rogers's (Standard Oil's) attempt to purchase most of the M. O. P. C. properties in Butte earlier in the month.

[36]Letter to Mrs. Otto Heinze, Sr., from her son, F. Augustus, May 30, 1898.

"People in Butte in those days said of F. Augustus that entirely unexpectedly, F. Augustus would take his bag some fine morning and go out a couple of miles and locate a mine where no ore had ever been found. Everyone would be amused at such foolishness, but suddenly a couple of years later that particular spot would turn out to be the key to the entire district; in mining F. Augustus was indeed very farsighted."[37]

The opposition's attacks had occasional, temporary success, despite this farsighted program. In such emergencies, the advances from Otto's dry-goods firm and from other credit sources sustained F. Augustus until production again rose. The Heinze brothers united to form a self-protecting nucleus which its opponents could not penetrate. The prime extensions from this nucleus were long tentacles which extended throughout the financial world to secure strong sources of credit. The Rogers-Rockefeller-Stillman-Lawson coalition found that it could not ruin the Heinzes as it had devastated A. S. Bigelow in 1899; the tripartite nucleus had a broad base.

---

[37]O. C. Heinze MS., p. 11.

Chapter VI

HEINZE'S COPPER WAR LITIGATION

The Heinze phase of the War of the Copper Kings (1896-1906) began when the Boston and Montana Mining Company, led by Albert S. Bigelow, challenged F. Augustus's Butte production. The battle subsequently (1899) became an opposition of Heinze and the Rogers-Standard Oil trust, the Amalgamated Copper Mining Company.[1] The Copper War strikingly resembled international warfare: periods of intense, destructive battle alternated with quiescent times during which the strategists refreshed themselves and planned new campaigns. Each side possessed an efficient headquarters from which coded orders emanated to the generals in the field, primarily by telegraph.

The events of this dramatic decade received national attention for two reasons. First, the financial maneuvers and the pitched physical and political battles were excellent fodder for sensationalistic newspapers and magazines. In addition, the Heinze phase of the Copper War featured persons eminent in high finance—H. H. Rogers, Thomas W. Lawson, Marcus Daly, James Stillman, A. S. Bigelow, W. A. Clark, the Heinze brothers, and others.

To explicate the role of F. Augustus Heinze in the War, several topical chapters are necessary. This chapter addresses several ingenious legal devices employed by F. A. and his attorneys, as well as three prime lawsuits. Chapter Seven presents, in greater detail, two other court cases—that of the receivership of the Boston and Mon-

---

[1]Please see résumés of the Boston and Montana, and Amalgamated companies in Appendix Two of the essay; see also the explanation of the two phases of the War of the Copper Kings, page 16, n. 6.

tana and that of the Parrot mine. The subsequent chapter summarizes several physical encounters of the War deep within the mines and Chapter Nine delineates the relation of politics to Heinze's career in Montana. A related topic—F. Augustus's withdrawal as a major Butte operator by means of his sale to the Amalgamated—is the subject of yet another chapter.

VI-A. Legal Devices:
The Johnstown Mining Company

Although he possessed substantial financial support, F. Augustus would not tolerate having his rich holdings become unproductive simply because of Rogers's and Amalgamated's injunctions. F. A. found it extremely vexatious to be enjoined from mining the Rarus, Michael Davitt, Minnie Healy, and other productive properties. Heinze employed a large legal staff—often as many as thirty-five attorneys who worked under the direction of his brother, Arthur—to extricate him from such situations, as well as to defend his interests in court. This staff developed three notable mechanisms: the Johnstown Mining Company transfer, the Copper Trust, and the Delaware Surety Company.

Amalgamated's injunctions against the Montana Ore Purchasing Company in the Michael Davitt case prohibited mining that property after the second trial in 1900.[2] Arthur Heinze then suggested the Johnstown Mining Company stratagem. The Johnstown Company had been organized in 1898 to fight the Boston and Montana's Pennsylvania suits.[3] Arthur simply suggested transferring all of the Montana Ore Purchasing Company rights in the Michael Davitt mine to the Johnstown Mining Company. The latter company was not restrained by the injunctions and the Johnstown stratagem's net effect was to permit Heinze to continue mining the Davitt.

---

[2]Please see a more detailed discussion of this case: Section VI-F.
[3]O. C. Heinze MS., p. 35.

Otto Heinze states that their plan was to use the firm,

". . . to buy, mine, or sell, such mines as we ourselves, through any of our other companies, did not wish to own for one reason or another."[4]

This explanation is more conservative than that accepted by most participants in the Copper War. Heinze transferred to the Johnstown Mining Company his complete title to the disputed ore bodies in the Davitt case. Then the Johnstown proceeded in mining Davitt ore. Amalgamated officials meanwhile became frantic with chagrin and real concern that they were being robbed.

Heinze's miners, formerly employed by the M. O. P. C., became employees of the Johnstown Mining Company and were subsequently paid through that firm. These miners raised large bulkheads to close openings into the enjoined sections. Through crosscuts from the Heinze-owned Rarus, they then removed the high-grade ore from which the M. O. P. C. was restrained, but from which the new company was not. F. Augustus knew the tremendous worth of the rich veins—Enargite and Windlass—in the Michael Davitt. A telegram of December 19, 1898, refers to certain rich veins and provides some picture of the intricacies of the veined system.

"Knowles modified Larkin Snohomish injunction limiting same to west 220 feet of the Snohomish and releasing balance of Windlass vein on the Never Despair and Michael Davitt; also granted injunction on Silver Queen on ground through veins already in Corra ground. It might change its dip and wriggle out again into the Silver Queen in its upward course."[5]

The Michael Davitt adjoined the Amalgamated's Pennsylvania; the ores extracted from the Pennsylvania could be hoisted through the Rarus shaft.[6] Heinze's miners consequently worked steadily to

---

[4]O. C. Heinze MS., p. 35.

[5]M. O. P. C. Telegram File, December 19, 1898. Wire from F. Augustus in Butte to the New York office. Note that the Windlass vein is within at least three mines.

[6]An interesting fact concerning the Butte mines is that the gallows frame—which the tourist sees or which the reader finds pictured in books as "the Minnie Healy mine,"

surface as much enjoined ore as possible before retaliation occurred. Amalgamated's miners in the Pennsylvania could hear the blasting and rumbling of the work. Some of these men were paid to spy on the Johnstown workers so Amalgamated could confirm its suspicions. While Amalgamated's lawyers tried, with little success, to obtain a hearing and, thereby, the right to send inspectors underground to investigate, the company's miners worked from the Pennsylvania until they faced the men within the Rarus. Dramatic underground combat began immediately.[7]

VI-B. Legal Devices:
The Copper Trust Company

The Copper Trust was an application of the cliche, "fight fire with fire." After 1899 the Amalgamated reduced the output of Heinze's mines because of the numerous injunctions it secured. In the spring of 1900 the Heinze brothers retaliated with a mechanism that demonstrated their co-ordination of mining and legal knowledge: the Copper Trust Company.

Historians concur in crediting F. Augustus Heinze with the discovery of this property. Otto Heinze, however, conflicts this judg-

---

"the Belmont mine," "the Mountain Consolidated mine"—appears to be a separate unit, removed by a considerable distance from other gallows frames. In fact, in the depths of the earth no such distinct division exists. The mining is extensive; drifts one hundred feet apart are connected by stopes (oblique, stepped passageways) through which the ores are reached and removed. It is possible to move from one mine to another underground, or to descend the shaft of one mine to one's employment in another mine. This practice is, of course, more common since the Anaconda Company became (1915) the one company operating on a major scale in Butte.

An experienced miner relates, "They gave me a gun one morning on the 1,300 [foot shaft level] of the Diamond and told me to go down with it and watch so Heinze wouldn't come through from the Corra. I quit then." The same miner recalls how Heinze's knowledge of the mines baffled others: "Once Heinze went down in the Corra and came up in the Moonlight; no one knows how; he had to go through the Diamond, the Old Bell and the Anaconda hill—probably through the Anaconda, the Never Sweat or the Parrot." He concludes with this tribute: "I worked for Heinze down in the Rarus mine blasting timber; Heinze was too God damned smart for any of them if he had kept going, but he sold out." (Interview by the author with William McNelis, Butte, Montana, June 14, 1945.)

[7]Please see Section VIII-A for a detailed discussion of this example of underground warfare.

ment. He recalls that his older brother, Arthur, was studying maps of the Butte Hill one winter afternoon late in 1896.

"Arthur noticed that there was a small space between the St. Lawrence mine and the Anaconda which seemed to have been left out [not claimed or filed by any party]. Careful examination convinced him that the locations of the several surrounding mines had left this small triangle territory open. He and Fritz Augustus went over the whole matter and concluded that a new mine could legally and properly be located there; they drew their lines, set up their posts, filed their papers and thus became the owners of this property, right in the very heart of Amalgamated mines, a terrible threat to those mines, as an injunction could properly lie against them until the owners could prove that large ore bodies below did not apex or partly apex in our new mine [the forty-square-yard Copper Trust]."[8]

F. Augustus decided to test the potential of the Copper Trust claim in the spring of 1900 because of the effective injunctions brought against his mines by Amalgamated. Judge William Clancy issued the necessary injunction and Amalgamated immediately closed its mines, which employed many thousands. A distressed futility betrayed none of the wily planning by Amalgamated's legal staff. The company's explanation concentrated the miners' wrath on Judge Clancy and talk arose of dealing violently with His Honor. Clancy's office was elective and the miners were voters; the Judge removed the injunction before the end of the day and Amalgamated resumed operations. Although F. A. had misjudged this situation—one of the few times he erred while in Butte—he did retain ownership of the

---

[8]O. C. Heinze MS., p. 37. One discrepancy in Otto's account is that he mentions only two adjacent mines, the St. Lawrence and the Anaconda. Three claims bordered the triangular Copper Trust; the third was the Never Sweat property. These three holdings were Marcus Daly's until 1899, when he sold them to the Amalgamated.

One should not overlook the cunning with which F. Augustus named his new properties. He seems to have selected names which would help to confuse the issue or would, as in the instance of the Copper Trust, be ironic. When he named the Johnstown Mining Company in 1898, he apparently borrowed the name from a Boston and Montana property which also lay near his Rarus.

Copper Trust Company and its potential of fomenting new trouble almost instantaneously. This fact did not contribute to the peaceful sleep of Amalgamated's strategists.

VI-C. Legal Devices:
The Delaware Surety Company

The Delaware Surety Company was incorporated in 1900.[9] It was the solution of Arthur Heinze and the Montana Ore Purchasing Company's legal staff to the Pennsylvania litigation begun by the Boston and Montana Company and subsequently assumed by Amalgamated. The apex theory was the crux of the case; the southwest corner of Heinze's Rarus mine cut the northeast section of the B. and M.'s Pennsylvania claim.[10] Heinze was permitted to mine in the Rarus under a bond to the State Supreme Court that he would reimburse the Pennsylvania owners to the amount of ores taken from the mine, if the court ruled in their favor.[11]

Worried by the extensive pirating of their ores, Boston and Montana executives brought evidence into court early in 1901 to prove that $1,257,934 of their ore had been mined. Heinze was under $950,000 bond which the court promptly raised to $1,300,000. F. A.'s opposition felt that he could not raise the difference of $350,-000 in the allotted time. On May 10, 1901, however, he presented the required bond.[12] The payment was issued through the Delaware Surety Company which Otto Heinze described as having been formed "to give bond for us in the litigations that were forced upon us; all legal points were carefully attended to."[13]

The adversaries of the Heinzes, however, described the company

---

[9]This firm was also recognized as: the Wilmington Bonding and Casualty Company.

[10]Please see statutes pertaining to the apex theory in Appendix Three.

[11]Robert G. Raymer, *Montana, the Land and the People* (Chicago: Lewis; 1930), I, p. 489.

[12]Raymer, *Montana*, I, p. 489; see also: C. P. Connolly, "The Fight of the Copper Kings," *McClure's*, XXIX (June, 1907), p. 217.

[13]O. C. Heinze MS., p. 34.

as having been incorporated merely to meet this single crisis. They identified its president as Otto Heinze's brother-in-law, its secretary as a stock clerk employed by Otto, and several directors as other employees connected with the dry-goods importation business.[14] One should note that the two explanations do not conflict directly; both can be correct. In any case, the Delaware Surety Company did assist F. Augustus at this time and its legality was recognized by the Montana Supreme Court which accepted its cash bond.

That same court, in ruling on the Pennsylvania case on December 24, 1902, granted Heinze the right to follow his veins beneath the surface of the Pennsylvania claim. In fixing the boundaries, however, the court refused to permit F. Augustus to collect $265,000 as the costs of the case. It further upheld the lower court's recognition of the extralateral-rights doctrine which allows the owner of a mining property to follow to its conclusion a vein that apexes in his surface.[15]

VI-D. Lawsuits:
The Estella Mine

F. Augustus Heinze was involved in extensive litigation during his years in Butte, especially in the second phase of the Copper War (1896-1906). His legal staff—numbering as many as thirty-seven in 1902—conducted dozens of actions simultaneously. Three representative cases pertain to the Estella, Minnie Healy and Michael Davitt claims.

F. Augustus was twice named in ownership suits and both times he was the victor. James A. Murray, a Butte citizen, was plaintiff in the Estella case. This suit began on January 10, 1893, in the Butte district court and involved the Estella mine, north of Butte. Murray's complaint charged that Heinze violated several terms of a lease agreement which he had negotiated with Murray on August 1, 1892.[16] The

---

[14]Connolly, "Fight," pp. 217-218.

[15]Anaconda *Standard*, December 25, 1902. See also, regarding the apex theory, Appendix Three of this essay.

[16]Anaconda *Standard*, January 11, 1893.

complaint asserted that F. Augustus had agreed not to remove any ores for treatment or other purposes without notifying Murray; this point had not been honored. In addition, Murray charged that F. A. had promised to erect a fifty-horsepower boiler; instead, he had installed a boiler of only thirty-eight horsepower. Finally, Heinze was accused of not having removed the ores in a "miner-like fashion."

"On the contrary, he so mined the ore as to unnecessarily and carelessly mix the ores with large quantities of waste and he thereby caused great damage to Murray."[17]

F. Augustus, according to the August 1 lease, was to pay Murray five cents per pound for copper extracted from the Estella and ninety percent of the market quotation for mined silver. The complaint asserted that, in October, November, and December of 1892, Heinze had removed large quantities of ore but had paid nothing to Murray. It also stated that F. A. had furnished, instead of the agreed monthly statement,

". . . what purported to be statements, but which the plaintiff alleges, on information and belief, were incorrect and untrue."[18]

In the second clause of the action it was contended that, although Murray had demanded the lease annulled and possession of the mine, Heinze was continuing to extract large quantities of ore; an injunction was asked against his activity during the pendency of the suit.[19]

After the matter was determined in his favor, F. Augustus referred to it in a letter to his mother.

"We have settled the old Murray-Heinze lawsuit over the Estella by Murray agreeing to accept one-half the money we offered him as his due before the suit commenced and he now feels most friendly toward us. A number of other small suits have been

---

[17]Anaconda *Standard*, January 11, 1893.

[18]Anaconda *Standard*, January 11, 1893.

[19]Anaconda *Standard*, January 11, 1893. See also, *Reports of Cases Argued in the Supreme Court of the State of Montana, Official Reports*, XVII, pp. 353-369.

settled as well and all things considered, I am commencing to regain faith in the belief that I was not born to fight everybody; but there have been times which I thought we were hoodooed, as they say in the South and West."[20]

VI-E. *Lawsuits:*
The Minnie Healy Mine

The second ownership case concerned the notorious Minnie Healy mine; it was initially tried in 1901. Tons of newsprint were used nationally to explain or distort the Minnie Healy story, depending upon the prejudices of the individual editors. Everyone talked of the Minnie Healy, but few knew anything about it.

". . . A friend of Heinze's in San Francisco one day wrote Fritz a letter saying, 'For Heaven's sake, my dear friend, do pay that black-mailing woman, Minnie Healy off; she is doing your reputation more harm out here than any amount of money is worth.' That was the way the Rogers's minions were falsifying the press accounts all over the United States; this was the way the terrific power of H. H. Rogers and his associates would practically falsify nearly everything about F. Augustus."[21]

Plaintiff in the original Minnie Healy suit was Miles Finlen, who had leased the mine from its owner, Marcus Daly.[22] The matter might have been settled amicably and early, if Finlen had not sold his right to the mine and the suit to the Amalgamated Copper Mining Company which planned to ruin and rout Heinze.

The lease, which originally Finlen held, gave him the option to buy the Healy for $100,000. Finlen had spent $54,000 in developmental work with little return; he welcomed Heinze's offer to assume

---

[20]Letter to Mrs. Otto Heinze, Sr., from her son, F. Augustus, May 30, 1898.

[21]O. C. Heinze MS., p. 36.

[22]"The Story of the Minnie Healy," *Reveille* (Butte), August, 1901, and July 28, 1902. For a less biased résumé of the case, see also: C. P. Connolly, "The Fight for the Minnie Healy," *McClure's*, XXIX (July, 1907), pp. 317-332.

his lease for a reimbursement of $27,000 in six months and another $27,000 within two years. The initial terms of the deal unfortunately were made orally and not written for about a month. F. Augustus wanted the mine to discover if the Gambetta and the Piccolo, Boston and Montana properties, apexed in it. He soon found, however, that the Minnie Healy itself contained a virtual fortune in unmined ores. Knowledge of the discovery leaked. Finlen learned that the mine had begun to pay and he moved to regain possession of it, claiming that he had never intended to relinquish the property. When Heinze refused, in what almost became a pitched battle between Finlen's and Heinze's men, Finlen sued. Before a court decision could be rendered, Amalgamated purchased Finlen's interest and continued the suit.

Judge Edward W. Harney, presiding in district court at Butte, gave the decision to Heinze (February, 1901). Amalgamated promptly appealed to the Montana Supreme Court and produced affidavits to show that Harney ruled in Heinze's favor because he had been bribed. In American court records it would be difficult to find a more sordid story than Amalgamated's attempt—in Butte's Thornton Hotel on the night of August 5/6, 1901—to bribe Judge Harney with $250,000 to swear that F. Augustus had bribed him. Heinze's newspaper, the *Reveille,* stated that H. H. Rogers ordered William Scallon, managing director of the Amalgamated in Butte, to secure Harney's favor for $125,000. In the course of the meeting with Harney, however, Amalgamated's representatives—D'Gay Stivers, Arthur J. Shores and Charles Clark—were forced to raise the bid to $250,000 before suspending the unsuccessful negotiations.[23] Harney refused to be purchased by Amalgamated.[24]

The State Supreme Court returned the Minnie Healy case to the district court in July, 1903, for retrial by Judge William Clancy. Clancy recognized the legality of the verbal agreement with Finlen and declared Heinze the owner of the Minnie Healy. This decision was rendered on October 22, 1903—the same day on which

[23]*Reveille,* July 28, 1902.
[24]Connolly, "Minnie Healy," pp. 324-328.

Clancy ruled in Heinze's favor in the Parrot suit. The judge's Healy opinion certainly enforced Amalgamated's decision to effect the momentous Shutdown of 1903. Amalgamated then continued the Minnie Healy litigation by again appealing the district court decision. The Montana Supreme Court, on April 20, 1905, ruled for Heinze by sustaining the lower court's decision. This victory ended six years of legal contest over the Healy.

In the majority decision of Supreme Court Justice William L. Holloway and in the Court's earlier statement upon the defendants' first appeal, several facts were revealed.[25] Finlen had secured leases and bonds from John Devlin, Devlin's wife and a Mrs. Reilly, in return for an accumulative three-fourths interest in the Healy, and from Caroline V. Kelley, for a one-twentieth interest. These agreements gave to Finlen the option to purchase the mine for $100,000 before February 3, 1900. Heinze's Johnstown Mining Company also held a one-eighth interest. In discussing the claim with Heinze, Finlen said that it would not justify work and that he wanted to dispose of it. On November 21, 1898, Finlen agreed in writing to assign all his leases and bonds to Heinze who would work the mine and, if it appeared worthwhile, would purchase it from Finlen for $54,000. From December 23, 1898, until February 24, 1899, F. Augustus worked the property and, by discovering new ore bodies, enhanced its value.

Finlen admitted only one agreement with F. A.: to institute a suit against the Boston and Montana Company to enjoin its removal of ore from the Piccolo and Gambetta claims, until it could be proved whether or not the claims apexed in the Minnie Healy. Heinze recognized this pact; he was to pay the costs of the suit and to realize any profits that would result. Finlen attempted to retake the property on February 24, 1899, but F. A.'s men forcibly ejected him. Heinze continued to work the mine until a court injunction closed the property in June, 1899.

The case was remanded by the State Supreme Court to the Butte

---

[25]The Montana Supreme Court ruled on the first Finlen-Amalgamated appeal on July 24, 1903; it ruled on the second appeal on April 20, 1905.

district court in July, 1903. A rehearing was necessitated by correspondence placed in evidence which indicated that Judge Harney had discussed the Minnie Healy case with a court stenographer and friend, Ada Brackett. The Montana Supreme Court judged that Harney's affidavit did not clearly vindicate him and directed that the case be reheard in the district court by Judge William Clancy. Clancy's decision also favored Heinze. After this second trial, the Supreme Court upheld the lower court (April, 1905).

Justice Holloway also injected some personal observations in his majority decision. He noted that the fact that Heinze had rendered the mine profitable after Finlen had found it unproductive did not entitle Finlen to retake it; F. Augustus's luck was integral to the risk of mining. Holloway also stated that, since Finlen had himself contemplated suing the Boston and Montana because of the Gambetta and Piccolo claims, one could not consider it champerty or collusion that he had instigated such a suit in Heinze's interest following their November, 1898, agreement.[26] In the second of the two ownership cases, therefore, defendant F. Augustus Heinze again emerged the victor.

VI-F. Lawsuits:
The Michael Davitt Mine

In February, 1897, a consolidation of mining companies prominent in Butte occurred. The Boston and Montana Mining Company and the Butte and Boston Mining Company united some of their assets and co-ordinated their management; although each company retained superficial independence, their boards of directors were interlocking and Albert S. Bigelow appeared to control both firms.[27] F. Augustus took this opportunity to offer Bigelow $250,000 for the Boston and Montana's Michael Davitt property. Heinze had previously leased this claim and knew that the B. and M. considered it

---

[26]*Montana Supreme Court Reports*, XXVIII, pp. 548-577, and XXXII, pp. 354-394.
[27]Please see Appendix Two for résumés of these two mining companies.

sterile of valuable ore. F. A., however, was motivated by more than an altruistic desire to avoid endless court action: "Of course Fritz did believe there were other ore bodies in it and was willing to take his chances."[28] Bigelow refused the Heinze offer and immediately ordered the B. and M. attorneys to begin suit against Heinze.

The first hearing of the Michael Davitt suit occurred in March, 1898, in the Federal District Court of the Ninth Circuit in Butte. The crux of this case was the apex theory:[29] was F. Augustus Heinze removing ore which apexed in his Rarus mine or was he extracting Michael Davitt ore? The Boston and Montana claimed it was Davitt ore, whereas Heinze insisted that it was Rarus ore, to which he was entitled under the apex theory. Judge Hiram Knowles directed a verdict for the Boston and Montana; the jury, however, determined for F. Augustus and forced a retrial. Pending the retrial, Judge Knowles issued an injunction which prevented Heinze from extracting the disputed ore bodies. This order reduced F. A.'s production, "for the time being, very considerably."[30]

In January, 1899, the Montana legislature passed H. B. 132 over the veto of Governor Robert Smith. This bill permitted the transfer of stock without the consent of minority stockholders. Simultaneously Henry Rogers, who controlled the majority of Butte and Boston stock and, therefore, possessed substantial power in the young consolidation of Boston mining firms, moved to depose A. S. Bigelow from effective power in the firms; although Bigelow was retained as president of the consolidation, Rogers and his Standard Oil associates gained complete control of the interlocking directorates.

On May 1, 1899, the Amalgamated Copper Mining Company, a holding firm for Standard Oil, which was incorporated in New Jersey in 1898, announced the formal purchase of the Anaconda Copper Mining Company. Marcus Daly was installed as the president of Amalgamated; the company's board of directors included: Daly, H.

---

[28]O. C. Heinze MS., p. 20.

[29]Please see statutes pertaining to the apex theory in Appendix Three.

[30]O. C. Heinze MS., p. 21.

H. Rogers, A. C. Burrage, Adolph Lewisohn, W. J. Riley, James P. Phillips, Jr., William G. Rockefeller, and James Stillman.[31] The year 1899 is, therefore, the year that Standard Oil, under the guise of Amalgamated, moved into Butte, both formally and informally. Amalgamated held the Anaconda Company directly as an operating firm; Rogers, functioning for Amalgamated, secured effective control of the Boston consolidation. During 1899 the copper factions in Butte regrouped and new battle lines were drawn for the second phase of the War of the Copper Kings. For all practical purposes, the War became F. Augustus Heinze and W. A. Clark versus Standard Oil's newly copper-plated octopus. After Clark's defection (1901), F. A. opposed the giant trust virtually by himself.

Commencing with the retrial in Helena of the Michael Davitt suit (1900), therefore, F. Augustus Heinze went into battle against Amalgamated, which had assumed the Boston and Montana's case. F. Augustus was young, eager, and apparently pleased that his adversary was sufficiently prominent to arouse public interest. F. A. endeavored to satisfy that interest immediately with news stories and other accounts in the Helena papers.

H. H. Rogers, William Rockefeller, and James Stillman of Amalgamated's board of directors were the basis of the great Standard Oil trust which, at the turn of the century, exuded a stench not entirely of petroleum. Standard Oil was being discredited nationally by the federal government's trust-busting movement. On this peg, Heinze's newspaper writers hung their stories. Throughout the six-week trial in 1900, Helena papers were never without their attacks on the oil corporation.[32]

Sympathy favored Heinze and again the jury returned a verdict in his favor. On the strength of its charge that the newspaper articles had influenced the jury, Amalgamated was granted the right to obtain a third trial, this one in the San Francisco circuit. As the litigation was to continue, the initial injunction which restricted F. Augustus

---

[31]George Walker, *Copper Mines of Butte* (New York: Boston Financial News; 1900), p. 17.

[32]Connolly, "Fight," p. 222.

from mining the Rarus-Davitt ore also continued. At this point, therefore, Heinze's victories were barren.

"Heinze won it twice even with Knowles sitting both times as judge; the juries gave it to him and eventually, after waiting for years, the Circuit in San Francisco gave it to him also. After doing his utmost to get the Court of Appeals to act, he took the bull by the horns and mined the ore which two juries had given him; this is the basis for the wild screams of theft which the Amalgamated Company's minions gave out."[33]

"Taking the bull by the horns," in this instance, indicates the use of the Johnstown Mining Company stratagem—a mechanism devised by Arthur Heinze and effectively applied to permit F. Augustus to mine the contested ore.[34] Although the original injunction against the Montana Ore Purchasing Company remained effective for years, Heinze mined the Rarus-Davitt vein through the Johnstown Company. The Amalgamated forced a hearing on this case and F. Augustus was fined $20,000 by Judge James H. Beatty of Idaho for contempt of court because he had resumed mining the enjoined property. Testimony revealed that he had extracted a million dollars' worth of ore. F. A.'s attorneys appealed this decision to the Federal Court of Appeals. The final consequence was the dissolution of the Davitt suit by virtue of Amalgamated's purchase of the Heinze holdings in 1906.[35]

These three mining suits—the Estella, Minnie Healy, and Michael Davitt mine cases—and the legal devices employed by Heinze's staff of attorneys to alleviate the situations are typical of the litigation of the Copper War. Two additional litigious sequences present a more detailed picture of this realm of the War of the Copper Kings: the case of the Boston and Montana receivership and the Parrot mine suit.

---

[33]O. C. Heinze MS., p. 36.

[34]Please see Section VI-A for a more comprehensive discussion of the Johnstown Mining Company.

[35]Anaconda *Standard*, February 14, 1906.

Chapter VII

MORE COPPER WAR LITIGATION

The two sequences of litigation which compose this chapter are contrastive; each, however, is illustrative of a type of combat basic to the War of the Copper Kings. The case of the Boston and Montana receivership had several phases and was quite lengthy. The initial action began in June, 1898, and the case was terminated only by the sale of F. Augustus Heinze's Butte holdings to the Amalgamated Copper Mining Company in 1906. F. Augustus was relatively successful in this litigation, but also resorted to some questionable devices to enhance this success. The second suit, that of the Parrot mine, best illustrates the trend of the Copper War after 1902. Following the defection of W. A. Clark to Amalgamated (1901), Heinze was virtually alone in his opposition to the Standard Oil trust. The outcome of this battle was predictable. The Parrot case, and the Shutdown of 1903 which it precipitated, formulated the context of F. Augustus's effective defeat. Both sequences of litigation are revealing; they expose the methods of Heinze's enemies, as well as his own manipulations.

VII-A. Lawsuits:
The Boston and Montana Receivership Case

A financial maneuver designed by Henry H. Rogers in 1898 precipitated the Boston and Montana receivership case.

"Mr. East, one of the lawyers for Standard Oil, conceived the idea that it would be a good move to give their judge, Hiram Knowles, jurisdiction over the litigation the Boston and Montana Company was involved in. . . . To accomplish this, the officers and directors of the Boston and Montana Company transferred all the assets of that company to a New York corporation which they also called the Boston and Montana Company and this without a single notice or word to the stockholders of the former company; only after this transfer had been made did they call a meeting of the old company stockholders to ratify that transfer. This, under the laws of the State of Montana, was an absolutely illegal act. MacGinniss and Lamm, our stockholders, went immediately before Judge Clancy, asking for a receiver and an injunction, and Clancy granted their pleas."[1]

The transfer occurred on April 6, 1898, although the stockholders were not informed of it until May 31, 1898. Boston and Montana executives, on the advice of Henry Rogers, called a meeting for June 6, 1898, so the stockholders could perform the necessary ratification of the transfer previously made by the directors.

Part of the Heinze brothers' strategic pattern was to buy some stock in the companies of their enemies, thereby securing "inside lines." On April 8, 1898, James Forrester of the New York legal staff of the Heinze interests, purchased one hundred shares of Boston and Montana stock. John MacGinniss, an executive of the Montana Ore Purchasing Company, also bought one hundred shares of the stock on May 16, 1898. Forrester and MacGinniss brought action against the stock transfer (June 4, 1898) two days prior to the stockholders' meeting; they also sought an injunction pending the outcome of the case. The Boston and Montana offered bond of $50,000—on the conditions that it would, when requested by the plaintiffs, buy the two hundred shares at the market price and that it would pay any damages that might occur as a result of the stockholders' meeting. The court refused to accept bond in lieu of the injunction.[2] The B.

---

[1]O. C. Heinze MS., p. 39. Otto errs in one instance: John MacGinniss's co-plaintiff in this case was James Forrester, not Daniel Lamm. Lamm was involved in a similar case, as a minority stockholder, with MacGinniss against the Parrot Mining Company. Please see Section VII-B.

[2]*Montana Supreme Court Reports*, XXI, pp. 544-572.

and M. appealed the case immediately to the Montana Supreme Court.

In November, 1898, Justice William T. Pigott, with Justices W. Y. Pemberton and William H. Hunt concurring, gave the majority opinion that it was legal for minority stockholders to enjoin ratification of the transfer. Justice Pigott held also that, although the stockholders acquired the stock after the transfer was made and waited until two days before the meeting of the stockholders to sue, they were within their rights and could seek the injunction; in common law, *all* stockholders must consent to such a transfer. The Justice further stated that the statutes on which the defendants relied (1887, div. 5, 8492-8494) did not give authority for the transfer.[3]

As a result of the Supreme Court order, the Montana Ore Purchasing Company office in New York received a message from MacGinniss.

"Supreme Court rendered decision in case John MacGinniss, Forrester vs. Boston and Montana Company affirming lower court. Congratulations. You should get this into the Boston papers."[4]

Strengthened by this court action, F. Augustus commenced the second step of litigation; he proceeded to secure a receiver for the Boston and Montana. F. A. wired to Butte on December 5, 1898.

"Think Boston and Montana people may transfer back all property to old company and immediately thereafter transfer anew

---

[3]Subsequently, the lobbyists for Amalgamated and others who wished to qualify for federal court jurisdiction—and thereby escape the rule of the Butte district courts—succeeded in persuading the 1899 Montana legislature to bring such transfer of property within the law. H. B. 132, or the Two-Thirds Act (1899) permitted a corporation to sell, lease, mortgage or exchange part or whole capital stock of any other corporation, its ground, smelter, and all assets, if two-thirds of the stockholders favored the move. The act passed over the veto of Governor Robert Smith. Please see: *Laws, Resolutions and Memorials of the State of Montana Passed at the Sixth Regular Session of the Legislative Assembly, 1899* (Helena: State Publishing Co.; 1899), H. B. 132. See also: Anaconda *Standard*, November 2, 1902.

[4]M. O. P. C. Telegram File, November 28, 1898. Wire from John MacGinniss in Butte to the New York office.

everything but some small piece of property to New York company. We desire to take action to prevent this at the earliest possible date."[5]

More explicit directions comprised his wire two days later.

"Butte and Boston and Boston and Montana both quoted much higher tonight, with rumors that Amalgamated's consolidation about completed. Think you should tonight proceed immediately to get receiver appointed, if possible, keeping matter secret. The reason for proceedings being ex parte is that appointment of receiver here should be simultaneous with appointment there. Your last telegram of today does not indicate that you have completely understood our plan, the desideratum being simultaneous tie up all around without previous notice to other side. If you can get order signed, send us verbatim draft by wire, also of former order continuing injunction, and such other information as New York Statutes would seem to require for our use here. Think time is of the utmost importance. Also advise us minutely."[6]

There was considerable compromise with ethics in the planning done by the Heinze legal staff—planning to which F. A. was, of course, a party. Precise fulfillment of the spirit and letter of the law, however, did not distinguish tactics of the growing corporations of the United States. F. Augustus conceded that certain of his activities were outside the law. He once stated, "My dear Mother, I cannot fight a band of robbers by singing hymns and sprinkling holy water."[7] Otto Heinze, while admitting that certain irregular activities were condoned, denies transgression of the law.

". . . however, we never did anything that was not lawful—that

[5]M. O. P. C. Telegram File, December 5, 1898. Wire from F. Augustus in New York to the Butte office.

[6]M. O. P. C. Telegram File, December 7, 1898. Wire from F. Augustus in New York to the Butte office.

[7]O. C. Heinze MS., p. 38.

H. H. Rogers would have welcomed with joy; he was that kind of man and attacked ferociously."[8]

The procedure followed by F. Augustus in the Boston and Montana receivership case appears extralegal. His objective, when the receiver was named, was to have exactly the same sequence of events simultaneously develop in Montana and New York. To effect this particular mechanism, F. A. directed the initial phases of the strategy from the Montana Ore Purchasing Company's New York office (December, 1898): early in 1899, he returned to Montana to oversee the specific implementation of the plan. This plan required that the full text of the legal papers issued in Montana be wired to the New York office where duplicates could be prepared and used in a New York State court. These copies could be complete, excepting the blanks left for the name of the judge, the receiver, the lawyer, the court clerk and others whose names would be telegraphed to the East at the moment they became definite in Montana.[9] F. Augustus designated the purpose of this device in his telegram of December 14, 1898.

"Tell no one of our intended proceedings at this end. This data [pertinent names for the blanks] needed here because our attorney must swear that his papers are exact copies."[10]

The Heinzes knew, as did other participants in the Copper War, that money talks and they acted to some extent on that principle. When, for instance, they thought they would need another stockholder in Montana to advance the B. and M. receivership case, they scanned their lists and discovered such a person.

"Stockholder referred to in your cable willing to act any way we desire for $1,000."[11]

[8]O. C. Heinze MS., p. 38.

[9]M. O. P. C. Telegram File, December 14, 1898. Wire from F. Augustus in New York to the Butte office.

[10]M. O. P. C. Telegram File, December 14, 1898. Wire from F. Augustus in New York to the Butte office.

[11]M. O. P. C. Telegram File, December 19, 1898. Wire from Butte office to New York office.

Another wire transmitted during the receivership period characterizes F. Augustus as a person unwilling to spare any expense, if the matter concerned were vital. Somewhat aghast at the order from F. A. in New York, the Butte office asked,

"Are we to understand today's telegram as calling for the telegraphic transmission [of] two orders referred to six typewritten pages?"[12]

Heinze's reply was instantaneous.

"We certainly think matter of sufficient importance for you to telegraph orders in code verbatim. . . . It is possible at any moment our position may be made untenable or otherwise altered by action from other side, when our parsimony would have resulted in irreparable damage. Under these circumstances we should do best possible, regardless of expense."[13]

The receiver of the Boston and Montana Company, Thomas R. Hinds, was appointed on December 15, 1898, by Judge William Clancy; the B. and M. sued immediately to nullify the receivership. The Montana Supreme Court denied this motion on February 27, 1899. The same court simultaneously denied a B. and M. request which would have permitted a lower court to review the case. At 1:25 P.M. on that day, F. Augustus wired news of the denials to New York.

"Supreme Court today dismissed writ of certiorari. You are at liberty to go ahead. Proceed."[14]

The Boston and Montana countersuits had prevented Hinds from immediately becoming receiver; on April 8, 1899, however, the firm recognized him. The B. and M.'s motive was to secure more favorable

---

[12]M. O. P. C. Telegram File, December 9, 1898. Wire from Butte office to F. Augustus in New York.

[13]M. O. P. C. Telegram File, December 9, 1898. Wire from F. Augustus in New York to the Butte office.

[14]M. O. P. C. Telegram File, February 27, 1899. Wire from F. Augustus in Montana to the New York office.

status with the Montana Supreme Court. Having surrendered to the receiver, the company immediately asked that the receiver be declared incapable of conducting the firm's business and argued that the B. and M. had abandoned its plan to transfer stock to New York. The 1899 Montana legislature assisted the Boston and Montana's interests by legislating the right to appeal from an order appointing, or refusing to appoint, a receiver—or refusing to vacate an order appointing or affecting a receiver. On April 13, 1899, the Supreme Court therefore ordered the receiver, Thomas Hinds, to return the property to the company. The Boston and Montana was ordered to post bond that it would pay all damages adjudged due the plaintiffs in the future. The Court did not, however, discharge the receiver until June 8, 1900, when it ordered the lower court to discontinue the receivership as of that date.[15] As Hinds was not formally discharged, the B. and M. continued to be hampered by Heinze—for example, it could not legally align itself with its informal leadership, the Amalgamated.

The two hundred shares of Boston and Montana stock which MacGinniss and Forrester had bought (1898) was the weapon which Heinze used to frustrate the original plan of the Standard Oil coalition to form a copper trust that would complement its oil trust. H. H. Rogers's plot designated that Amalgamated would first formally acquire the Boston companies and then buy the holdings of Clark and Daly, before purchasing the mines of Michigan and Arizona. The tandem Boston and Montana cases dismembered that plan: the first suit by contesting the transfer to New York, and the second, involving Hinds, by postponing the B. and M.'s merger with Amalgamated.

The first case is the more significant. Instituted in 1898, it effectively bound the Boston properties for almost two years. During that period the Hinds receivership enforced the restriction of B. and M. activity. For this reason, Henry Rogers and his associates altered their original plan and, in May, 1899, purchased Marcus Daly's Anaconda Copper Mining Company.

---

[15]Anaconda *Standard*, November 2, 1902.

Daly dealt from a position of power in his negotiations with the Rogers coalition. He realized that the Rogers group required an immediate cornerstone for its projected copper trust and that, because of F. Augustus Heinze's litigation, the Boston and Montana was legally unavailable—although Rogers controlled both the Boston and Montana, and the Butte and Boston companies. Daly possessed another apparent advantage: Heinze's receiver, Thomas Hinds, was a former associate of Daly; perhaps Daly could influence Hinds' personal actions in the B. and M. litigation. As a result of this situation, Marcus Daly received *his* price for the Anaconda property; Daly was also designated the first president of the Amalgamated Copper Mining Company.

"During the summer preceding the legislative session of 1899, which elected William A. Clark to the United States Senate, Marcus Daly, H. H. Rogers and their associates had framed the incorporation of the Amalgamated Copper Company. Their first plans contemplated the purchase outright, either for cash, stock in the Amalgamated, or both, of all the properties on the Butte Hill which they might be able to acquire; and their entrance into the field was undoubtedly intended to serve tacit notice on all independent operators that it would be the part of wisdom to enter the alliance rather than be compelled to succumb after inevitable struggle."[16]

Otto Heinze's account of the situation complements Connolly's description:

"This decision of Clancy [appointing Hinds to be receiver] was absolutely in accordance with the laws of the State of Montana. Our opponents—recognizing that it might take a long while to unravel this situation and having made their plans in many different directions for the flotation of the Great Copper Trust (which was to rival the Standard Oil Company) and not being

---

[16]Connolly, "Fight," p. 5.

willing or ready to acknowledge that their foe, F. Augustus Heinze (whom they had constantly been belittling as hardly of any importance) had suddenly thrown a crowbar right into their plans—turned to Marcus Daly and, abandoning their original plan of making the Boston and Montana Company and the Butte and Boston Company the first units of their Copper Trust, made a deal with Daly, by which the Anaconda Company was to become the cornerstone of that trust.

"Marcus Daly knew the exact situation; his man, Thomas R. Hinds, was the receiver of the Boston Companies and Rogers and his associates were practically at his mercy. Daly told them what he would do, fixed his price—it is said, an enormous one —nominated himself for the presidency of the Amalgamated Copper Company (Rogers was originally to have been that) and told these wonderful men in New York exactly what they were to do and they, realizing their own position, met his views most cordially; and, thus, at the start, H. H. Rogers got a blow from F. Augustus which unsettled all of his original plans; he never forgave him."[17]

Otto Heinze's assessment of the effect of F. Augustus's litigation with the Boston and Montana Company is equally revealing.

"This was the first stone we threw into the path of the supposedly invincible Rogers, Rockefeller, Stillman combination. It was, indeed, quite a surprise to them. We knew exactly what we were doing, as Mr. Rogers, when he had his first meeting with Fritz (I was present at that meeting), told us what he intended to do in the formation of his worldwide copper trust. He was very pleasant and quite frank with us."[18]

The financial manipulation, however, which floated Amalgamated's stock at a private valuation of thirty-nine million dollars and a public appraisal of seventy-five million dollars was not a product

[17]O. C. Heinze MS., pp. 38-39.
[18]O. C. Heinze MS., p. 24.

of Marcus Daly's mind. He was widely known for his personal integrity. The sale of Amalgamated's stock was planned by Thomas W. Lawson, legendary Eastern manipulator, and was directed and approved by H. H. Rogers. The method used resembled the tactics which constantly enriched Standard Oil and established its independence in dealings with railroad companies and its own competitors.[19]

On July 23, 1901, John MacGinniss initiated another action in the Butte district court. He requested that the court appoint another receiver for the Boston and Montana Company, enjoin the Amalgamated from acquiring any control of the B. and M., and declare Amalgamated a trust or monopoly. Judge Edward Harney issued the necessary injunction and ordered the Boston and Montana to show cause why a receiver should not be named. Federal District Judge Hiram Knowles subsequently permitted (January, 1902) two Boston stockholders and two New York stockholders to become receiving parties with MacGinniss.[20] Amalgamated's attorneys legally forestalled the charge that the defendant firm was a trust or monopoly, but were forced to face the same charge in the later Parrot suit —with significantly different effects.

By means of the series of legal actions which F. Augustus Heinze directed against the Boston and Montana Mining Company, he was able to alter the Rogers-Standard Oil scheme to form a vast copper trust. F. A.'s attack was especially devastating, as it affected Amalgamated in its initial stage of development. The specific elements of Heinze's strategy in the Boston and Montana case were sufficiently successful that his legal staff employed similar tactics in the Parrot mine litigation (1903). In the two-year period between these cases, however, Amalgamated gained both economic strength and legal sagacity in Montana. The effect of the Parrot suit was to end F. Augustus Heinze's dramatic career in Butte.

---

[19]T. W. Lawson, *The Crime of Amalgamated*, Vol. I of *Frenzied Finance* (New York: Ridgeway-Thayer; 1905) pp. 283-375.

[20]*Engineering and Mining Journal*, LXXII, p. 614; as quoted in Raymer, *Montana*, I, pp. 490-491.

VII-B. Lawsuits:
The Parrot Case and the Shutdown of 1903

John MacGinniss and Daniel Lamm, minority stockholders in the Parrot Mining Company, instituted a suit against that firm in 1903. They charged that Amalgamated was a trust formed to control the supply of copper. The two plaintiffs cited the fact that the Parrot Mining Company, a direct subsidiary of Amalgamated, was managed for the benefit of the Amalgamated's other operating companies and against the interest of Parrot stockholders, who did not participate in the trust.[21]

On October 22, 1903, Judge William Clancy acted on the matter. He ruled that: 1) *the Amalgamated Copper Mining Company was a trust which had no lawful status in Montana;* 2) *therefore, Amalgamated's subordinate corporations were enjoined from paying dividends to the holding company.* F. Augustus had finally neutralized legally the mammoth copper trust, if only momentarily. To augment F. A.'s victory, Clancy also adjudged the Minnie Healy case on the same day. He ruled that the Heinze-Finlen agreement was binding and he awarded F. Augustus ownership of the property. Clancy's Healy ruling was subsequently sustained by the State Supreme Court (April 20, 1905). Of the two decisions, however, the Parrot judgment was the more immediately significant.

In retaliation for Judge Clancy's Parrot decision, the Amalgamated nobly declared that, as the court endeavored to outlaw it, it would cease all activity in Montana. Amalgamated closed all of its Montana operations, except its newspapers, on October 22, 1903. Just as the winter season approached, 11,000 Butte men who worked for Amalgamated found themselves unemployed. By 1903 the Standard Oil trust had extensive business affiliations in Montana—from lumber companies to railroads to retail stores; most of those concerns which were not partially or wholly owned by Amalgamated, relied on the trust to purchase their products. Three-fourths of the state's wage earners were unemployed within a week.

---

[21]Connolly, "Minnie Healy," p. 328.

There was a facet to Amalgamated's shutdown other than its attempt to turn public sentiment against F. Augustus Heinze and, thereby, destroy one basis of his Montana operations. The company possessed a huge supply of copper—reputedly 150,000,000 pounds —which it was withholding from the market to maintain the copper price at seventeen cents per pound. An extensive Butte shutdown would reduce copper production and, therefore, the amount of copper on the world market. Amalgamated could then sell its reserve supply at a figure which it could quote.[22] This "secret" was generally recognized in the financial centers of the copper world. It was not realized within Montana, where the majority of families faced the more immediate problems of food and shelter and where the Amalgamated-controlled press assessed the shutdown only as an unfortunate situation forced upon the company by F. A.'s dastardly legal maneuvers.[23]

---

[22]O. C. Heinze MS., p. 38.

[23]The use of Montana newspapers to control or shape the information disseminated to the state's citizens is a facet integral to the entire Copper War (1888-1906). In the first phase of the War, W. A. Clark's personal organ, the Butte *Miner*, directly and vitriolically opposed the Marcus Daly-owned Anaconda *Standard* on virtually all issues.

Prior to his success in Butte, F. Augustus Heinze recognized the advantages of possessing one's own newspaper. He effected his coup against the Canadian Pacific largely by means of his Rossland (British Columbia) *Miner*. In 1899 F. Augustus installed his *Miner* editor, Pat O'Farrell, as the executive editor of his Butte paper, the *Reveille*. In the same year, the *Standard* became an Amalgamated publication, purchased with the rest of Daly's Montana properties. The *Standard* was the nucleus of Amalgamated's extensive Montana press chain. Early in the second phase of the Copper War, the *Reveille* joined the Butte *Miner* against the *Standard*.

After Clark's defection (1901) and during the height of the second phase of the War, the *Reveille* stood virtually alone against a network of dailies and weeklies which smothered the state. Standard Oil had also learned the vital importance of formulating public opinion by manipulating news. A September, 1902, alignment of some state newspapers appeared in the *Reveille:*

	Anaconda *Standard*
	Butte *Inter-Mountain*
	Dillon *Tribune*
	Great Falls *Leader*
	(24 lesser Republican papers)
	Butte *Miner*
Heinze's *Reveille* vs. Amalgamated's:	Virginia City *Madisonian*
	Missoula *Democrat*
	Bozeman *Chronicle*
	Dillon *Examiner*
	Great Falls *Tribune*
	Helena *Independent*
	(6 lesser Democratic papers)

F. Augustus agreed that ulterior motives forced the massive shutdown. On the day of the closure, he issued a statement.

"The action of the Amalgamated Copper Mining Company in ordering a shutdown of all mines of Butte controlled by their subsidiary companies has no actual connection with the decision handed down by Judge Clancy.

"His order does not necessitate a closedown. As far as the receivership suit against the Butte company is concerned, there has been no change for two years past. An application for appointment of a receiver has been pending that long and today's order simply puts the matter in shape for the Supreme Court.

"In my opinion this evening's closedown is due entirely to an attempt to affect the price of Amalgamated copper stock in Wall Street. Mr. H. H. Rogers and his many associates in the Standard Oil Company thought Judge Clancy would appoint a receiver.

"Mr. Thomas Lawson of Boston, one of the chief brokers of Amalgamated stock, yesterday issued a bulletin there that a receiver would be appointed. All preparations had been made to close down in line with the threats heard in the city for several weeks past.

"The decision came to them in the nature of a surprise. They had been selling stocks in anticipation of a big drop in the quotation, when they could buy back much lower than they sold. Under these circumstances, as they actually occurred, it became necessary to do something that would bring conditions in the stock market as nearly as possible corresponding to what would

---

After 1901 F. Augustus was simply outclassed and outfinanced by the massive trust in the newspaper realm of the Copper War—just as he was in most other facets of the confrontation during this period. Amalgamated's control of the state press is probably best exemplified by the Shutdown of 1903 and its subsequent developments. Although a degree of exasperated anger existed, there was generally popular support for the extra legislative session and for the acts which it passed. The majority of unemployed Montanans, who were allowed to hear only Amalgamated's side of the controversy, began to react favorably to the saturation. The *Reveille* fell with Heinze to the Amalgamated in 1906. There was no serious threat to Amalgamated's newspaper chain or to its control of the news well into the twentieth century.

have occurred if Clancy had acted with less moderation, and so when Mr. Rogers was advised of the occurrences at the court-house he immediately sent word to Brother Scallon to close down everything."[24]

Amalgamated may have profited from the partial sale of its copper reserves, but the Montana wage earner did not make a cent after the shutdown. To compound the impact on the Butte miner, there had been a closure during the previous June which had similarly severed his source of income. The situation became critical for the Montana citizen: his expenses were increased because the new school term demanded clothes, shoes, and supplies for his children; the approach of the cold weather also required purchases of coal and other fuel. In addition he had to meet his regular expenses for rent and food. Amalgamated had the economic whip hand and began its move to ruin F. Augustus Heinze.

Amalgamated—joined by Senator W. A. Clark for no reason, un-less personal animosity, or jealously of Heinze, or the desire to appear the Good Samaritan to the miners—offered, on October 25, to lend sufficient funds to the Miners' Union to buy the shares of stock held by Lamm and MacGinniss at two-and-one-half times that price which they had paid for them. The union would, of course, be forced to agree not to prosecute the suits. MacGinniss preferred to allow F. Augustus to handle the matter; he left Butte so no offer could be made to him. When the union committee of five approached Heinze, F. A. stated, "I will give you my answer at four o'clock tomorrow from the courthouse steps."[25]

F. Augustus Heinze addressed the assembly on the afternoon of October 26, 1903, promptly at four o'clock, from the steps of the Silver Bow County Courthouse. Tall, handsome, a superior actor and fine speaker, Heinze effectively read the highly emotional situation. The occasion was tinged with genuine sentiment for him: his roots

---

[24]Butte *Miner*, October 23, 1903. "Brother Scallon," is a reference to William Scallon, the managing director of Amalgamated's operations in Butte.

[25]Connolly, "Minnie Healy," p. 328.

were deep in Butte and his expulsion, Amalgamated's avowed objective, would be pleasant neither for him, nor for his attackers.

"Heinze's speech from the steps of the Butte courthouse has been described in most of the books about the great copper war, but the courage and determination it took on the part of F. Augustus to step up before a mob of ten thousand miners desperate and armed, nearly every one of them, has not been stressed. One drunken miner and one single shot would have started the bloodiest kind of a battle and Fritz would have probably been one of the first victims. There were a thousand of our miners there, all armed to the teeth, but he himself carried no weapon of any kind. The fact is that during his residence in Butte he never went armed and, although many times threats went around that his enemies were going to shoot him, he was never attacked; he had superb courage both mentally and physically and never any fear of anybody or anything."[26]

There were between ten and twelve thousand men employed in Butte at this time and, since the shutdown had kept them from work, most of them appeared to hear F. Augustus's oration. The best paragraphs of F. A.'s speech, pertinent to content and emotional appeal, reveal overtones of William Jennings Bryan's "Cross of Gold" masterpiece.[27] An excerpt best illustrates the personality of the orator and the tone of his address.

"My friends, I could have met the committee of the miners' union in my private office, but as a free American citizen, rely-

---

[26]O. C. Heinze MS., p. 39. Butte residents, especially older miners, deny that there were many armed men in the crowd and that the Heinze thousand were carrying guns. Guns and bullets were not common possessions of miners. For the most part, Butte miners were not adventurers, but family men who would consider the possible consequences before firing to kill. Nor was the situation worth such violence to them individually, although it was temporarily critical. If Heinze were unarmed, he was, in that respect, no different from his average listener.

[27]Bryan's speech would apply to the Butte situation not only in tone, but also in content. Note, for example, the defiant peroration of the address: "You shall not press down upon the brow of labor the crown of thorns, you shall not crucify mankind upon a cross of gold."

ing on the justice of his cause and not afraid to place it before the people of Silver Bow County, I preferred to meet that committee here in public.

"The statement has been made that I am hounding the Amalgamated Copper Company in the courts of this county and state. Six or seven years ago, these gentlemen came to me and said, 'You must leave the state. If you don't get out, we'll drive you out.' They have been trying to do that ever since. They have injunctions against me at this time which, if removed, would make it possible for me to give employment to two thousand extra men. They have fought me in every possible way. They have beaten me a dozen times in one way or another, and I have taken my defeats like a man. I fought my own battles, explaining them to the public when I had the opportunity, and asking their support at the polls. I will stake my life on the statement that there are, within the sound of my voice, a hundred men, now in my employ, who have been offered bribes ranging all the way from a thousand to ten thousand dollars to commit perjury for the purpose of defeating me in my lawsuits.

"My friends, the Amalgamated Copper Company, in its influence and functions, and the control it has over the commercial and economic affairs of this state, is the greatest menace that any community could possibly have within its boundaries. That stock of Mr. MacGinniss is a bulwark to protect you and others here in Butte, miners and merchants, from the aggressions of the most unscrupulous of corporations, the Standard Oil Company. Rockefeller and Rogers have filched the oil wells of America and in doing so they have trampled on every law, human and divine. They have ruthlessly crushed every obstacle in their path. They have wrecked railroad trains and put the torch to oil refineries owned by their competitors. They entered into a conspiracy with railroads, by which competitors were ruined and bankrupted. Sometimes they were caught in the act, but they bought the judges and saved themselves from prison stripes and punishment. The same Rockefeller and the same Rogers are seeking to control the executive, the judiciary, and the legislature of Montana.

"I am responsible for John MacGinniss leaving the state. Mr. MacGinniss is not going to let any man point a gun at his breast and say, 'If you don't take this price, you take your life in your hands.'

"It is true that I am deeply interested in the outcome of this struggle. My name, my fortune, and my honor are at stake. All have been assailed. You have known me these many years. You are my friends, my associates, and I defy any man among you to point to a single instance where I did one of you a wrong. These people are my enemies, fierce, bitter, implacable; but they are your enemies, too. If they crush me today, they will crush you tomorrow. They will cut your wages and raise the tariff in the company stores on every bite you eat and every rag you wear. They will force you to dwell in Standard Oil houses while you live, and they will bury you in Standard Oil coffins when you die. Their tools and minions are here now, striving to build up another trust whose record is already infamous. Let them win and they will inaugurate conditions in Montana that will blast its fairest prospect and make its very name hateful to those who love liberty. They have crushed the miners of Colorado because those miners had no one to stand for their rights.

"In this battle to save the state from the minions of the Rockefellers and the piracy of Standard Oil, you and I are partners and allies. We stand or fall together."[28]

Heinze further explained his case and advanced five points for the Amalgamated to meet—in return for which he would drop the Mac-Ginniss-Lamm action against the Parrot Company. These points were: 1) that the MacGinniss-Lamm shares would be sold to the Union, not at the price offered, but at cost, plus the interest on the

---

[28]Connolly, "Minnie Healy," pp. 330-331. Heinze's "courthouse speech" was not entirely virginal; sections of it were lifted from a speech which F. Augustus had made on November 6, 1900.

investment—provided the Amalgamated would pay the cost in Heinze's lawsuits; 2) that the Amalgamated would sell to him, at its original cost, the five thirty-sixths it had in the Nipper mine, the other shares already being his; 3) that the Amalgamated keep its Butte mines operating for at least a year; 4) that the Amalgamated pay the existing wage scale for three years; 5) that, if the Amalgamated failed to keep this agreement, a board would be appointed to arbitrate the dispute.[29]

Amalgamated had no intention of settlement on Heinze's terms. The trust determined to win—and win it did, by securing an extra session of the state's legislature. Amalgamated bluntly bargained with Montana's reluctant Governor Joseph K. Toole: Toole would call a special legislative session; the legislature would pass a law providing the guaranty of a fair trial in civil suits; Amalgamated would end the shutdown.[30] Governor Toole stated that he would rather continue the shutdown indefinitely than establish the precedent of a corporation dictating the conditions for a special legislative session. Toole, asked, however, if Amalgamated would resume work when the session was called, rather than when the legislature passed the acts which Amalgamated demanded. Amalgamated agreed and Toole immediately convened (November 10) the legislators; work resumed in Amalgamated's properties.

The legislature passed laws which allowed the Montana Supreme Court to review cases in equity and which permitted a change of venue, or the transfer of any case to another judge if either party felt it would not receive fair treatment from the presiding judge.[31] The legislative session was legal, but the evil that Governor Toole feared was not eliminated. Henry Rogers, Standard Oil, and Amalgamated dramatically demonstrated that their economic power in Montana could readily be converted to political strength.

[29]Connolly, "Minnie Healy," p. 332; see also: Butte *Miner*, October 26, 1903.

[30]W. McLeod Raine, "The Fight for Copper," *Leslie's Magazine* (February, 1904), p. 28.

[31]*Laws, Resolutions and Memorials of the State of Montana Passed at the Eighth Regular and Extraordinary Sessions of the Legislative Assembly, 1903* (Helena: State Publishing Co.; 1903), c. XXXXII, p. 61-65.

The special legislative session of 1903 signaled the ultimate defeat of F. Augustus Heinze in the War of the Copper Kings; the session was Heinze's last great stand against Standard Oil's strength of capital and strategy. Even with extensive credit reserves, no one could singly battle a force that could dictate so openly and boldly to a state's elected governor and its legislators. While the legislature was in session, however, Heinze led the opponents of Amalgamated in forming the Anti-Trust political party in Helena. Six hundred delegates—cattlemen, sheepmen, miners, lumbermen, businessmen, railroad workers —attended the convention.[32] It planned to campaign against the Standard Oil-Amalgamated trust, but was embarrassingly unsuccessful.

Thomas Lawson, often a Standard Oil spokesman, summarized the events of the autumn of 1903.

"We have demonstrated that the 70,000 voters in Montana who are dependent upon Amalgamated can be made to think through their stomachs better than through their brains. We have solved the Heinze problem by the only reasonable method."[33]

Ruthless as the remark is, it demonstrates that Heinze had been a substantial hindrance to Standard Oil's Montana manipulations; it concedes that F. A. had forced Amalgamated to desperate measures. To F. Augustus Heinze, however, such recognition was small consolation.

---

[32]Raine, "Fight," p. 28.

[33]*Reveille*, October 28, 1903.

Chapter VIII

WARFARE WITHIN THE HILL

The second phase of the War of the Copper Kings (1896-1906) pitted F. Augustus Heinze against the Amalgamated and its operating companies in various spheres. The most physically violent of these contests occurred deep within the Butte Hill between Heinze's miners and those men who worked for the Amalgamated. In two specific instances, the Michael Davitt and Minnie Healy properties, miners faced each other with any available weapon—including dynamite and water stores—to secure rich veins. Underground warfare was not uncommon from 1900 to 1904; several deaths were attributed directly to the fighting and innumerable physical injuries were inflicted on the participants.

The underground combat complemented the constant legal battles in the courts of the state and the nation. In both cases virtually any tactic was permitted and the lives of men were ruined by battle. F. Augustus Heinze proved as adept a general in the mine fighting as in the courts: he could attack quickly and decisively, hold a line against opposing Amalgamated forces with strength, utilize the surprise tactic effectively, and render the battlefield useless to his enemy when necessary. In some respects, F. Augustus was more successful in the underground warfare than he was in the "more dignified" battles on the surface.

VIII-A. Warfare in the Mines:
The Michael Davitt

Underground combat involving F. Augustus Heinze first resulted from Michael Davitt litigation. By the spring of 1900, juries had twice decided the Davitt case in Heinze's favor.[1] Until a higher court could finally determine the legal right to the disputed ores, however, both Heinze and the Amalgamated-controlled Boston and Montana Company were enjoined from mining the Davitt. In this situation the Johnstown Mining Company stratagem was applied (1900)—Heinze assigned his Montana Ore Purchasing Company rights to the Johnstown.[2] Under the auspices of the Johnstown Company, which was not restrained by any court order, Heinze's men periodically extracted ore from 1900 to 1904. The mining periods precipitated several phases of underground warfare.

Operating from the Rarus, the Johnstown miners erected large barriers across every opening which could admit miners from the Amalgamated's Pennsylvania mine. They then mined openings into the enjoined ore veins of the Davitt. These openings were a maze of passageways whose terminal point no one could determine without following their labyrinthine course; they appeared to be only corridors within the Rarus. After ore was extracted from the Davitt sections and surfaced through the Rarus shaft, Heinze's miners filled the excavation with unmarketable rock and cemented the surface walls to seal the waste. This work could not be done in silence; the blasting, the excavation, and the rapid movement could not remain a secret. Amalgamated, already suspicious of F. Augustus, acted quickly when it received reports from its Pennsylvania miners of the extensive, twenty-four hour activity which they could hear in the enjoined sections.[3]

In 1901 a federal court granted permission for Amalgamated to

---

[1]Please see Section VI-F for a more comprehensive discussion of the Davitt litigation.

[2]Connolly, "Fight," p. 222. Please see Section VI-A for a detailed presentation of the Johnstown Mining Company stratagem.

[3]Connolly, "Fight," pp. 222-224.

inspect the Michael Davitt workings. Heinze therefore doubled his force of men to speed the removal of the ore, through the Rarus shaft, to his smelter. His workers refused to allow Amalgamated's inspectors to enter the mine or to acknowledge the court order. The United States court that issued the permit of inspection had meanwhile adjourned, so Amalgamated's advantage was nullified.

Amalgamated, no more scrupulous than Heinze, began mining from the Pennsylvania into the Davitt. A confrontation was inevitable; when it came, the workers of the opposing sides battled. Initially the Johnstown miners used the huge pipes which carried air into the depths of the Butte mines. Under Heinze's direction, they filled the pipes with slaked lime and repulsed the opposition's sally. Temporarily halted, the Pennsylvania crew retreated. It soon returned with high-pressure hoses for water and steam with which to neutralize the lime dust and to make the contest unpleasant for the foe. Falling debris, buckets of lime and rock, burning rags and electrified turn sheets became weapons.[4]

Simultaneously, F. Augustus's men mined the Davitt. Amalgamated's directors and legal staff chafed because of their inability to keep Heinze from removing the ore and because they could not secure adequate evidence of the quantity of ore being removed. "Stolen" was Amalgamated's word for the action; "mined" was Heinze's term, because of the two jury verdicts in his favor. A mile and one-half of the subterranean network continued to be the battlefield.[5]

Amalgamated attempted to shift the battlefield to the courts. Its lawyers asked Federal Judge Hiram Knowles to give them at least an equal chance. Their chief attorney, John F. Forbis, made an appeal to the court.

"There are eight bulkheads and if we are compelled to force our way underground, it will be necessary for us to run a blockade. By a cunning move, they have encroached upon the Michael Davitt ore bodies, and will leave the mine a shell unless relief

---

[4]Butte *Miner*, January 13, 1904.
[5]Butte *Miner*, January 13, 1904.

is shortly granted. If we cannot stop this, the Government might better abandon its courts and leave litigants to determine their rights by the shotgun. Your Honor should dissolve the order enjoining us from working this ground, and let us go in there and fight for our ore."[6]

Judge Knowles agreed, but Heinze could not be found to serve the court order on him. The United States Court of Appeals finally sent Judge James H. Beatty of Idaho to Montana to hear the case. He fined F. Augustus $20,000 and his superintendents, J. H. Trerise and Alfred Frank, $500 each for contempt of Judge Knowles's order. He gave the defendants a choice: pay the fines and go to jail, or admit Amalgamated's inspectors.[7]

In 1903 the inspectors were admitted, led by H. V. Mitchell, Amalgamated's leading geologist. The examiners reported that, at one location alone, ore valued at $300,000 was removed, and that the richest fissures of the Michael Davitt were gutted.[8] Before the inspectors could measure the exact loss of ore, however, Heinze's miners dynamited the basically disputed section.[9]

> "Above ground, in the courts and in the markets, Amalgamated was crowding full sail into its warfare against him [Heinze], injuring his credit wherever possible and setting afloat, through the many channels in which it was powerful, constant rumors of his impending insolvency."[10]

---

[6]Connolly, "Fight," p. 225.

[7]Connolly, "Fight," p. 225.

[8]In view of the subsequent production from the mines which Amalgamated purchased from Heinze and the total production from the Butte Hill, it is unlikely that any mine by 1903 was left "a shell," as Forbis maintained. In fact, on the day that the Heinze sale to Amalgamated was reported (February 14, 1906), the Anaconda *Standard* (an Amalgamated paper) stated that there were "some tremendous rich ore bodies" in the Davitt and also that the total ore reserves released by injunctions being voided was fifty million dollars or more.

[9]Destroying evidence by exploding a section of a mine was a tactic utilized by Amalgamated as well as by Heinze. Connolly ("Fight," p. 10) reports that Amalgamated miners went into the Heinze property, took ore in violation of an injunction, and dynamited the raided section. Amalgamated's officials were subsequently fined by Judge William H. Hunt of the United States Court of Appeals for violating the court order.

[10]Connolly, "Fight," p. 225.

The combat continued sporadically through 1903. It again reached an extreme when the Amalgamated, under Knowles's permit, attempted to discover how its rich Enargite vein in the Michael Davitt had fared. In the fighting, two Pennsylvania miners, Samuel Oleson and Fredolin Divel, were killed by a blast on January 1, 1904. The Amalgamated charged that Johnstown miners caused the explosion; Heinze maintained that it was the work of the Pennsylvania's men.[11]

Judge Beatty returned to Montana to hear the testimony and to assess Heinze's continued activity in defiance of Judge Knowles's order. Beatty refused to accept F. Augustus's claim that the Johnstown Company, which executed the extraction, was not enjoined. He blistered the Heinze legal staff.

"I cannot think of the Johnstown Mining Company and the Montana Ore Purchasing Company as two independent companies, working each in its own separate interest. They were working harmoniously together, and with such harmony as to indicate that they were under the same influence, controlled by the same power. In thirty-two years of experience, I have never known of so flagrant a violation of a court's order."[12]

Judge Knowles fined F. Augustus $20,000 and his superintendents $1,000 each—a minute amount in comparison to F. A.'s profit from the extracted ore. The judge also announced that any further contempt of court orders would precipitate larger fines and imprisonment. This decision ended the warfare in the Davitt and rendered the mine's ore enjoined until 1906, when the Amalgamated's purchase of Heinze's properties nullified all pending litigation.[13]

---

[11]Connolly ("Fight," p. 226) states that the widow of one of the miners subsequently received a judgment of $25,000 against F. Augustus. Otto Heinze states that this report is incorrect, to his knowledge; he classifies the charge (O. C. Heinze MS., p. 40) as ". . . another of the lies that were circulated by our enemies."

[12]Connolly, "Fight," p. 226.

[13]Anaconda *Standard*, February 14, 1906.

VIII-B. Warfare in the Mines:
The Minnie Healy

Underground combat in the Minnie Healy mine was equally spectacular and dangerous as that in the Michael Davitt. Amalgamated was enjoined (1901) by Judge William Clancy from extracting ore in a particularly rich section of the Heinze-controlled Healy called the Firing Line. Amalgamated wished to assure that, if Heinze did receive the court decision, he would get no ore. The trust, therefore, mined the area from its adjacent Leonard claim by the shrewd device of issuing leases to individuals for parts of the enjoined bodies.[14] In this Firing Line, between the Leonard and the Minnie Healy, Amalgamated forces would explode any crosscut as soon as Heinze's miners opened it. On one occasion when Clancy ruled a lucrative stretch of vein to F. Augustus, Amalgamated's miners, on signal from the company's office building, dynamited and destroyed the entire section. At the conclusion of the litigation, the section ironically was recognized as Amalgamated's.[15]

Under F. A. Heinze's direction, his miners resorted to pouring water from huge hoses into Amalgamated's Leonard territory. The trust's tacticians, however, were equally resourceful in skullduggery. They built a dam within the mine, filled it, and then drilled a hole through which they released the water into the Minnie Healy shaft. Word swept through Butte that the Healy's miners were being drowned. A crowd gathered at the shaft which was primarily composed of the horrified and distraught wives and children of the men in the mine. Heinze, however, had been warned to evacuate the miners and all survived.

This encounter marked the climax of the Healy's subterranean war. The likelihood of death on a major scale, of a wholesale loss of life, became imminent. On the following day the opponents arranged a gentleman's agreement and effected a truce. This action eliminated

---

[14]Connolly, "Fight," p. 220.
[15]Connolly, "Fight," pp. 227-228.

personal combat in the Healy and minimized the tension which had gripped the city.[16]

VIII-C. *Warfare in the Mines:* Other Incidents

Some minor events, which were part of the mosaic of war in the earth, reveal that the mine contest had many facets. In the summer of 1902, fire destroyed the Heinze concentrator in Meaderville.[17] As a result, F. Augustus leased the concentrator of the Boston and Bay State Mining Company at Basin (October, 1902); he negotiated an option to buy it within four years at $345,000.[18] F. A. subsequently reduced first-class ore at the Montana Ore Purchasing Company smelter and sent the low-grade ore to Basin.[19] The pertinent newspaper accounts of the fire do not admit foul play as a cause; Otto Heinze however, refers to an earlier, unsuccessful attempt to burn the smelter.

"There are some things, which were suddenly sprung, which were very serious and had to be met immediately and which the public accounts do not mention; as for instance, the fire in our smelter one cold winter night. Informed of the blaze at four different places in our smelter, F. A. rushed there and found that there was no water to be gotten from the city water mains. The water supply had been cut off; only attaching our hose to our pumps in the Rarus mine enabled him to succeed in putting out the fire and saving our smelter; as it was, considerable damage was done, which it took some time to repair. We never found out who set the fires."[20]

---

[16]Connolly, "Fight," p. 228.

[17]Anaconda *Standard*, December 21, 1902.

[18]Anaconda *Standard*, October 9, 1902.

[19]Anaconda *Standard*, December 21, 1902.

[20]O. C. Heinze MS., p. 41.

Otto Heinze relates other unpleasant, serious matters which arose during the period of underground warfare.

"Our letters and telegrams were opened, our miners and foremen were frequently bribed to mine waste instead of ore and to lose the vein. Every mine we bought was attacked, the same with every company we formed. Women would appear making all sorts of claims, breach of promise, etc., who were entire strangers to F. A. and whom he had never seen before; rumors were constantly circulated that F. A. was bankrupt and would collapse. In fact, it was the regular propaganda as now used by all the nations in war. Efforts were made to bribe judges; laws were introduced in the legislature and also in Congress in Washington to affect our title or litigations. In short, anything and everything went on; it was an endless string of calumny and hatred and never-ending, garbled and entirely false reports in the newspapers all over the country."[21]

---

[21]O. C. Heinze MS., p. 41.

Chapter IX

F. AUGUSTUS HEINZE, POLITICIAN

F. Augustus Heinze was a party to many lawsuits and underground battles—both of which required a significant degree of general public support, if he was to be successful. It was natural, therefore, that he engage in politics. F. Augustus did not, however, have any part in one of Montana's most glaringly corrupt political farces, the election of W. A. Clark to the United States Senate by the 1899 legislature.[1] In his political forays, Heinze was primarily concerned with the election of district court judges, justices of the State Supreme Court and, occasionally, members of the state legislature. F. A. nevertheless exerted his greatest influence, and received his most satisfactory results, within Silver Bow County. Heinze's enemies were most prone to the claim that especially District Court Judge William Clancy was his vassal. These men, however, ignored the fact that Marcus Daly— and not F. Augustus Heinze—was responsible for the bargain which effected Clancy's initial election victory in 1896.[2] F. Augustus, in fact, took no active part in the campaign of that year or in the 1898 campaign. It was in 1900 that Heinze moved into the political arena with force; he retained that strength through three campaigns.

---

[1] C. P. Connolly, *The Devil Learns to Vote* (New York: Covici Friede; 1938), pp. 121-212; an excellent monograph which devotes the cited section to the election of W. A. Clark and the subsequent Senate investigation.

[2] Connolly, *Devil*, p. 185. See also Connolly, "Fight," p. 14.

IX-A. Politics:
The Campaign of 1900

Heinze made his debut as an effective manipulator of candidates, especially district judges, in 1900. Senate aspirant W. A. Clark was equally as intensely interested in this campaign: he desired himself elected in a manner that could not be contested in Washington. Each in the interest of his own objectives, Heinze and Clark joined forces. Both agreed on their prime opponent: the Amalgamated Copper Mining Company or, more correctly, the Standard Oil Company. Their basic, insurmountable tactic with which to gain votes in 1900 was the grant of the eight-hour day in their own mines and smelters. They emphasized by contrast the difficulties of Amalgamated's miners whose request for the shorter day had been rejected by the trust's New York office. Heinze and Clark appealed to Butte's clerks and other workers, in addition to the city's miners, by advocating a shorter day for all mining company employees. Particular jibes were also directed at the D. J. Hennessy Mercantile Company, an Amalgamated subsidiary, which had refused the clerks' request for shorter working hours.[3]

All those factions that opposed Standard Oil's practices and personnel became part of the Fusionist Party which championed the Heinze-Clark ticket in Silver Bow County during the 1900 campaign. The Fusionists were diverse: Republicans who did not like trusts; Democrats who, for one reason or another, did not like local Democratic leader Marcus Daly; surviving Populists; advocates of the eight-hour day; and the undecided who liked the dramatic show which Heinze and Clark staged. F. Augustus personally carried the burden of the fight, giving stump speeches throughout the state.

During the 1900 campaign, Heinze's newspaper, the *Reveille*, was read widely. Its relentless theme was an attack on Standard Oil and on Amalgamated, as its bastard child. Pat O'Farrell, who had written for F. Augustus's Rossland (British Columbia) *Miner*, edited the

---

[3]Connolly, "Fight," p. 11.

paper and penned most of its virulent articles. Otto Heinze was happy neither with O'Farrell nor with his methods.

"The hatred engendered by the savage attacks made in that campaign are still, I believe, responsible for much of the hatred against F. Augustus, although P. A. O'Farrell wrote most of the articles."[4]

Part of the *Reveille's* consistent attack on Standard Oil was a series of woodcuts. These early cartoons invariably depicted the weary Amalgamated miner toiling in the "hot boxes" of the earth for ten long hours, while Heinze and Clark miners had an eight-hour shift at the same wage that they received previously for ten hours.[5]

The campaign was no small carnival—it was a huge, three-ring circus. Its vaudevillian features were directed by W. A. Thompson, formerly of the Boston Lyric Opera Company. Cissy Loftus, the sweetheart of the moment, was brought to Butte at considerable expense to sing at election rallies. Everyone liked the rhythm and ridicule of her anti-Standard Oil parody of "The Wearing of the Green:" "We must down the kerosene boys / We must down the kerosene." F. Augustus also addressed these rallies, sometimes in English, other times in German, both of which he spoke fluently.

"[He] told with real oratorical genius the story of Amalgamated's attempt to drive him from the state. When he had concluded, men who did not dare to cheer for fear of losing their bread went away full of unyielding antagonism to Standard Oil. They had the Australian ballot and they meant to use it."[6]

No political orator would defend Standard Oil or Amalgamated because of the popular feeling; rather, Amalgamated's speakers condemned Heinze for looting the company's property. This charge F. Augustus answered with subtle and double-edged references to Amalgamated's "honesty" and with the assertion that, if he did not attack

---

[4]O. C. Heinze MS., p. 34.
[5]*Reveille*, September-November, 1900.
[6]Connolly, "Fight," p. 12.

Amalgamated in every quarter, he would soon find himself without wealth and the population without a champion.

" 'Drive Standard Oil out of the State' became the rallying cry. . . . So masterfully had Heinze arrayed facts against Standard Oil, that his larceny of Amalgamated ores was forgiven in the belief that he was fighting a battle royal against a coterie of public enemies and judicial bribers, and was therefore justified in the use of any weapons. The public eye was focused on the young, daring, resourceful freebooter. They little cared how selfish his motives might be—his fight was their fight. They admired his boldness and sympathized with his unequal struggle against a powerful clique that had forced so many other struggling competitors to walk the plank."[7]

Heinze and Clark won the November election overwhelmingly. This result signified that at the polls Amalgamated's men had cast their votes for the Heinze-Clark Fusionist slate. Clark was assured that those legislative candidates elected would give him the "vindication" he sought. F. Augustus secured the Butte district judgeships for Edward Harney, William Clancy, and John D. McClernan. Such an elaborate, extensive campaign, however, was expensive.

"It is claimed that Clark put up a great deal of money . . . but F. A. put up an awful lot of money also; maybe not so much as Clark, but Heinze never was a man to let the other fellow do all the paying. He always did his share and usually a great deal more, frequently all."[8]

In addition to securing the election of the judges he desired, F. Augustus accelerated social legislation in Montana. The first major bill passed by the Seventh Legislative Assembly (1901) provided an eight-hour day in mining and smelting. Another bill—precipitated by Heinze's contemptuous description of the "company store" during

---

[7]Connolly, "Fight," pp. 12-13.
[8]O. C. Heinze MS., p. 23.

the campaign—made it illegal for workers to be paid in anything but real money, thus outlawing script.[9] The Heinze-Clark speeches and the Fusionist platform also advocated two elements of direct legislation—the initiative and the referendum—which became constitutional in Montana in November, 1906. F. Augustus Heinze supported these two measures vociferously in the campaign of 1902, possibly his most successful foray into politics.

IX-B. Politics:
The Campaign of 1902

The campaign of 1902 was momentous for F. Augustus Heinze, but it also presented some problems.

"That campaign showed politicians in other states how these large combinations of capital could be curbed and defeated. It was necessary to have a man brave enough to face these predatory interests, publish the facts ruthlessly, give the public all the necessary information on which the charges were based and the majority of voters would inevitably respond at the polls. I may even say that the eyes of the entire United States were directed by this campaign to Montana, but, of course, it cost us a fearful amount of money. We halved the expenses of the 1900 campaign with Clark; in the campaign of 1902 we not only had to fight his well-known methods but also those of H. H. Rogers, which were not less well-known."[10]

Throughout the month prior to election day (November 4, 1902), the Anaconda *Standard*—originally a Daly enterprise but, after 1899, Amalgamated's prime mouthpiece—prophesied the victory of the

---

[9] *Laws, Resolutions and Memorials of the State of Montana Passed at the Seventh Regular Session of the Legislative Assembly, 1901* (Helena: State Publishing Co.; 1901), H. B. 1, p. 62; S. B. 85, p. 147.

[10] O. C. Heinze MS., p. 34. Proof that Otto is correct in referring to the national interest in the election is the telegram of congratulation from C. W. Barron, head of the Boston News Bureau, which he sent to F. Augustus in November, 1902: "My sincerest congratulations upon your victory, the greatest of the national election and the greatest defeat of the most dangerous industrial conspiracy lawless millionaires ever planned." (M. O. P. C. Telegram File, November 6, 1902.)

Democrats and the defeat of the Fusionists and Republicans. Headlines, degrogatory cartoons, and sneering accounts of Heinze's campaign were featured. The cartoons always represented F. Augustus in a top hat and tailed coat; his nose was beak-like and he was endlessly puffing a huge cigar.

A full-page Sunday cartoon sequence showed Heinze dreaming blissfully of the election; its successive pictures depicted him being brought favorable court decisions and several mines. It then concluded with his unpleasant awakening to discover that the November 5 headline reported an election victory in landslide proportions for Amalgamated's slate. The front-page cartoon of October 2, 1902, depicted voters rushing in large numbers to a big tent on a circus grounds which represented the Democratic Party, while F. Augustus vainly hawked tickets to the "Heinze side show." On October 18, the *Standard's* artist pictured F. A. in the boxing ring, knocked out by Montana's State Democracy; it was entitled, "The Stars Heinze Will See Next November." In a derisive feature story in the October 6 edition of the same paper, Heinze's party was called by the ludicrous name of the "Heinzeantitrustboltingdemocraticlaborpopulist ticket."

A principal development on the 1902 Montana political scene was Senator Clark's affiliation with the Amalgamated. Clark was heavily indebted to Heinze for the campaign results of 1900 which made possible the achievement of his burning ambition to be United States Senator from Montana. Clark had little of the political skill which F. Augustus demonstrated, nor was he as popular a speaker as Heinze. In their joint campaign of 1900, F. A. was the one who secured votes, the campaigner par excellence, the "Napoleon of Politics," as the *Standard* jeered. Almost immediately following the election, however, Clark entered the Amalgamated camp. He explained this repudiation to Heinze by saying that Henry H. Rogers had threatened to unseat him in the Senate, if he did not desert F. Augustus. Clark believed that Rogers was not bluffing when he asserted that he controlled thirty Senators in Washington.[11]

---

[11] O. C. Heinze MS., p. 33. See also Connolly, "Fight," p. 9.

F. Augustus Heinze (1889), upon graduation from the Columbia School of Mines and immediately prior to his arrival in Butte.

All illustrations courtesy of Montana Historical Society

Butte from the Southwest, circa 1890: Note the haze and lack of vegetation—the effects of the reverberating concentration method.

Butte from the West, circa 1900: After F. Augustus Heinze had pioneered the cupola concentration method.

Typical Butte mining crew, 1890's.

Use of the revolutionary compressed-air drill in the Butte Hill.

F. Augustus Heinze (right) mapping battle strategy with one of his mining engineers, George H. Robinson.

F. Augustus Heinze's "independent," M. O. P. C. smelter.

F. Augustus Heinze's Montana Ore Purchasing Company plant.

Marcus Daly, President of the Anaconda Company and, later, the Amalgamated.

The Anaconda Copper Mining Company in Butte, nucleus of the Amalgamated copper trust.

Standard Oil magnate Henry H. Rogers, director of Amalgamated's strategy and F. Augustus Heinze's basic opponent in the Second Phase of the War of the Copper Kings.

Senator William A. Clark, the initial opponent of Marcus Daly. Clark allied himself with F. Augustus Heinze temporarily, before defecting to Roger's Amalgamated camp (1901).

The Rarus mine complex; F. Augustus Heinze's first Butte success.

The gallows frame and several surface buildings of United Copper's Corra mine.

Miles Finlen, F. Augustus Heinze's initial opponent in the Minnie Healy litigation.

The Minnie Healy mine, basis of extensive litigation and underground warfare.

The notorious Butte Judge William Clancy (right)—for whom F.
Augustus Heinze campaigned arduously and was duly rewarded—
speaking with "Swede" Murphy.

Judge Edward W. Harney (left)—F. Augustus Heinze's other judicial stalwart in the Butte mining litigation—pictured with the contemporary historian C. P. Connolly.

A portion of the ten to twelve thousand Butte residents gathered to hear F. Augustus Heinze's "Courthouse Speech" (October 26, 1903), which followed Amalgamated's shutdown of its Montana operations.

F. Augustus Heinze (bareheaded, at lower left) speaking from the steps of the Silver Bow County Courthouse. Although F. A. won this battle, he effectively lost the Copper War to the power exerted by Amalgamated in the shutdown of 1903 and the Legislature's subsequent extraordinary session.

F. Augustus Heinze (spring, 1907) as President of the Mercantile National Bank—immediately prior to the Panic of 1907, from which he never recovered, physically or financially. ARCHIVES AND SPECIAL COLLECTIONS, MANSFIELD LIBRARY, UNIVERSITY OF MONTANA.

As a political campaigner, Heinze was successful and dramatic. He used excellent diction, possessed a fine voice, and could appeal to the emotions and prejudices of his audience. Some of his speeches were delivered from the balcony of the Butte Hotel, where he maintained rooms. Crowds congregated in East Broadway Street below and impeded the regular schedule of the city trolley cars. These trollies were owned by W. A. Clark, and F. Augustus would delight his hearers with the taunt, "Move back, boys, and let the corporation go by."[12] This ability to gain political advantage from the immediate incident was valuable to Heinze, the politician.

W. A. Clark not only deserted F. A. Heinze, he worked actively against him. In late October, 1902, Clark delivered an address to a Helena crowd. For more than an hour he related his story of F. Augustus's treachery to those who had been his friends and of Heinze's attempt to control the State Supreme Court and the legislature.

"I cannot consent to allow this man who has more than 150 suits in the courts of this state . . . to place the courts where they cannot be used in the interest of justice for all comers, but must be used only to this man's selfish interests."[13]

Derided by his erstwhile collaborator, Clark, and openly attacked in Amalgamated's press campaign, F. Augustus persevered and seemed to thrive on the pre-election activity and excitement. One newspaper gibe which recurred was that Heinze's Fusion candidates were grafters, interested not in the office, but only in the opportunity it might afford for self-aggrandizement. Another *Standard* article exploited the same theme. It ridiculed the situation of the Fusionists —having not one, but five, separate campaign headquarters; it explained this phenomenon by saying, "five hands are better than one."[14]

---

[12]O. C. Heinze MS., p. 34.

[13]Anaconda *Standard*, October 25, 1902.

[14]Anaconda *Standard*, October 8, 1902.

When the election results proved the extent of F. Augustus's victory, the Anaconda *Standard's* editorial meekly admitted: "In Silver Bow County victory for the Heinze ticket takes in practically everything." A news story's second-deck headline declared:

"FUSIONISTS ELECT ENTIRE LEGISLATIVE TICKET"[15]

F. A. found that winning an election in Montana was difficult and expensive; he also discovered that one's problems did not cease with the election victory.

"In many cases no sooner had Heinze elected a man to office than he would go into the camp of our enemies and this is the sort of thing that had to be watched continually. We even had to keep an eye on Congress in Washington. That all cost an immense amount of money.

"We not only had lawyers in Butte and Helena, but also in Washington, California, New York state and city, and at times, in other states such as Pennsylvania and Colorado. Our legal expenses were enormous. But so long as the Montana Ore Purchasing Company made its million or million and a half a year we could take it."[16]

IX-C. Politics:
The Campaign of 1904

The election of 1904 had many of the characteristics of the 1902 campaign. F. Augustus Heinze again was extensively active; he again staged a big show at his own expense. It also differed from the earlier contests in some ways. As the special legislative session had passed the Fair Trials Bill (November, 1903), securing the election of particular district judges would have no special value. After the Shutdown of 1903 and Heinze's "courthouse speech," it was also evident to F. A. that he could not continue to vie successfully with Amalga-

---

[15] Anaconda *Standard*, November 6, 1902.

[16] O. C. Heinze MS., p. 33.

mated; he could afford no Pyrrhic victories. Despite the fact that his heart could hardly have been in the campaign, F. Augustus exemplified the actor's precept, "the show must go on."

On May 1, 1902, Heinze merged his complete Montana interests in the United Copper Company which he had incorporated in New Jersey for tax purposes. This action was grist for Amalgamated's political mill; incongruously, the trust berated F. Augustus for his extra-Montana corporation. An early reference to the election is indicative.

"The only corporation this year in politics is Heinze's . . . working on the assumption that it takes a trust to catch a trust. . . . The purpose is the making of the Heinze county ticket."[17]

Throughout October, 1904, a crusade was conducted in the editorial columns of Amalgamated's newspapers throughout the state to convince the people that they should vote their own ticket and "Have no Traffic with Outsiders."[18] Editors attacked Heinze's corporation slate as one opposed to the Democratic and Republican. An October 6 editorial explained that there was no difference in principle among the five Fusion parties: "All are opposed to any corporation but United Copper, which all seem to like."[19] Clark's newspapers tried to discredit F. Augustus by insinuating that he was not paying his taxes.[20] The *Standard* criticized Heinze's speeches for telling the people how to vote; throughout its own columns, however, were fillers advising, "The Democratic ticket is the first column on the ballot—vote it straight."[21]

W. A. Clark's leading paper, the Butte *Miner*, in its coverage of election returns during the days immediately following the balloting,

[17]Anaconda *Standard* editorial, September 30, 1904.

[18]Please see page 77, note 23, for a more detailed discussion of the newspaper alignment as a facet of the second phase of the Copper War (1896-1906).

[19]Anaconda *Standard* editorial, October 6, 1904.

[20]Butte *Miner*, November 4, 1904.

[21]Anaconda *Standard*, November 6, 1904.

is an excellent study in hope. The first day's issue (November 9, 1904) declares a Democratic victory in all local offices, and the defeat of the Fusionist candidates.

> "Heinze and his party fall to defeat in Silver Bow County—the self-styled Savior of Montana is rejected by the voters; politically F. Augustus Heinze is 'dead as a doornail.' "[22]

On November 10, the *Miner's* headline lost some of its exultation. This issue notes the retarded rate of the count and reassesses the box score.

> "Judges and several county offices are certain for the Democrats, with others in doubt. Fusionists probably elect entire legislative ticket."[23]

On the following day (November 11), ballot tricks and bribery are described to discredit Heinze—the alibi begins to appear.

> "Judge, Clerk of the Court, Coronor go to the Democrats; three are doubtful; the remainder goes to the Fusionists. Evidence exists of an attempt to steal the count for Heinze."[24]

Finally, in the November 12 edition, the *Miner* returns to its position of "normalcy." It presents two editorials which pertain to the election. The first belittles Heinze's victory, states that it is nothing really, and declares that the state and Butte are suffering seriously from Heinze's political debauchery. The other, entitled "Burden of Heinzeism," credits the defeat of certain candidates to the fact that Heinze had supported them.[25]

F. Augustus Heinze's endorsement of a candidate in Silver Bow County, however, generally assured his election. Even as late as 1910, candidates seeking office tried to profit from an association with F. A. and circulated material reputedly bearing his endorsement. In

[22]Butte *Miner*, November 9, 1904.
[23]Butte *Miner*, November 10, 1904.
[24]Butte *Miner*, November 11, 1904.
[25]Butte *Miner*, November 12, 1904.

one instance, F. Augustus sent a message to his superintendent in Butte, M. W. Bacon.

"Your telegram received. Circular purporting to quote me is a fabrication. I have not made, nor authorized any statement with reference to any ticket or candidate in Silver Bow County in this campaign."[26]

It is to F. Augustus Heinze's credit that he was effective in the Montana political realm. He was a stirring speaker and a realistic campaigner. Further, he was able to cover—and thereby sustain—his mining activities by means of his political victories. H. H. Rogers, Standard Oil, and Amalgamated learned some facets of Montana politics from Heinze. In the extraordinary legislative session of 1903, they combined this knowledge with their extensive economic power and effectively foreshortened F. Augustus's mining career in Butte.

---

[26] Anaconda *Standard*, November, 1910.

Chapter X

HEINZE SELLS OUT

One of the more interesting sequences of events in the life of F. Augustus Heinze pertains to the sale of his Butte properties to the Rogers-Amalgamated coalition of Standard Oil. Two distinct chapters exist in this story. In the first, as Amalgamated moved to effect its copper trust, F. Augustus blocked the attempt by binding in litigation the Boston and Montana Company, the projected nucleus of the trust. At this point (1898) Rogers tried to purchase Heinze's properties, and lawsuits, for $500,000—strictly because they were a nuisance. There is evidence also that Rogers, working through an intermediary, multiplied his offer ten times within several months to gain F. Augustus's holdings. Heinze would not sell.

Rumors persisted from 1899 until after the Shutdown of 1903 that Heinze's sellout to Amalgamated was imminent. The second chapter of the story, however, does not begin until late in 1904, when F. A. entered negotiations with the trust's representatives. This bargaining continued until the spring of 1906, at which time the sale of Heinze's United Copper holdings was announced. This chapter of the story elicits mixed emotions. F. Augustus Heinze at once was defeated—deposed from his position as an eminent Butte copper magnate—and victorious—having forced the mammoth Standard Oil trust to assent to his terms. The sale itself is also a pivotal event in F. Augustus's life: whereas it concludes one phase of his career, it initiates another which is equally exciting.

X-A. *Heinze and Amalgamated:* Early Negotiations

Henry H. Rogers of Standard Oil and his prime associates, William Rockefeller and James Stillman, knew the advantage of establishing a copper trust. Fortunately for F. Augustus Heinze, his operation was relatively small in 1898, when the copper-trust concept was projected by these men. The directors of Standard Oil, therefore, planned to secure his properties—with those of other small operators—only after they had coerced and purchased most of the nation's large copper productions. Thomas W. Lawson, Boston broker and publicity agent in the flotation of the copper-trust plan, revealed the original scheme.

"We had agreed that the first companies to go into our consolidation would be Butte and Boston, Boston and Montana, Calumet and Hecla and any other of the long-established properties of which we could get hold. It would be difficult, we knew, to purchase the control of the Calumet and Hecla, for its owners thought too highly of their investment to part with it, but if we accumulated less than a majority of the shares we could easily resell at a large profit. I began my operation with Boston and Montana stock, buying cautiously and obtaining it at fair prices."[1]

Possibly most significant is the tacit assumption of the members of the Rogers coalition that it was just a matter of time before they could establish the copper trust. One must realize, however, that this same group had successfully effected just such a monopoly in oil. Against this type of beast, an unknown twenty-nine-year-old from a small, mountain town in Montana was to do battle.

As the Rogers coalition moved to purchase control of the Boston companies—the Boston and Montana, and the Butte and Boston—an apparently minor item arose.

---

[1] Lawson, *Crime of Amalgamated*, p. 240. Note Lawson's intimation that, if he was not the sole originator of the copper-trust concept, he was one of its co-creators. Subsequently H. H. Rogers categorically denied this contention.

"A great friend in common attempted to scare Mr. Rockefeller and Mr. Rogers by informing them that the title to the copper properties were defective and that a man, then unknown, named Heinze, who had made himself very strong with the Montana courts, was about to confiscate them."[2]

Lawson was summoned to New York City to consult with Rogers and confidently succeeded in "satisfying Standard Oil as to the facts."[3]

Despite Lawson's assessment of the situation, Rogers was forced to recognize F. Augustus Heinze. Late in 1898 Rogers attempted, without success, to negotiate the purchase of Heinze's properties, primarily because of their nuisance potential. Heinze was in Montana when he received the invitation from Rogers. On November 3, 1898, Otto Heinze advised F. A. regarding the Standard Oil offer.

"Your telegram to Rogers first class. Telegraph him you cannot come here owing to press of business. Refer to me; I act in your behalf. We can exchange views. I know more than he of present state of affairs; therefore I will not be at disadvantage. I will keep you well informed, telegraphing progress negotiations; if later advantageous you can come here at once; telegraph me your decision. Do not buy Butte and Boston Mining Co. stock."[4]

Amalgamated's attempted acquisition of the Boston companies proceeded simultaneously under Rogers's auspices. There was some concern in Otto Heinze's mind that its consummation might preclude a settlement with F. Augustus.

"It is reported that Burrage and A. S. Bigelow were conferring here with Rogers Monday. I think it not safe to hold off from negotiations with Rogers. You must appoint myself as agent. If

---

[2]Lawson, *Crime of Amalgamated*, p. 256.

[3]Lawson, *Crime of Amalgamated*, p. 256.

[4]M. O. P. C. Telegram File, November 9, 1898. Wire from Otto Heinze in New York to F. Augustus at the Butte office.

you have decided not to negotiate at all it may lead to business between Rogers and A. S. Bigelow."[5]

Rogers wanted to purchase the Boston companies substantially prior to obtaining Heinze's properties. Amalgamated, or Standard Oil, was obviously negotiating to secure the Boston and Montana, and the Butte and Boston, which, after February 18, 1897, had interlocking directorates and were one company practically. There was much activity in copper during this period, but that which occurred was not obvious to all participants. F. Augustus Heinze was approached by the Boston and Montana Company—as well as by Rogers—but, throughout the early negotiations with the B. and M., the exact relationship between Rogers and the Boston company was ambiguous to the Heinzes.

The brothers took no risks; Standard Oil was considered in any move. For example, on November 4, 1898, Otto Heinze informed F. Augustus that he would advertise one hundred shares of the Montana Ore Purchasing Company stock for sale at auction—to see what factions were interested in their operations. He added, "I will myself surely buy these 100 shares at the November 9th auction."[6] This news, corroborated in another telegram from Stanley Gifford, prompted the legal mind of Arthur Heinze to offer some advice from Butte.

"Otto C. Heinze should withdraw the 100 shares advertised and advertise the large number in one lot. What we wish to accomplish would be knocked out by advertising in separate lots. Either Boston and Montana or Rogers probably would be willing to pay anywhere from $50,000 to $100,000 for 100 shares Montana Ore Purchasing Company so as to cause trouble. They

---

[5]M. O. P. C. Telegram File, November 9, 1898. Wire from Otto Heinze in New York to F. Augustus at the Butte office. "Burrage" is a reference to A. C. Burrage, a member of the Standard Oil legal staff.

[6]M. O. P. C. Telegram File, November 4, 1898. Wire from Otto Heinze in New York to F. Augustus at the Butte office.

might hesitate to pay so large a price for 1,000 shares. Make no mistake in this matter as it is of vital importance to us."[7]

In December, 1898, F. Augustus, then in New York City, was contacted personally by H. H. Rogers. He was also given the opportunity to name his terms of settlement for his Butte properties. F. A. informed John J. McHatton, his chief counsel in Butte, of the reception of his terms.

"Still conferring with Standard. Have proposed Butte and Boston, and Montana Ore Purchasing together should have control of consolidation between three companies, and we should get 56% of apportionment for Butte and Boston, and Montana Ore Purchasing. Think parties control Boston and Montana as well as Butte and Boston. They state our demands are altogether unreasonable. The whole matter is now at a standstill."[8]

Four days later F. Augustus again wired the Montana Ore Purchasing Company in Butte.

"Butte and Boston people have reopened negotiations. Have appointment for afternoon December 8th."[9]

The talks that F. Augustus had with Rogers and his intermediaries occurred simultaneously with a stage of Heinze's litigation to secure a receivership for the Boston and Montana Company. This fact was not ignored by F. A.'s opponents. They realized that a suit was pending as a result of the action brought by John MacGinniss and James Forrester to enjoin the transfer of the company's assets to a New York

[7]M. O. P. C. Telegram File, November 9, 1898. Wire from Arthur Heinze in Butte to the New York office. The corroborating telegram was sent by Stanley Gifford in the New York office to Arthur Heinze at the Butte office, November 7, 1898. Another telegram from Gifford, on November 9, to the Butte office stated: "O. C. Heinze bought the 100 M. O. P. No outside competition."

[8]M. O. P. C. Telegram File, December 2, 1898. Wire from F. Augustus in New York to McHatton, through the Butte office.

[9]M. O. P. C. Telegram File, December 6, 1898. Wire from F. Augustus in New York to the Butte office.

company of the same name.[10] On December 15, 1898, Judge William Clancy named as receiver of the B. and M., Thomas Hinds. The following day Boston and Montana stock dropped twenty-eight points on the Boston exchange.[11]

F. Augustus met with Rogers on the next day, December 16, 1898. Fritz was aware of both developments—the receivership and the stock drop—as he was informed immediately by his Butte office and by his Boston connections respectively. Rogers learned of these events only after he left the fruitless session with Heinze. Rogers then commented on his meeting with F. A.

"That is as cool a devil as one will ever meet in his life. He must have had that decision in his pocket through all the hours he was sitting in front of me, and he never showed it in look or act."[12]

Heinze's own account of the negotiations is also interesting.

"Rogers yesterday, before he received news of receiver, offered us 5,000 shares of Boston and Montana for Montana Ore Purchasing properties, including Sullivan, Minnie Healy, Rock Island, Corra and Silver Queen. Last evening, after receipt of news, Lawson called upon me and offered, if I was willing, to try to get for me 13,300 shares of Boston and Montana stock, guaranteed value $225. Boston and Montana quoted today $229."[13]

---

[10]Please see Section VII-A for a more extensive discussion of the Boston and Montana receivership case.

[11]Connolly, "Fight," p. 216. Connolly states that it was generally believed on the Boston copper exchange floor that F. Augustus and his associates were playing the market short and that the stealthy appointment of a receiver was made to bring heavy decline in the price of B. and M. stock. F. Augustus telegraphed the Butte office of his M. O. P. C. (December 16, 1898) concerning this occurrence: "A rumor has been circulated here to the effect that the Lawson attack has ruined the entire Bigelow crowd. Lawson has stated that they had to borrow $2,000,000 from Rogers." Therefore, Lawson—and not Heinze—appears to be the culprit. F. Augustus definitely was not working with Lawson at this time. Ultimately then, the stock drop can be credited to Rogers and Standard Oil, manipulating through Lawson.

[12]Connolly, "Fight," p. 216.

[13]M. O. P. C. Telegram File, December 16, 1898. Wire from F. Augustus in New York to the Butte office.

Otto Heinze met with F. Augustus in New York City after the latter's meeting with Rogers on December 16. F. A. told his brother that Rogers was pleasant and frank, but he characterized the offer of five thousand shares at par value of one hundred dollars—or a total proposal of $500,000 for the M. O. P. C. properties—as "contemptible." Fritz did not dignify that offer by giving Rogers an answer. Although the brothers did not display their feelings to the Standard Oil magnate, they were disgruntled.

"We were indeed sore to think that we should have been valued at so low a price, particularly as our Montana Ore Purchasing Company was at that time making at least a million a year. The offer was not an offer; it was nothing more or less than an effort to steal our property."[14]

The negotiations with Rogers and Standard Oil continued through January, 1899, and into February. Early in the latter month, an apparently tactical element was added to the mosaic of corporate bargaining. On February 4, 1899, a man named Foxwell telephoned from Philadelphia to Stanley Gifford, a chief associate of the Heinzes in the M. O. P. C., in New York City. Foxwell asked if F. Augustus would be in New York on February 6, and stated that he had a definite proposition "from Boston." He also requested a complete list of property and suits which Heinze could convey and promised conclusion of the deal within ten days.

The Heinzes did not know whom Foxwell represented—one of the Boston companies or Rogers's trust-oriented group. Gifford wired his opinion to F. Augustus, who had returned to Butte after Christmas to direct his mining operations there.

"I think he represents Bigelow side and not Rogers. Unless you are negotiating with Burrage think we should begin negotiations with him, even if you are positive receiver will stick. Cable full instruction immediately for guidance of Otto C. Heinze and Stanley Gifford. Hope you recollect details my conversation

---

[14] O. C. Heinze MS., p. 24.

with Captain while you were here. Think his proposition will be $5,000,000 or $6,000,000, half cash, half stock, but know nothing definite."[15]

The general concensus among the brothers, however, was that Foxwell was a Rogers intermediary and that Rogers effectively, if informally, controlled the Boston companies.[16] Otto Heinze made the contact with Foxwell. Otto proposed three terms for the sale of the M. O. P. C.'s holdings: 1) the Heinze interest should have twenty-seven percent of the Butte and Boston, Boston and Montana, and Montana Ore Purchasing Company consolidation; 2) C. H. Batterman should be discharged;[17] 3) F. Augustus Heinze should become general Western manager. Otto doubted that a deal could be completed, but he requested instructions for its conclusion from F. A., in the case that their terms were accepted. Otto noted that Foxwell had made no offer to date.[18] F. Augustus was eager neither to compromise nor to sell to either group: Rogers's Amalgamated or Bigelow's Boston and Montana. He sent a pertinent telegram from Butte on February 6, 1899.

"We will make no further proposals. Either Rogers or Bigelow

---

[15]M. O. P. C. Telegram File, February 4, 1899. Wire from Gifford in New York to F. Augustus at the Butte office. "Burrage" refers to A. C. Burrage, a member of the Standard Oil legal staff. The "Captain" is H. H. Rogers.

[16]The Heinzes' opinion that Rogers informally controlled the Boston companies proved correct. In March, 1899, it became evident that Rogers possessed the majority of Butte and Boston stock. At this time, he forced A. S. Bigelow from the effective leadership of the young Boston consolidation and, henceforth, ruled the two Boston companies—informally—as subsidiaries of Amalgamated. Only F. Augustus's court action against the B. and M. kept Rogers's control from becoming formal. Please see Appendix One for a better chronologic perspective of Rogers's gradual consumption of mining corporations to satisfy his copper-trust scheme.

[17]Batterman is the engineer whom F. Augustus left in charge of the M. O. P. C. operations in Butte while he was in British Columbia, directing his operations there. In 1896 Batterman defected to the Boston and Montana Company with the majority of the M. O. P. C.'s maps and mine reports. For a more detailed discussion of this incident, please see Chapter IV.

[18]M. O. P. C. Telegram File, February 6, 1899. Wire from Otto Heinze in New York to F. Augustus at the Butte office.

know well what we have. If they wish to offer, they can do so. We are not worrying."[19]

Foxwell attempted to strengthen his case with the assertion that Marcus Daly of the Anaconda Copper Mining Company had joined with Rogers against Heinze.[20] The intermediary offered $5,500,000 for the Heinze properties, $500,000 of which was to be his commission. If, as the Heinze brothers strongly suspected, Foxwell was Rogers's agent, then Amalgamated's offer of $5,000,000 was tenfold Rogers's quotation of December, 1898—less than two months earlier. The Heinzes concluded that the Standard Oil trust was becoming anxious to launch its copper monopoly;[21] F. Augustus's lawsuits against the Boston and Montana were preventing the Amalgamated from securing the designated nucleus of the metal trust, the young Boston consolidation.

Foxwell tried another tack. He claimed that within ten days Amalgamated would consummate a $500,000,000 consolidation. If F. Augustus did not join the organization immediately, he would be forced from business, as had so many of Standard Oil's petroleum competitors.[22] Both Otto Heinze and Stanley Gifford accepted Foxwell's statement as genuine and wired to Butte for instructions. F. Augustus severed all negotiations with the Boston companies and with the Rogers coalition by means of his courageously blithe reply, "Tell them to guess again."[23] Although Foxwell returned to Boston to secure a larger offer, no sale of the Heinze properties was concluded, nor did the Boston companies join the Amalgamated's copper trust at this time. When an attempt was made in 1901 to merge the

[19]M. O. P. C. Telegram File, February 6, 1899. Wire from F. Augustus in Butte to the New York office.

[20]M. O. P. C. Telegram File, February 20, 1899. Wire from Stanley Gifford in New York to the Butte office.

[21]M. O. P. C. Telegram File, February 21, 1899. Wire from F. Augustus in Butte to the New York office.

[22]M. O. P. C. Telegram File, February 24, 1899. Wire from Otto Heinze and Stanley Gifford in New York to the Butte office.

[23]M. O. P. C. Telegram File, February 25, 1899. Wire from F. Augustus in Butte to the New York office.

Boston and Montana with Amalgamated, John MacGinniss—as a minority stockholder in the B. and M.—sued to prevent alignment.[24] Rumors of a great copper combine appeared in the national press during the spring of 1899. The estimates set a valuation from $350,-000,000 to $500,000,000 and indicated that the consolidation would be an international concern.[25] The foreign associate was to be the Rothschilds, who had recently acquired the Rio Tinto mines of Spain.[26]

On May 1, 1899, Henry H. Rogers and his Standard Oil associates moved to establish this copper trust. They secured the Amalgamated's first major property, the Anaconda Copper Mining Company. The Anaconda was largely the property of Marcus Daly, James B. Haggin, and the George Hearst estate. Its management had been almost completely in the control of Daly. Daly became the first president of the Amalgamated.[27]

Possibly the most significant point demonstrated by Amalgamated's purchase of the Anaconda, as the nucleus of its proposed copper trust, was the strength of the shepherd in this David-and-Goliath contest. F. Augustus Heinze sufficiently manipulated events to alter Standard Oil's scheme for the launching of a copper trust to rival its oil monopoly. First, he rejected the offers of Rogers which would have provided him with a profit, but also would have eliminated him from the scene. Second, he practically immobilized by litigation the originally designated foundation of the trust, the Boston and Montana Company. The Rogers-Standard Oil-Amalgamated complex was forced, therefore, to acquire a less desirable company around which to build the trust.

Marcus Daly realized the plight of the complex and bled it for the presidency of Amalgamated, as well as for an almost unrealistic price

---

[24]Please see Section VII-A for a more comprehensive presentation of this element of the Boston and Montana receivership case.

[25]Anaconda *Standard*, April, 1899.

[26]O. C. Heinze MS., p. 48.

[27]Please see Section VII-A, pp. 72-74, for a closer integration of Daly's sale and the position of Amalgamated in the complex situation.

for his properties. Time was pressuring the Rogers coalition—it had to begin consuming copper producers. Time and F. A. Heinze's actions coalesced to alter the trust's program and to benefit Marcus Daly. David had staggered the giant, but not killed him. In one sense, the second phase of the War of the Copper Kings (1896-1906) is the story of Goliath lumbering after the boy, finally (1903) cornering and bludgeoning him, and then (1906) purchasing his slingshot for a handsome price.

X-B. *Heinze and Amalgamated:*
The Sale

In historical perspective, the sale of F. Augustus Heinze's Butte properties to the Amalgamated was inevitable—from that point at which he refused Henry H. Rogers's indirect offer of $5,000,000 and entwined the Boston and Montana in litigation. F. Augustus, however, was both fearless and nearsighted; he met each opponent directly and fought each battle as if it were the entire war. During the period from the spring of 1899 to the autumn of 1904, when he commenced negotiations with Amalgamated, F. Augustus pursued the many ramifications of his mining business. In addition to directing matters of litigation, underground warfare, and politics, he continued to build a copper empire. To this end he created the United Copper Company and purchased additional properties. He constantly faced rumors, however, that his sellout was imminent. *In fact*, it was impending only after the Shutdown of 1903.

On May 1, 1902, F. Augustus Heinze and his associates in the Montana Ore Purchasing Company merged that organization and its auxiliaries in the United Copper Company, with an authorized capital stock of eighty million dollars. Five million was preferred stock at six percent accumulative and seventy-five million was common stock. Only forty-five million dollars worth of common stock was to be issued with the preferred.[28] The Heinze brothers transferred *all* their

---

[28] O. C. Heinze MS., p. 44.

Montana assets to United Copper which, except for an initial reversal, prospered until F. Augustus sold his complete Butte holdings (1906).[29]

F. A. was always interested in broadening his field of mining activity. In 1904 he purchased the Lexington mining complex in Walkerville, north of Butte, from its French owners. These associated properties included the Wild Rat, Louisa, Angelo, Wappelo, and Allie Brown mine and mill sites, among others.[30] The owners had suspended operations and returned to Paris. To handle this new enterprise, the Heinzes organized the La France Copper Company; in the autumn of 1904, Otto Heinze personally floated the new company's stock on the Paris market. He had little success, except to exchange the original French bonds for La France bonds. F. Augustus retained the Lexington mine complex in Walkerville after he sold his Butte properties to the Amalgamated in 1906. Otto Heinze explained this retention simply: "Amalgamated was not willing to pay the price F. Augustus set upon them."[31]

During the period from December, 1898 (when Henry H. Rogers offered F. Augustus $500,000 for his Butte holdings), through February, 1899 (when Rogers, through Foxwell, proposed $5,000,000 —or ten times the original offer—for Heinze's properties), F. A.'s enemies constantly sought to weaken him by rumors that he would sell, or already had sold surreptitiously, his mining assets in Montana. Again, in December of 1902, this report gained sufficient circulation to prompt the Anaconda *Standard* to comment on the situation.

"For a week or ten days all sorts of rumors of a proposed settlement of differences of Amalgamated and Heinze have been fly-

---

[29]O. C. Heinze MS., p. 44. In this source, Otto Heinze relates the first attempt to launch the United Copper Company (1902), which was unsuccessful. He believes that the difficulties encountered in floating the stock—for which he was personally responsible —are attributable to Rogers's surreptitious manipulations of the market and the public media. After a period of reassessment, the stock was successfully refloated and the United successfully relaunched (later in 1902); the subsequent record of this company is quite prosperous.

[30]O. C. Heinze MS., p. 44. See also, Anaconda *Standard*, February 19, 1906.

[31]O. C. Heinze MS., p. 44.

ing thick and fast. But if the Boston News Bureau's account of December 23 is true, there is no truth in them:

" 'We can state authoritatively that rumor of a settlement between Amalgamated and Heinze is untrue.

" 'It is true that internationally prominent bankers of United Copper are restless because of lack of promise of a settlement. These bankers are dissatisfied because the copper business is not as profitable as they supposed.' "[32]

The rumor was unfounded, but it caused significant talk and constraint in the copper world. The *Economist*, published in London, carried an editorial (April, 1903) which stated that Amalgamated was losing its advantage by its attempt to *force* other producers to join with it in an effort to fix the price of copper; it noted further that the Standard Oil trust had, by a series of blunders, benefited its competitors at its own cost. The editorial concluded that, if an utter collapse were to be averted, the Heinzes should be offered a better price and, thereby, induced to join the Amalgamated.[33]

The price of copper gradually declined during the second half of 1902; in November electrolytic copper was 11.2 cents per pound. Amalgamated stock sold low throughout the autumn and was 53 in mid-November. It rallied slightly in the spring of 1903, when the copper price reached 14.4 cents per pound; Amalgamated then sold at 71. Between May and August of 1903, however, copper prices dove to a low of 12.9, which correspondingly reduced copper-stock value. On August 5, Amalgamated was quoted at 37 and the small speculators who had purchased it at 100 were justifiably alarmed.[34]

Critics of the copper market believed that the Rogers-Standard Oil-Amalgamated monopoly was making its move—forcing prices down to eliminate its weak competitors and to induce those opponents who

---

[32]Anaconda *Standard*, December 29, 1902.

[33]The *Economist*, April, 1903; as cited in Raymer, *Montana*, I, p. 497. Whether the point is causal or not, one should remember that the Heinzes had extensive lines of credit in Europe, including London.

[34]Raymer, *Montana*, I, p. 497-498.

survived to sell to the trust at a minimum price. As these critics believed F. Augustus's credit was ephemeral,[35] even with a sound market, they forecast his sellout as imminent. "Surprisingly," Heinze's Butte operations increased production during the early autumn of 1903.

The Shutdown of (October) 1903 further aggravated the fears of independent speculators. The closure, however, was of short duration and, when operations resumed, the market rose; Amalgamated paid its second-quarter dividend. The Russo-Japanese War (February, 1904, to April, 1905) subsequently created the best market that the copper interests had ever experienced.[36]

Throughout the election campaign of 1904, the opposition's newspapers—specifically W. A. Clark's Butte *Miner* and Amalgamated's Anaconda *Standard*—carried the refrain of wishful thinkers: "Heinze has sold out." Thomas W. Lawson, Standard Oil publicity agent, kept the rumor alive in Eastern financial centers. The stories were similar in one respect: they pictured Heinze as seeking to sell. None, however, presented Amalgamated as desirous of buying. A Sunday front page of the Anaconda *Standard* (November 6, 1904) featured a letter to H. H. Rogers from J. W. Gates, of the Charles G. Gates and Company firm of New York, in which the writer assured Rogers that Heinze had offered to sell his properties for eight million dollars.[37]

Another story (November 5, 1904) related an interview that the Butte *Miner's* Boston correspondent had secured with Lawson in which the trust's publicist challenged, "The Heinzes don't own United Copper."[38] In answer to this statement, F. Augustus displayed his United Copper stock certificates in the window of his Butte bank, with the sign:

---

[35]Please see Chapter V for a detailed rebuttal of the popular belief—maintained by participants in the Copper War and, subsequently, by historians—that F. Augustus's credit was transitory.

[36]Raymer, *Montana*, I, p. 498.

[37]Anaconda *Standard*, November 6, 1904.

[38]Butte *Miner*, November 5, 1904.

"HERE IS THE CONTROL OF THE UNITED COPPER
COMPANY EXHIBITED BY F. AUGUSTUS HEINZE."[39]

Opposition factions seized the phraseology of "exhibited by"; they
tortured from their reasoning the argument that, if Heinze had not
sold his Butte properties, he would have written "owned by," rather
than "exhibited by." The logic concluded that the certificates were
forged, not genuine.[40] On the following day, a red-banner, *Miner*
headline trumpeted:

"CHAIN OF EVIDENCE AGAINST HEINZE IS COMPLETE."

A complementary news story stated that Gates's letter to Rogers was
verified, that Lawson had exposed the United Copper bluff, and that
Heinze had sold to the Amalgamated and would leave the state.[41]

A month later, when election returns demonstrated that the rumor
had alienated few Heinze-Fusionist voters, the *Miner* noted that
Amalgamated stock had risen to 81 and was expected to reach 90
by January. The ascent was credited to the repetitious observation.

"It is generally believed in Eastern centers that Heinze has made
arrangements to turn over his properties to Amalgamated and
that the long and bitter copper war will stop."[42]

Equally repetitive was the weak analysis involved in citing this "fact."
In this particular case, the faulty analysis was exposed within three
days by the market's action, although the basic rumor was perpetu-
ated.

"The stock market was demoralized during the greater part of
the session today and many fortunes were cut or swept away
before the excited speculators could save them. Most of the

---

[39]C. P. Connolly, "Heinze and Lawson, a Contrast," *Donahoe's Magazine* (January,
1905), p. 67. Tear sheets of this article are bound in the Heinze file at the Montana
State Historical Society Library, Helena, Montana.

[40]Butte *Miner*, November 7, 1904.

[41]Butte *Miner*, November 8, 1904.

[42]Butte *Miner*, December 5, 1904.

active stocks lost from two to three points. Amalgamated was the principal sufferer, going off 8¾ points. *It was said that a party, of which Augustus Heinze is the chief member, had thrown over its Amalgamated Copper holdings at 80.* Gates's following was also selling copper in large amounts. Trading was on a large scale and the tone was extremely nervous. All metal shares went down rapidly."[43]

Otto Heinze also recalls this situation, although he errs regarding the date. Otto explicates that event which market critics interpreted as a devious, anti-Standard plot.

"During the summer and fall of 1905 [i.e., 1904] we did a big business not only in our own stock but in many others. F. Aug. sent on some very large orders to buy Amalgamated stock, selling around 100. One afternoon, going over our purchases, I found that we had bought for him nearly one hundred thousand shares which we were carrying in about ten or fifteen other houses, margined to the extent of about one million dollars. If Rogers and his crowd dropped the price of Amalgamated overnight 50%, which they could do, we would have lost five millions of dollars. I immediately telegraphed F. A. that he must immediately sell at least half the stock, as I was not prepared to run such a risk. He was very angry and consented only when I insisted. To have sold it through the firms who were carrying the stock for us would have been disastrous; we therefore employed other brokers to sell and instructed them to borrow the stock so as to make it appear that these sales were what is called short sales and in this way disposed of the entire lot, delivering our long stock in place of the stock we had borrowed on our short sales. Rogers and others had sold us our long stock. Of course, they did not know who had bought it; they had also bought our supposedly short stock. Rogers told one of his friends that there were some fools who were selling Amalgamated

[43]Butte *Miner*, December 8, 1904. In presenting this report, the *Miner* used the following date line: "New York, Dec. 7;" (Italics are mine).

short; he would some fine day make them pay dearly for it. We were much amused to think how he felt when we delivered our long stock, which he had thought had been definitely placed, a difference in his market transactions of about ten millions of dollars.

"I was tremendously relieved when we had this transaction completed, but F. A. was still very angry. I am afraid that was the beginning of our separation later on, although contrary to his expectation Amalgamated did not go much, if any, higher after the settlement was announced."[44]

It was inevitable that F. Augustus Heinze would eventually sell his M. O. P. C. properties. Conditions for him were becoming intolerable in the Silver Bow district; he had managed to thwart personal attacks and rumors, but he had no adequate weapon against the power that Amalgamated revealed in the Shutdown of 1903 and the subsequent special legislature. F. A. was not a person to expend his energy on the quixotic flailing of windmills. He could find profitable business where Amalgamated was not a competitor.

"No one human being could carry the weight of this war upon his shoulders for an indefinite period, against the unending power of money, controlled by H. H. Rogers and his associates. With every year it cost more and more money and, in the end, maybe not for many years, if no compromise could be reached, it was bound to break down any human being mentally or financially, the more so if not loyally supported by the people of Montana and the miners of Butte."[45]

The rumors of a Heinze sellout, which had been incessant while F. Augustus viciously battled Amalgamated, were strangely absent during the actual negotiations. Both Heinze and the Amalgamated

---

[44]O. C. Heinze MS., p. 47. The "separation" to which Otto refers is the dissolution of the brothers' business and personal partnership, which was one of F. Augustus's real strengths in his Butte operations. The break was quite evident by 1907.

[45]O. C. Heinze MS., p. 51.

demanded absolute secrecy through the months of arrangement. The negotiations themselves proceeded for approximately fifteen months —from the early winter of 1904 into the spring of 1906. F. A. possessed no friendship for William Scallon, initially one of Marcus Daly's Butte attorneys who subsequently became the Amalgamated's managing director. Otto Heinze believed that Fritz would conduct business neither with Scallon directly, nor with H. H. Rogers.[46] When Scallon resigned as managing director (1904), he was succeeded by John D. Ryan, whom Otto Heinze described as, "an extremely nice man";[47] another observer of Montana personalities, however, does not agree.

"Organized greed could teach him [Ryan] nothing in selfishness and no awakening conscience disturbed the dreams of avarice. He combined a pleasing personality with the arts of dignity. He reinforced plausible argument with flattering persuasion, and possessed, to the full extent of its power, that peculiar combination of talents which enables the distinguished kings of finance to entice enemies and fleece friends with equal skill and unction."[48]

Nevertheless, the relationship between F. Augustus and Ryan was friendly and it was possible for them to negotiate. Their first discussion occurred in Butte; the remainder were conducted in New York City to maximize secrecy.

"There was not the slightest effort at bluff or coercion; they, he and F. A., just sat down and talked the whole trouble over in a perfectly friendly way and Ryan suggested that they go over every mine and all other property and value each and every thing fairly and squarely and then see if a deal could not be made. After a year to eighteen months and many conferences giving a

[46]O. C. Heinze MS., p. 35.
[47]O. C. Heinze MS., p. 35.
[48]Murphy, *Comical History*, p. 64.

fair and reasonable value to our mines, the sale was consummated."[49]

A significant problem of the early negotiations was finding a person to hold the stakes whom both parties could trust completely. Until the deal was concluded, F. Augustus would not relinquish his deeds and transfers; neither would Henry H. Rogers, Amalgamated's president for whom Ryan acted, deposit his money in Heinze's coffers. Yet the trust's attorneys would have to approve the legality of F. A.'s property deeds. Both parties feared an unforeseen incident that might precipitate litigation and delay. A neutral party was required to hold the Heinze papers and the Amalgamated's millions. If the negotiations miscarried, the neutral had to be trusted to return the properties to their respective owners.

Each side suggested persons for the position and each rejected the names originally submitted by the other. The two parties finally concurred. William H. Porter, president of the Chemical National Bank of New York, undertook the responsibility, with the consent of his board of directors. He performed his duty to the mutual satisfaction of his employers, each of whom paid one-half of his fee of $300,000.[50]

Given the stature of the negotiators, the intensity of the second phase of the Copper War, and the prevalence of "sellout" rumors, that absolute secrecy was maintained throughout the negotiations is nothing less than miraculous. No word which could be substantiated reached the public; in fact, other copper magnates were ignorant of the conferences. Although the Heinze-Ryan transactions were concluded to mutual satisfaction on February 1, 1906, not until February 14 did the public learn that F. Augustus had sold his Butte assets to the Rogers-Standard Oil-Amalgamated coalition. The extreme secrecy that was maintained is as admirable as it was improbable; the denouement of the second phase of the Copper War assumed a relative degree of respect.

On February 14, the negotiators released the news of their trans-

[49]O. C. Heinze MS., p. 35.
[50]O. C. Heinze MS., p. 50.

action simultaneously to the Montana, New York, and Boston papers. The Anaconda *Standard* restricted its edition of that date, as did most Montana newspapers, to the dramatic bombshell. It employed a traditional reference in its column-one headline.

"OLIVE BRANCH NOW REPOSES UPON THE HILL
"CARNIVAL OF LITIGATION IS APPARENTLY AT AN END"[51]

In another opposition paper, the Butte *Miner*, a three-column, ten-inch picture of F. Augustus Heinze greeted the reader. An accompanying eight-column, red banner proclaimed the news.

"HEINZE SELLS HIS BUTTE COPPER PROPERTIES"[52]

Despite these dramatic presentations, the initial news reports lacked many details, primarily regarding the amount which F. Augustus had received. The papers agreed, however, concerning the facts that had been released.

"There is no mistake or slip about it this time, for already all the properties, mines and smelter of Mr. Heinze and the United Copper Company in Butte have passed into the possession of new owners.

"Telegrams officially announcing the transfer of interest were received in Butte both from John D. Ryan, managing director of the Amalgamated Company, and from F. Augustus Heinze. . . . All the property of Mr. Heinze and the United Copper Mining Company was turned over to Arthur C. Carson, representing Thomas F. Cole [president of the North Butte Mining Company of Butte].

"Mr. Cole has taken title to the property for a new company [the Butte Coalition Mining Company] in which the Amalgamated Copper Company, North Butte Mining Company, and United Copper Company interests will be associated.

"Property transferred includes the Minnie Healy, Rarus, Johns-

---

[51] Anaconda *Standard*, February 14, 1906.

[52] Butte *Miner*, February 14, 1906.

town, Corra, Belmont and Nipper mines among the big properties of United Copper; the Johnstown Mining Company, the Hy-
pocka Mining Company, Guardian Mining Company, Nipper
Consolidated Mining Company, Belmont Mining Company,
Minnie Healy Mining Company, Montana Ore Purchasing Company and smelter, in addition to a large number of other properties that are not now productive. Among the latter are the
interests large and small in the Highland Chief, Mountain Chief,
Tramway, Snohomish, Little Ida, Dayton, Black Diamond, Wild
Goose, Hasley, Pompey, Montana, Clinton, Scottish Chief, Lion-
ess, Kinkaid, Taffy, Silver King, A. J. P., the Robert Emmett 1
and 2, Nipper, Snoozer, Chief Joseph, Fairmount, Balm, L. E. R.,
and several others.

"The settlement is due to John D. Ryan . . . who, with attorneys
A. J. Shores, S. J. Campbell, and L. O. Evans, has been in New
York since early last November negotiating with Mr. Heinze,
who was represented by Charles R. Leonard of Butte and several
New York attorneys."[53]

As the release states, Heinze did not sell directly to the Amalgamated; he transferred his property to Arthur C. Carson, who functioned as agent for Thomas F. Cole, president of the North Butte
Mining Company of Butte. The agreement stipulated that a new firm,
the Butte Coalition Mining Company, would be founded to control
the operations of the Heinze properties and that this company would
be a subsidiary of Amalgamated.[54] This indirect transfer saved face

---

[53]Anaconda *Standard*, February 14, 1906.

[54]New York *Commercial*, February 17, 1906; as quoted in the Anaconda *Standard*,
February 18, 1906. The following description of the newly conceived holding company
is a paraphrase of the article: "Butte Coalition Mining Company, Montana," *The
Copper Handbook, A Manual of the Copper Industry of the World*, ed., Horace T.
Stevens (Houghton, Mich.: Stevens; 1906), VI, pp. 294-295.

   The Butte Coalition Mining Company was organized on February 24, 1906,
under the laws of New Jersey. Its president was Thomas F. Cole and its vice-
president was John D. Ryan. The company was capitalized at $15,000,000. It
ostensibly began operations with $4,000,000 cash. The B. C. M. C. owned the
Red Metals Mining Company, which was Amalgamated's intermediate holding
company for its mining operations in Montana.

for both F. Augustus and H. H. Rogers. Neither officially capitulated to the other.

In effect, Amalgamated created a new position in its lineage of direction for the B. C. M. C. Although the geneology of Standard Oil's corporate complex rivals—if not surpasses—in convolution and confusion the most intricate example of European ancestral structure, perhaps the diagram below can demonstrate the trust's mechanical assumption of Heinze's properties through the Butte Coalition Company.

To consume and align these properties, Standard Oil subdivided its "intermediate holding company" level, created the Butte Coalition Company, and made its only former "intermediate holding company," Red Metals, an immediate subordinate of the B. C. M. C. With only this minor adjustment, Amalgamated enveloped F. Augustus Heinze's holdings.

One should remember that the diagram is constructed merely to demonstrate the mechanics of the merging process. He should not be misled by its extreme simplicity.

AMALGAMATED'S REALIGNMENT: FEBRUARY, 1906

LEVEL 1:

(STANDARD OIL)
(supreme trust)

LEVEL 2:

AMALGAMATED
(supreme copper trust)

LEVEL 3:

ANACONDA
(prime holding company)

LEVEL 4-A:

←——————— **BUTTE COALITION**
(prime intermediate holding company)

LEVEL 4-B:

RED METALS——————→
(subordinate intermediate holding company)

LEVEL 5:

PARROT——————→ ←——— **NIPPER CONSOLIDATED**
(subsidiary holding company)

LEVEL 6:

ST. LAWRENCE——————→ ←——————**RARUS**
(operating company)

As the newspapers had no facts regarding the amount paid to F. A., they could only speculate. Most papers set the price too high—remarkably so, given the rumored estimates at the turn of the century. The most common guess was $25,000,000—quoted, for example, by the Anaconda *Standard*.

"How little is known of the details or the consideration paid is indicated by the statement of so reliable a firm as C. G. Gates and Company that the United Copper Company interest received $25,000,000, one-half cash and the remainder in securities, while other oracles multiplied the figure by two, three and four."[55]

The Chicago *Record-Herald's* account was no more accurate than the reports that appeared in smaller papers.

"The seven years' war of the copper magnates in Montana which has filled the courts with lawsuits in which $400,000,000 were involved and which has been one of the greatest financial struggles on record came to an end today. The treaty of peace between F. Augustus Heinze, the spectacular, and Amalgamated was the direct result of the deals which have resulted in the formation of a giant copper trust, the details of which were outlined recently in the *Record-Herald*.
"United Copper Company receives $25,000,000, part cash and part stock in the new company; the proportion of cash is placed at $15,000,000 to $20,000,000."[56]

The New York *Commercial* was closer to the actual amount in its guess.

"While it was stated yesterday, on what purported to be good authority, that $25,000,000 had been paid to the United Copper Company, it may be accepted as true that the figure is nearer

---

[55] Anaconda *Standard*, February 15, 1906.

[56] Chicago *Record-Herald*, February 14, 1906. A typescript of this account is contained in the F. Augustus Heinze file at the Montana State Historical Society Library, Helena, Montana.

one-half of this amount, and from this latter has been deducted an amount sufficient to work out the mortgage indebtedness standing against the United Copper Company's property."[57]

In fact, Otto Heinze states that F. Augustus sold his Butte holdings for,

". . . ten and a half million for his mines and another million and a half for machinery, plants, smelter and equipment [total sale price: $12,000,000]. . . .

"In setting his price he had taken into consideration reasonable expectation for future development. He supposed he might have charged even more but, as he also wanted to make the deal and be done with the Copper War, he did not want to ask for too much. The price we got was magnificent at the time."[58]

Although he retained the United Copper Company to control the remainder of his assets, the sale to Amalgamated officially ended F. Augustus Heinze's career as a major operator in Butte; he had reason to survey that career with pride. In seventeen years he had made a deep impression on the mining city. F. A. had entered Butte (1889) as an unknown, nineteen-year-old college graduate whose first job returned $250 a month. He left the Hill (1906) at thirty-six, a renowned figure with twelve million dollars, in addition to active mining interests which he retained in Montana and the West. F. Augustus personally, however, did not fade unobtrusively into the background. He remained energetic and powerful in the world of mining. In an interview on February 15, 1906—the day following the announcement of the Amalgamated transaction—he clarified that he was not restricted by any private agreement from opposing, on any level, the new company that had been formed—the Butte Coalition Mining Company. F. A., however, could not foresee any conflict with the B. C. M. C.

---

[57] New York *Commercial*, February 17, 1906; as quoted in the Anaconda *Standard*, February 18, 1906.

[58] O. C. Heinze MS., pp. 35 and 51.

"There is no further possibility of conflict over the properties taken over by the holding company. I will continue as an important producer, but the properties I still control outside the new holding company are so far to one side of the hitherto disputed claims that there is not the slightest possibility of any dispute. The disputes are all over claims that interlaced—cases where the copper veins crossed from one claim to another. All such have been settled for all time by the formation of the new company with Mr. Cole at its head."[59]

The peace desired by most parties concerned—from Boston copper investor to Butte miner—descended with the conclusion of the Heinze-Amalgamated litigation.

"Eighty lawsuits with aggregate claims for nearly one hundred million dollars damages were dismissed in the state courts, and twenty-three lawsuits were dismissed in the United States courts, thus cleaning up the protracted and costly litigation between the Amalgamated and the United Copper Company interests."[60]

The four-score cases pending in the district courts were dismissed en masse on March 3, 1906. L. O. Evans, a legal representative of Amalgamated interests, and James Denny, an attorney for F. Augustus and United Copper, appeared first before Judge John D. McClernan and petitioned to dismiss the cases pending there. In the afternoon, Evans and Denny entered the court of Judge George M. Bourquin to conclude the nullification procedure. Each suit was read by number and title, and a motion was made for dismissal of the case as settled; each party paid its own court costs.[61] Arson, bribery, calumny, perjury—all were entwined in these cases, many of which were no nearer settlement in 1906 than they were upon institution, as early as 1897.

---

[59]Anaconda *Standard*, February 17, 1906; a portion of an interview that the *Standard's* New York correspondent conducted with F. Augustus in his suite at the Waldorf-Astoria.

[60]"Butte Coalition Company," *Copper Handbook*, VI, p. 294. See also: Anaconda *Standard*, March 4, 1906.

[61]"Butte Coalition Company," *Copper Handbook*, VI, p. 294.

Quite anticlimactically the most extensive, turbulent, and dear litigation in the history of United States mining ceased.

The litigation of the second phase of the Copper War (1896-1906) was severed with F. Augustus Heinze's sale to the Amalgamated—as were the devastating underground warfare, the dramatic political campaigns and manipulations, and the excitement of the David-Goliath confrontation which disseminated throughout the nation from Butte. That period of F. Augustus Heinze's life was completed. The intense personal and professional emotions engendered by the confrontation, however, dictated the course of F. Augustus's remaining years. *The Nation's* comment on the second phase of the Copper War, which was intended to be somewhat cynical, is found to be preternaturally prophetic.

"It is not because of any obvious commercial or moral gain that a truce in the Copper War was to be welcomed. That struggle has been attended from the first, however, by so notorious a debauching of courts, voters, and legislatures and by such utter demoralization of the business communities in the tainted district that anything was better than its continuance. Nobody comes out of the contest with clean hands but, at any rate, there is now hope of ending it. Whether the acquisition of the so-called 'Heinze' mines will tempt Amalgamated to throttle the copper trade again, as it did five years ago, may be doubted. . . . But the promoters of the Amalgamated scheme will doubtless continue busy, chiefly in working *a much more valuable mine than the Boston and Montana, the Butte and Boston, or even the Anaconda, whose daily discoveries of new and unprecedentedly rich veins of copper have, for some weeks past, enlivened financial discussion. The richest veins which these explorers have as yet opened up have been found in Wall Street.*"[62]

---

[62]"National News," *Nation*, LXXXII (February 22, 1906), p. 149. (Italics are mine.)

Chapter XI

F. AUGUSTUS HEINZE, FINANCIER

Fresh from the sale of his Butte properties to the Amalgamated in February of 1906, F. Augustus Heinze possessed more working capital than ever before in his life. He chose the complementary realms of the stock market and national finance in which to manipulate that capital. In effect, he traded his natural battleground, the Butte mines, for the territory of his bitter enemies, Wall Street. Fritz's enemies—the Rogers-Standard Oil-Amalgamated complex—utilized their advantage.

The final eight years of F. Augustus's life (1906-1914) compose a tale of dissipation. Dissipation of his fortune; dissipation of the close relationship with his brothers; dissipation of his competitive spirit; dissipation, finally, of his health. He left his environment and it killed him. It was a slow, almost deliberate, certainly pathetic, process—but it killed him.

F. Augustus's physical death, however, seems strangely anticlimactic to the financial murder of which he was a victim in the Panic of 1907. The Panic becomes a symbolic block to which Fritz's enemies led him, carefully positioned his head, and smugly lopped it from his body. This financial upheaval is the nucleus of his dissipation—a dissipation all the more dramatic because of the strength and vitality with which F. Augustus assaulted the financial world in 1906.

XI-A. Transition:
Butte to Wall Street

In the spring of 1906, F. Augustus Heinze's assets included the twelve million dollars that he had acquired from the sale of his Butte properties, the United Copper Mining Company, the La France Mining Company, the Davis-Daly Estates Mining Company, and the Ohio Mining Company. This list is quite imposing, but can easily be overestimated. For example, following the February settlement, the New York *Herald* described the United Copper Company's condition.

"As it stands today, the United Copper Company is in practically the same position as the Northern Securities Company was after it was compelled to transfer and distribute its holdings of Great Northern and Northern Pacific stocks. The Northern Securities Company owned a few stocks, but the great holding company was nothing but a shell. Similarly with the United Copper Company, its properties have been sold and its treasury has been reimbursed with cash. . . . In this way the $80,000,000 mining company known as United Copper becomes, for the moment, a shell with its valuable assets sold and the cash paid for their control in its treasury."[1]

The status of another asset, the La France Company, was as dubious. Otto Heinze stated that the firm was not transferred to the Butte Coalition Company because Amalgamated was unwilling to pay F. Augustus's price for it. Other sources, however, assert that F. A. did not have complete title to the company.

"The property of the La France Company, constituting the mines of the Lexington Company and the concentrator in Basin known as the 'Heinze' plant, was not included in the sale because Mr. Heinze does not own it and could not sell. He has a lease and bond on the property . . . and on the concentrator from the

---

[1]New York *Herald*, February 20, 1906; as quoted in the Anaconda *Standard*, February 21, 1906.

Boston and Bay State Mining Company which built the plant and a smelter in Basin several years ago."[2]

The latter argument is apparently more correct, for, when Heinze acquired the Basin property (October, 1902), the Anaconda *Standard* reported that he had also secured an option on the Basin concentrator —to buy it within four years at $345,000.[3] F. Augustus did not exercise that option. The La France, further, was not an especially profitable venture.[4]

Even before negotiations with Amalgamated were completed, F. Augustus planned the restocking of United Copper with new operating companies. After the February sale, he assumed control of the Davis-Daly Estates Copper Company (Montana) and the Ohio Copper Company (Utah). The latter proved the more successful acquisition.

On January 12, 1906, Heinze organized the American Consolidated Copper Company under the laws of Maine. The specific purpose of this firm was to consolidate the copper lands held by the estates of A. J. Davis and Marcus Daly.[5] Once these properties were partially secured, F. Augustus launched (May 29, 1906) the Davis-Daly Estates Copper Company. This firm was capitalized at $10,-050,000, again under the laws of Maine. F. A. immediately removed himself from public direction of the company; under the supervision of his agent, Charles R. Leonard, the Davis-Daly began to work southwest of Butte, in mines which had been abandoned since approximately 1890.[6]

The company did not prosper. Several somewhat questionable financial maneuvers were employed by Leonard and the Davis-Daly

---

[2]Anaconda *Standard*, February 19, 1906. One should remember that the *Standard* is an Amalgamated paper at this time; for a discussion of the role of the newspapers in the War of the Copper Kings, please see Chapter VII, p. 77, n. 23.

[3]Anaconda *Standard*, October 9, 1902.

[4]Please see: "La France Copper Company," *Copper Handbook*, ed. Horace J. Stevens (Houghton, Mich.: Stevens; 1908), VIII, pp. 856-857.

[5]"American Consolidated Copper Company," *Copper Handbook*, VIII, p. 294.

[6]"Davis-Daly Estates Copper Company," *Copper Handbook*, VIII, pp. 618-619.

president, J. A. Coram, to keep the firm apparently afloat from 1906 to 1908. With creditors and shareholders converging, F. Augustus reorganized the project into the Davis-Daly Copper Company in the autumn of 1908, and became the firm's president.[7] The Davis-Daly, however, was doomed to failure; it never did make the "strike" that its directors promised. In 1914, the year of Heinze's death, the stockholders were still paying assessments to meet the company's expenditures, which consistently exceeded receipts.[8]

F. Augustus's second attempt to restore the strength of his United Copper Company involved an established firm, the Ohio Copper Company of the Salt Lake district, Utah. In the summer of 1906, F. A. purchased about two-thirds of the Ohio's stock and forced the company's reorganization under the laws of Maine early in 1907; the Ohio's capitalization was increased to $10,000,000 with the reorganization, and raised to $15,000,000 the following year.[9] Heinze directed this company's operations personally during the autumn of 1906 and subsequently advised the Ohio's manager from New York City.

Fritz's activity in Utah resembles somewhat his earlier venture in British Columbia (1894-1898). The Ohio property had been a poor producer from 1903 to 1906; F. A. described it to his brother, Otto, as "a low-grade proposition with a mountain of ore."[10] To reduce expenses and increase volume, Heinze built a tunnel through a mountain and laid the Bingham Central Railroad in the tunnel, thereby connecting the company's concentrator with its mines. The Ohio shortly became a profitable enterprise.[11]

F. Augustus increased this list of "assets" by utilizing a portion of

---

[7]"Davis-Daly Estates Copper Company" and "Davis-Daly Copper Company," *Copper Handbook*, VIII, pp. 618-620. Copper critics generally felt the original firm to be a hoax, promoted by the company's directors solely for their personal profit. A summary in the cited source concludes with the remark: "The Davis-Daly Estates Copper Co., is a swindle and, were justice done, the people responsible for the frauds would be jailed."

[8]Raymer, *Montana*, I, pp. 512-513.

[9]"Ohio Copper Company," *Copper Handbook*, VIII, pp. 1065-1066.

[10]O. C. Heinze MS., p. 55.

[11]O. C. Heinze MS., p. 55.

the twelve million dollars. Newspaper accounts of the sale to Amalgamated surmised that a new company would be formed to operate the Heinze properties; some papers—obviously recalling the Marcus Daly-Amalgamated deal of 1899—also suggested that F. A. would be the executive officer of the new corporation. They were correct concerning the new firm, the Butte Coalition Mining Company, but totally incorrect in forecasting Heinze's position. The New York *Herald* revealed F. Augustus's actual relationship to the B. C. M. C.

"The good will of the Heinzes will also be maintained by the fact that they will be stockholders to a considerable extent in the new company Mr. Cole is forming."[12]

Of the twelve million dollars that he had received from Amalgamated, F. Augustus immediately invested two million in the Butte Coalition corporation.[13]

The *actual* assets of F. Augustus Heinze in the spring of 1906, therefore, included the remainder of the profits from the Amalgamated sale, stock in a company owning his former, proven copper properties, and control of a potentially profitable enterprise in Utah. These assets, however, could not immediately return the income that his Butte properties had provided. F. A. realized that the remaining millions in cash would be the basis of any project; in the autumn of 1906, he began contemplating lucrative endeavors other than mining and smelting.

Against the advice of Otto, the financial expert in the brothers' earlier operations, F. Augustus selected banking. His choice was influenced by two men whom he met after the Amalgamated sale, Charles W. Morse and E. R. Thomas. Morse was president of the Bank of North America, located in Exchange Place, New York City;[14]

---

[12] New York *Herald*, February 20, 1906; as quoted in the Anaconda *Standard*, February 21, 1906.

[13] O. C. Heinze MS., p. 54.

[14] O. C. Heinze MS., p. 55. See also "The Panic," *Literary Digest*, XXXV (November 2, 1907), pp. 631-633.

Thomas was associated with the Hamilton Bank, the Consolidated National Bank, and the Mercantile National Bank, all of New York City.[15] Otto Heinze states that the two men,

". . . courted F. Augustus assiduously and suggested that he also acquire one of New York's banks and join them in their operations."[16]

In addition to his own bank, Charles Morse had interests in other sound New York banks; it was rumored than he planned a national banking chain. He also had several significant businesses in the region. For example, he possessed a practical monopoly of New York's ice trade through his profitable Knickerbocker Ice Company. He also had established the Consolidated Steamship Company which controlled virtually all American ships on the East Coast.[17] This shipping organization, a sixty-million-dollar enterprise, had earned for Morse the enmity of powerful J. P. Morgan, who controlled the New York, New Haven, and Hartford Railroad. Consolidated Steamship interfered with Morgan's acquisition of a monopoly of New England transportation. Moreover, Morse was closely aligned with Tammany Hall which virtually dictated to New York City at the time.[18] Although both F. Augustus and Arthur Heinze were very favorably impressed with Morse, Otto always regarded him with some suspicion.

After little deliberation, F. Augustus joined Morse and Thomas in the banking business—he purchased the Mercantile National Bank of New York City. Noted financier Edwin Gould held the controlling interest in the Mercantile, for which he asked one million dollars.

---

[15]O. C. Heinze MS., p. 55. See also "Panic," *Digest*, p. 632.

[16]O. C. Heinze MS., p. 55.

[17]"The Story of Morse," *Current Literature*, XLVIII (February, 1910), pp. 151-153.

[18]O. C. Heinze MS., p. 56. See also: "Panic," *Digest*, pp. 632-633; Alfred O. Crozier, "The Recent Panic and Deadly Peril to American Prosperity," *The Arena*, XXXIX (March, 1908), pp. 272-275; "Morse's Comeback," *Literary Digest*, XLVI (June 28, 1913), pp. 1438-1440.

Heinze could have paid the full sum in cash, but he did not. He, instead, paid $350,000 in cash and gave Gould his note for $650,-000.[19] Otto Heinze provides an insight to this transaction. He states that F. A. made the purchase jointly with Morse, who did not want his name used as he was not friendly with Gould. Their bargain was that Morse would give a note for $500,000 to Fritz and would pay it when Heinze's note to Gould matured. Gould, therefore, retained as collateral most of the Mercantile stock that F. A. had purchased.[20]

At the annual meeting of the Mercantile National Bank (January, 1907), the board of directors was elected and F. Augustus Heinze assumed the bank's presidency.[21] Otto Heinze was emphatic in explaining his refusal to become one of the directors of the bank. One can perceive in Otto's statement the degree to which the brothers' former, tripartite relationship had dissolved.

"I said I for one did not wish to have anything to do with the bank; unfortunately my judgment was correct in this particular. The main reason for F. A.'s downfall was his being president of the Mercantile Bank. During all these discussions I could not see why he should want to take this position; his being president of a New York bank could not, according to my way of thinking, add anything to his prestige. I never did understand why he was so dead set on taking the position and I never got him to give me his real reasons."[22]

F. Augustus proceeded to expand his base in the realm of banking.

---

[19]Anaconda *Standard*, October 18, 1914.

[20]Gould's testimony at the subsequent investigatory trial (October, 1914) does not entirely complement Otto Heinze's account. Gould stated that he had heard (1906) that Heinze had bought stock in the Mercantile and, with Morse, was trying to gain control of the bank. He protested to Morse that, if Heinze controlled the bank, he would want no part in it. As a result, Morse negotiated to buy from him, for Heinze, eight thousand shares of Mercantile stock. For these shares Morse gave $350,000 in cash and Heinze's note for the balance, for Gould did not want to take Morse's own note. See: Anaconda *Standard*, October 15, 1914; O. C. Heinze MS., p. 57.

[21]O. C. Heinze MS., p. 58.

[22]O. C. Heinze MS., pp. 57-58.

Early in 1907 he joined Morse and Thomas as directors of a national financial chain which included six national banks, ten or twelve state banks, and five or six trust companies. This chain was the third such coalition of closely allied interests which effected vast financial transactions. Their organization was also the newest and, therefore, the least hampered by outmoded banking traditions. The enterprise was formed in much the same manner as that used by Edward H. Harriman to build a complex of railroads. Morse was the principal operator. The method was to buy control of one bank, then to use its stock as collateral to borrow funds for the purchase of another bank; this process could be repeated to the desired magnitude.[23]

Otto Heinze violently opposed his younger brother's entry into banking and he wanted the third brother, Arthur, to assist him in dissuading F. Augustus. To Otto's "disgust," Arthur regarded the enterprise favorably and encouraged F. A.'s participation in the banking coalition.[24] By the late spring of 1907, the foundation had been laid for the greatest debacle of F. Augustus Heinze's career. F. A.'s financial difficulties began almost immediately and they were inextricably involved with the dramatic financial Panic of 1907.

---

[23]"Review of the World," *Current Literature*, XLIII (December, 1907), pp. 585-599. The other two, similar financial coalitions were: 1) the Standard Oil group, dominated by Rockefeller, Rogers, Frick, and Harriman, with the National City Bank as their chief financial company; 2) the Morgan group, dominated by Morgan, Hill, and Ryan, who controlled five national banks and eight trust companies. This account comments upon the new financial coalition, "Having secured a chain of banks, they [Morse, Heinze, Thomas] could proceed to do some dazzling financial work."

[24]Arthur Heinze and Charles Morse had been involved previously in a speculative business relationship. In 1904 they formed a stock pool in which Arthur exchanged 30,000 shares of United Copper stock for shares of comparable value in the Knickerbocker Ice Company. Both Otto and F. Augustus were consenting parties to this transaction which was programmed to extend for two years. In 1906, when the original pool matured, Arthur wanted the brothers to engage in an identical pool with Morse. Otto and F. Augustus refused, but Arthur, who had legal direction of United Copper stock after 1905, launched the second pool. The two brothers, however, could not escape indirect participation in the pool: both owned United Copper stock and the Otto C. Heinze Company was a credit source for Arthur's directorship of the stock. Otto could not cancel the involvement of his company in the pool, because Arthur had been a partner in that firm since 1897. (O. C. Heinze MS., p. 58.)

XI-B. Transition:
The Panic of 1907

Business conditions in the United States were generally prosperous from 1897 to 1907, with the exception of the commercial slump of 1901.[25] Industry expanded, railroads proliferated, and the swelling labor market encouraged heavy immigration. Burgeoning industrialization formed a partial basis for the imperialism manifested in the Spanish-American War. Commerce was profitable, corporate speculation abounded, and capital was often overextended. The demand for money exceeded the supply and, consequently, money was dear.[26] This combination of circumstances classically precedes an economic recession; perhaps the combination *would have* precipitated such a decline in the American economy in 1907. Evidence exists, however, to indicate that the Panic of 1907 was deliberately instigated.

Senator Robert La Follette of Wisconsin believed that the Panic was consciously created. Speaking on the floor of the Senate in 1908, he stated that a diligent study of the financial crisis would show that it had been planned and executed, "insofar as such proceeding is subject to control, after once in motion."[27] He described conditions on the New York Stock Exchange on the day of the most serious crisis, October 24, 1907.

"How perfect the stage setting! How real it all seemed! But back of the scenes Morgan and Stillman were in conference. They had made their representations at Washington; they knew when the next installment of aid would reach New York. . . . They awaited its arrival and deposit. Thereupon they pooled an equal amount and held it. Interest rates soared . . . Wall Street was in a frenzy.

"Two o'clock came and interest rates ran to 150%. The smash-

---

[25]F. S. Mead, "The Panic and the Banks," *Atlantic Monthly*, CI (February, 1908), pp. 273-276.

[26]Lord Welby, "The American Panic," *Contemporary Review*, XCIII (January, 1908), p. 1.

[27]"La Follette's Theory of the Panic," *Literary Digest*, XXXVI (April 4, 1908), p. 470.

ing of the market became terrific. Then at precisely 2:15 the curtain went up with Morgan and Standard Oil in the center of the stage with money—twenty-five millions, giving it away at ten per cent.

"And so ended the panic. How beautifully it all worked out. They had the whole country terrorized. They had the money of the deposits of the banks of every state in the Union to the amount of five hundred millions. It supplied big operators with money to squeeze out investors and speculators . . . taking the stock at enormous profit. . . . Their course was that of men who were playing with the credit of the country for a purpose."[28]

Senator La Follette further demonstrated that, because of the consolidation of the trusts during the Panic, fewer than one hundred men subsequently controlled the credit of the entire nation.[29] He traced quite specifically this condensation of power.

"Two fights had much to do with it: the first was between the Clearing House banks and the trust companies; the second was between F. Augustus Heinze and his allies and the Standard Oil group which organized the Amalgamated Copper Mining Company."[30]

The relationship of each of these quarrels to the Panic is pertinent, since F. Augustus Heinze was involved in each. As one of the new financiers, he was not welcomed by the established Clearing-House bankers. During this period, the trust companies were less restricted by federal banking legislation than were the national banks. The trust institutions could also attract more money, for they were able to pay a higher rate of interest on deposits; consequently, they had more capital for investment.[31] Otto Heinze commented regarding this situation.

---

[28]"La Follette's Theory," *Digest*, pp. 470-471.

[29]"La Follette's Theory," *Digest*, p. 471.

[30]"Story of Heinze," *Current Literature*, p. 35.

[31]Mead, "Panic and Banks," p. 275. See also: Welby, "American Panic," pp. 1-2.

"There was a feeling of irritation between the sedate and old-time national banks and the younger and newer financiers who were forming trust companies and competing for the business and deposits of the old-line bankers. The laws governing trust companies were more liberal than those governing the national banks and they were going ahead fast."[32]

The national-bank complex realized that, if it could make an example of one trust company, it might solidify and facilitate its argument for more sympathetic banking legislation, in both New York and the United States.[33] The fate of the Knickerbocker Trust Company signifies that it was the sacrifical goat. This trust and its president, Charles D. Barney, had been quite successful for a young organization—"one of the largest and strongest [trusts] in the land."[34] Otto describes Barney as, "a very fine man, but very close to Charles Morse."[35] As a result of F. Augustus's dealings with Morse, F. A. was "close," if not "very close," to Barney.

At this juncture, the fate of the Knickerbocker Trust Company and its President Barney, and the demise of the Mercantile Bank, F. Augustus, Charles Morse, and E. R. Thomas become interlaced with the stock-market activities of Otto and Arthur Heinze. When the Heinzes launched the first United Copper stock pool (1904), they purchased, at $96,000, a seat on the New York Stock Exchange for the firm of Otto Heinze and Company. The importation business was subsequently reduced and the firm engaged primarily in banking.

In 1906 United Copper stock sold at $70 a share and had secured listing on the Paris curb market. The tightening of money in the fall of 1907, however, weakened the market and brought United Copper to $40 per share. At this stage Arthur Heinze alone was conducting the second U. C. stock pool. In an effort to support United Copper's price, he purchased large quantities of the stock and placed it on mar-

[32]O. C. Heinze MS., p. 56.
[33]Crozier, "Recent Panic," pp. 273-274.
[34]Crozier, "Recent Panic," p. 274.
[35]O. C. Heinze MS., p. 56.

gin with many brokerage houses—"a most dangerous thing to do; he had created for himself an indebtedness of two million dollars."[36] In October, 1907, constant calls for greater margin from brokers were eliminating the Heinze assets.

Arthur Heinze then discovered, in a precise stock audit, that nearly 100,000 shares of United Copper had been sold to him—*in excess of the number which actually existed.* This revelation indicated that the brokerage houses had sold the shares to him surreptitiously, instead of carrying them. Such indirect dealing by the holding brokers was normally a maneuver to lower the stock's price. If a call upon the brokers to deliver the stock that they were holding for Arthur Heinze found them unable to comply, a corner would be created in United Copper. The brokers would then be forced either to ask a settlement with the Heinzes or to buy at any price at which they could get the stock. In either case, the brothers could make a substantial profit from the transaction.

Arthur and Otto Heinze knew that to create a corner was their only recourse, for it was only a matter of time before they could not pay the margin calls.[37] Brokers who had held the stock and who delivered it when asked would have to be paid immediately. To acquire money for these payments, Otto Heinze went to F. Augustus on October 9, 1907. F. A. refused assistance, stating that he could not jeopardize his own position or that of the Mercantile Bank. He explained further that there had been a silent run on his bank for four months and that four million dollars in deposits had been withdrawn for no apparent reason. He had been forced to call his outstanding loans and could make no substantial advance to anyone.

Two days later it was evident to Arthur and Otto Heinze that further margin calls would eliminate completely the brothers' liquid reserves. An inability to meet these calls would effect the failure of

---

[36]O. C. Heinze MS., p. 60.

[37]One should remember that, although neither F. Augustus nor Otto were directly involved in the second United Copper pool, they were concerned in this situation because both held U. C. stock and did not want it to decrease in value. The pool was also using the credit of the Otto Heinze and Company business firm.

the Otto Heinze Company, its suspension from the Stock Exchange, and the complete devaluation of United Copper. Otto again approached F. Augustus, who arranged a meeting with Charles Morse, E. R. Thomas, and Charles Barney. Whereas all participants agreed that the collapse of the Otto Heinze firm would be disastrous, they denied assistance for the legitimate reason that they held little liquid cash and that their banks were suffering the same silent run that plagued the Mercantile.

Although Otto Heinze could not obtain the funds to cover the demands of the brokers, he nevertheless met (October 16, 1907) with Kleeberg of the Stock Exchange firm of Gross and Kleeberg. Otto asked him to arrange to notify the various brokerage houses regarding delivery of all United Copper stock certificates. This act steadied and increased the value of the copper stock; between ten o'clock and noon, United Copper rose thirty points. The delivery notices returned 30,000 stock certificiates and required payment of $630,000 which had to be made by 2:15 p.m., according to Stock Exchange rules.

These developments placed Arthur Heinze in a more favorable position. With a United Copper price of $60, he only needed approximately one-third of the value of his security to reimburse the brokers. Otto made a third visit to F. Augustus; it brought results. After F. A. had secured the approval of Charles Morse, the Mercantile Bank lent the required $630,000.[38]

The improvement was transitory. The newspapers of October 17 reported that copper prices had hit a record low on the preceding day. Amalgamated had reached 49, its lowest quotation of the year. They further stated that, whereas all coppers were affected, the sensational activity was in United Copper. On October 15, that stock had been advanced to $60 on "wash sales," but fell to $10 on October 16.

Brokers said that United Copper had been held at artificial prices and that those investors owning it had been advised to sell. The declining price would indicate that they were selling. By the close of

---

[38]O. C. Heinze MS., pp. 62-63.

the market on October 16, however, the price had rallied somewhat to $15. A release from the brokerage house of Hayden, Stone and Company said that the firm of Otto Heinze and Company, as well as the officers of United Copper, declined to make a statement. The house, however, conveyed the news that "other circles" were saying that the sensational movement of the stock was the result of manipulation by "insiders," a substantial short interest, and a bungling method of forcing shorts with reaction on the "insiders." The Hayden, Stone release concluded that banks had recently called loans on United Copper stock.[39]

The relevant news story in the Helena *Independent* of October 23, 1907, emphasized the "woman in the case" aspect of the Heinzes' compounding financial difficulties. It explained that F. Augustus Heinze had talked too freely to a young "woman friend" who lived near the Waldorf-Astoria on Thirty-third Street. He supposedly had told her of the overextension of the United Copper pool and she, in turn, had related the information to two "woman friends." None of the women apparently realized the need for extreme secrecy and each discussed the matter freely. A detective firm learned of the talk, checked it, and paid the women for the information.[40]

Amalgamated's men were, of course, tremendously interested and they hired the detectives to continue the investigation for them. The specifics of the situation were secured by having the young woman who first learned of the copper deal find someone close to F. Augustus who would know the complete details—and would reveal them, for a price.

---

[39]Anaconda *Standard*, October 17, 1907. The sudden drop in the price of United Copper stock, just as the pool seemed a success, would indicate that someone had entered the market with a large block of stock. The Heinzes accused Charles Morse of feeding the market ("Comeback," *Digest*, 1439), although he had agreed not to sell his U. C. shares. The brothers never did determine conclusively who had wrecked their cornering movement.

[40]Helena *Independent*, October 23, 1907. The *Independent*, like the vast majority of dailies in Montana during this period, was an Amalgamated-Standard Oil paper; one, therefore, should not expect an account which is sympathetic to F. Augustus's plight. Please see page 77, note 23, for a more detailed discussion of the Montana newspaper alignment during the Copper War, and after 1906.

"With all this knowledge in their possession, the men, who had in Montana and in New York tried to break Heinze, began operations."[41]

It was necessary to find one of the pool members who could be persuaded to betray the others by breaking his portion of the "gentleman's agreement" and, thereby, to ruin the corner in United Copper stock. When the "woman friend" located this member of the clique and induced him to betray the other members, he poured his stock on the market and the corner was immediately smashed. The *Independent's* article cynically concludes that, "The young women have not been seen in their accustomed haunts since the corner has been smashed."[42]

The validity of the "woman friend" slant to the situation is ultimately immaterial, for the financial mechanics are sufficiently correct to reveal the dissipation of the copper corner. Events then began to snowball for the Heinzes. Otto Heinze admits that the corner which had been created in United Copper accelerated the runs on New York banks—especially F. Augustus's—but he views the sequence of events philosophically.

"Corner or no corner, the end result would have been the same; the panic had long since been decreed and prepared and was inevitably on its way. After all, the downfall of the Otto Heinze and Company firm was just an incident—the main victims to be destroyed were the new financiers, their banks, and their trust companies."[43]

The corner of United Copper stock was smashed, the stock devaluated rapidly, to below its previous bottom of $10, and the Otto Heinze firm—a credit source for U. C.—declined. The financial panic began to gain momentum seriously. Concerted runs began on many New York banks; they *continued* on F. Augustus's Mercantile National.

---

[41]Helena *Independent*, October 23, 1907.

[42]Helena *Independent*, October 23, 1907.

[43]O. C. Heinze MS., p. 63.

On October 16, 1907, F. A. applied to the Clearing House committee for aid. Five accounts of the subsequent series of events coalesce to present a revealing pastiche of American business in crisis. The first report is one filed by the Associated Press on October 17.

"Sensations followed each other in rapid succession in the financial district today as a result of the projected corner in United Copper and the suspension of a prominent brokerage firm [Gross and Kleeberg] yesterday.

"The firm of Otto Heinze and Company was suspended on the exchange.

"F. Augustus Heinze, the Butte copper magnate, resigned as president of the Mercantile National Bank of New York.

"Amalgamated Copper, at its directors' meeting, cut its quarterly dividend from 2% to 1%.

"Boston and Montana directors declared a dividend of $6, instead of the former $12.

"Failure of the Haller, Seehle and Company of Hamburg, Germany [a substantial investor in American mining, including Amalgamated and United Copper], with liabilities that may reach $7,000,000 was announced.

"The State Savings Bank of Butte, in which the Heinzes are principal stockholders, suspended operations.

"As a result, the market was halting and irregular.

"The suspension of the Otto Heinze firm was due to a complaint of the Gross and Kleeberg Company that they had bought 3,211 shares of United Copper stock at the order of the Otto Heinze Company, but that the Heinze firm refused to pay the $600,000 owing them. The Heinze firm announced that it was solvent.[44]

---

[44]The Otto Heinze firm did refuse to buy stock (October 16, 1907) which Gross and Kleeberg had purchased. Otto Heinze states (O. C. Heinze MS., p. 63) that Kleeberg asked him for a check for five thousand shares of United Copper stock which he had bought at $50 a share; this would total $250,000. As he had particularly told Kleeberg to "not do anything in the market, to not buy or sell for my account, I would not accept or pay him." Kleeberg had his lawyers bring the matter before the Stock Exchange (October 16) and on the following day the firm of Otto Heinze was suspended and a receiver appointed by the court (October 17). Three years later the

"The resignation of F. A. Heinze was decided on at a night meeting at the home of C. W. Morse, who is largely interested in the bank. Mr. F. A. Heinze explained that he was resigning in order to spend his time straightening the business of his brothers' firm. He said he was not giving up his control in the bank; the control would remain the same."[45]

The second account was issued by the Butte office of Paine, Webber and Company, a brokerage firm, on October 18, 1907.

"As a condition of coming to the assistance of the Mercantile National Bank, the New York Clearing House today demanded the resignation of every director of the bank. The resignations were immediately signed and delivered to the Clearing House. Comptroller W. B. Ridgely has decided to accept the presidency of the Mercantile National Bank."[46]

The third report commences dramatically and is included in a contemporary article which develops the thesis that the Amalgamated and Standard Oil had attempted to ruin F. Augustus Heinze since the early Butte days. Of the Clearing House incident, the article concludes, "They think that they have him now."

" 'Sell and get out or take the consequences.' That ultimatum was delivered by the Clearing House committee in New York to F. Augustus Heinze sitting in his office in the Manhattan

---

receiver was dismissed and it was announced that the Otto Heinze Company had not been bankrupt when the receiver was appointed. This judgment, however, did not help the firm, which Otto says, "could never be resurrected." There were two other petitioners for the receiver, in addition to Gross and Kleeberg: a brokerage firm with a claim for $3,000, and a stationery company with a claim for sixty cents for office paper.

Another source—Harold J. Howland, "Standard Oil," *Outlook*, LXXXVI (September 28, 1908), p. 171—gives a different amount as claimed by the brokerage firm, Gross and Kleeberg: "Otto Heinze and Company, the agents for the insiders, refused to meet their buying obligations and a firm of brokers who held such contracts to the amount of $400,000 was forced to suspend while a movement was set on foot to have the Otto Heinze Company expelled from the Stock Exchange."

[45] Associated Press dispatch (New York City), October 17, 1907; as quoted in the Anaconda *Standard*, October 18, 1907.

[46] Anaconda *Standard*, October 19, 1907. Ridgely subsequently declined the position.

[i.e. Mercantile] National Bank, New York, a few weeks ago. At last the financiers of New York City had Heinze on the hip and he knew it. He was afraid to take those 'consequences,' so he sold and got out of the presidency of the bank. The bank was saved, but the panic was started."[47]

The fourth example comprises a retrospective view of the situation from London.

"October 20 [sic], the storm broke. The Mercantile Bank applied to the New York Clearing House for aid, and the Clearing House, after examining its affairs, called on the board of directors to resign. The resignation of the presidents of the Knickerbocker Trust and of other banks with which the Mercantile had been connected followed. The banks had been misusing their deposits in order to promote their own speculative schemes."[48]

Otto Heinze contributes the fifth, and final, element of the montage of American business.

"By the middle of the week a number of runs were developing, particularly on Morse's Bank of North America and F. Augustus's Mercantile Bank. There were some others which had already been helped out by the Clearing House committee. F. A. decided to apply to the committee. Examiners were sent into the bank and found it sound. But the Clearing House refused to give assistance unless the control of the bank were turned over to them and F. A. immediately resigned its presidency. He could do nothing else. The bank was assisted, remained open and every depositor received his money in full. Exactly the same thing happened to C. W. Morse when he had to call on the Clearing House committee; his bank also went through the panic and paid its depositors in full also. But the stocks of these two banks took a perpendicular drop of fully 50% or more."[49]

---

[47]"Story of Heinze," *Current Literature*, p. 36.

[48]Welby, "American Panic," p. 1.

[49]O. C. Heinze MS., p. 64.

Evidence substantiates Otto Heinze's assertion that the Mercantile National Bank was always solvent.[50] The bank was reorganized on October 20, with Seth M. Milliken, "one of the best known New York capitalists," as its president. Milliken's son, Gerrish, and William Skinner, a director of the New York, New Haven, and Hartford Railroad, became the Mercantile's new vice-presidents. Immediately following the reorganization, the Clearing House announced that the bank was *officially* solvent. With the permanent resignations of the concern's former directors—including F. Augustus, Morse, and Thomas—the Clearing House proclaimed its readiness to lend all necessary funds to any New York bank.[51] Financiers believed this action would preclude any crisis in New York banking circles.[52] The entire nation hoped that the Clearing House had rectified the "inequities" which had appeared on the banking scene and that the stock market would hold a relatively firm line. The Rogers-Standard Oil-Amalgamated complex, however, was not finished with F. Augustus Heinze; the upstart financier's bank was nullified, but he also was a partner in the trust chain with Morse, Thomas, and Charles Barney.

On October 22, 1907, the Knickerbocker Trust Company applied to the National Bank of Commerce, its regular agent with the New York Clearing House, to approve an $8,000,000 draw. The National Bank refused.[53] "Almost at once the news broke forth in scare headlines across the nation"—one of the largest trusts in the country was in trouble.[54] This news, however, was suspect. It was no secret to the business world that the directors of the national banks and those executives of Standard Oil also controlled Western Union and a number

---

[50] When the New York State Treasurer, Julius Hauser, and a number of other state officials visited the Mercantile National to investigate its condition—after F. Augustus's resignation—Milliken assured them that the bank was solvent and he advised them to leave in the bank those funds which the State had on deposit there, approximately $600,000 (Anaconda *Standard,* October 20, 1907).

[51] O. C. Heinze MS., p. 65.

[52] Anaconda *Standard,* October 21, 1907; from an Associated Press dispatch, New York.

[53] Crozier, "Recent Panic," p. 275.

[54] B. O. Flowers, "Popular Rule or Standard Oil Supremacy—Which Shall It Be?" *The Arena,* XXXIX (March, 1908), p. 340.

of newspapers with membership in the Associated Press. These men also owned chains of newspapers in the regions in which they had business interests—for example, the Amalgamated chain in Montana.[55] A case of "news management" was a possibility, to injure the Knickerbocker trust.

Many of the Knickerbocker's clients were not privy to this newspaper knowledge; they panicked and rushed to demand their deposits.

"The Knickerbocker Trust paid out four million dollars in a couple of hours; the Clearing House refused to help and the trust had to close its doors. Charles Barney, its president, shot and killed himself that night and runs started on nearly every bank and trust company in New York."[56]

At this point the real impact of the Panic of 1907 was felt. The financial maneuverings designed for specific victims could no longer be controlled and the financial decline was almost completely nondiscriminatory; especially the small investor who entered the market on margin was injured.

Public confidence, however, was restored somewhat when the large Trust of America Company and the Lincoln Trust met all obligations to their depositors during this hectic October week. Ultimately— near the turn of the year—the market stabilized, with the result cited by Senaor La Follette: fewer than one hundred men controlled the credit of the entire nation; they had eliminated their competitors and their enemies.

The Panic of 1907 accomplished three objectives so concentrated that they lend credence to the charge that the calamity was artificially or deliberately caused.

---

[55]New York *Post*, November 2, 1907; as quoted in the Anaconda *Standard*, November 3, 1907. This newspaper, in analyzing the causes of the Panic of 1907 blames, ". . . the recklessness with which newspaper headlines started the serious run last Wednesday and the dastardly use of newspaper advertising columns by the notorious Boston tipster [Thomas W. Lawson, the Standard Oil publicity agent]."

[56]O. C. Heinze MS., p. 64.

1. F. Augustus Heinze—an anathema to Standard Oil and Amalgamated Copper financiers, and one who dared, perhaps unwisely, to compete in their preserve of finance after having checkmated their plans in mining—was driven from the realm of national finance.
2. Charles W. Morse—whose extensive shipping business challenged the completion of a New England transportation monopoly under the aegis of J. P. Morgan—was routed and his national banking chain was rendered innocuous.
3. Public confidence in the newer trusts, banks, and bankers was weakened by the Knickerbocker Trust failure; the established financiers could then seek the desired legislation with a fair assurance of success.

A single incident possibly best exemplifies these three consequences of the Panic of 1907. Quite coincidently, one of the two new vice-presidents of the Mercantile National Bank—William Skinner—was a director of the Morgan-dominated New York, New Haven, and Hartford Railroad.

After the acute phase of the Panic had passed, in December, 1907,[57] F. Augustus Heinze assessed his situation. His complete financial venture was a shambles; he had lost his bank, his position in the Morse-Heinze-Thomas national financial trust, his profit from the United Copper shares, and the majority of his fortune. This decimation is vividly illustrated by the relevant entries in *Who's Who in America*. The volume for 1910-1911,[58] compiled during 1907, lists F. A.'s associations with the Mercantile National Bank, the Consolidated National Bank, the Mechanics and Traders Bank, the State Savings Bank (Butte), the Utah National Bank (Salt Lake City), the

---

[57]Some steps taken by men of authority in the national financial realm to restore confidence and financial security included: the issuance of Clearing House certificates which the banks agreed to accept instead of cash for the obligations that they owed to each other; the policy that savings and deposit banks would require thirty days' notice before the withdrawal of deposits; the United States government's issuance of bonds which were drawn on its power to borrow for the construction of the Panama Canal.

[58]"F. Augustus Heinze," *Who's Who in America*, ed. Albert N. Marquis (Chicago: Marquis; 1910), VI, p. 881.

Provident Savings Life Assurance Society, and the Cosmopolitan Fire Insurance Company. The volume for 1912-1913,[59] however, cites none of these relationships. F. Augustus's banking interests had been destroyed. The Rogers-Standard Oil-Amalgamated complex had accomplished in the civilized confines of Wall Street that which it had failed to achieve upon, and within, a copper mountain in the primitive wilds of Montana: the financial ravage of F. Augustus Heinze.

XI-C. Transition:
Wall Street to Butte—and Beyond

There were, of course, other factors which made the financial situation of 1907 susceptible to a panic, regardless of personal vindication. The economic recession was more extensive than the lives and fortunes of a score of men whose hatred had gradually intensified. The laxity which legally existed in stock-market transactions was itself a cause. One could speculate by presenting a margin payment which was but one-tenth or one-fifteenth of the investment. The customer who placed such a small deposit hoped to win many times that amount; the small deposit often represented his entire cash resources. Unfortunately brokers and bankers accepted the precept that an outsider or amateur who speculated heavily in the market would lose; they often implemented this "law."

A prime, resultant suggestion for market reform—with the hope of preventing future crises, especially among the small investors— was that no margin less than one-fifth of the total face value be accepted for the sale of securities.[60] Reforms were also necessary, on both state and national banking levels, which would provide greater protection and strength for banks through centralization. Relevant reformational suggestions were made by President Theodore Roosevelt, Secretary of the Treasury George B. Cortelyou, Controller of the

---

[59]"F. Augustus Heinze," *Who's Who in America*, ed. Albert N. Marquis (Chicago: Marquis; 1912), VII, p. 1076.

[60]"The Abuse of Speculation," *American Review of Reviews*, XXXVII (June, 1908), pp. 750-751.

Currency William Ridgely and Governor Charles Evans Hughes of New York. Several investigatory commissions were established by these men.[61]

In terms of F. Augustus Heinze's career, the unfortunate element of the Panic of 1907 was the business tradition that permitted speculative activity of the type therein exposed. Men with money, desirous of acquiring more money by broadening their transactions, utilized the lack of economic restraints. Testifying in his own defense in a subsequent court case (1914), F. Augustus said that he had never inspected the books of the Mercantile National Bank and that he was so busy with the affairs of his twenty or twenty-five mining companies that he had left the operation of the bank to a vice-president who had been retained from Gould's staff. If this statement is correct, and the facts support it, immediate reform of the banking situation was certainly necessary.

Billions of dollars were lost by American investors in the debacle of 1907. The average citizen, as he does when periodically his pocketbook is pinched or shrinks, emitted a bloodcurdling cry of angry frustration and gesticulated savagely the urgent command: "the government should do something."

Several investigations commenced in the autumn of 1907 and during 1908. In the most publicized one, District Attorney Wise of New York seized all the business papers of the Heinzes, the accounts for the Mercantile National Bank, and the records of the Otto Heinze Company. He was not able, however, to secure the records of United Copper. The books for that organization had disappeared and F. Augustus refused to produce them. Heinze's enemies charged that the books had been mutilated, that thirty-seven pages were missing from one of the ledgers. This accusation cannot be substantiated, as the ledgers were never presented during the subsequent court trial. F. Augustus insisted that the demand for them was simply a circuitous attempt to obtain an account of his business affairs.[62]

---

[61]"Editorial: The Panic," *American Review of Reviews*, XXXVII (June, 1908), pp. 12-13.
[62]*Reveille*, May 28, 1909.

The court indicted Charles W. Morse and F. Augustus Heinze separately.[63] Morse was tried on two counts of grand larceny and was sentenced to fifteen years in the federal penitentiary at Atlanta, Georgia. Specifically the sentence penalized him for failure to protect a note for $500,000.[64] Heinze was first charged in January, 1908, for endorsing notes used to assist the Otto Heinze Company, which had inadequate collateral. He later received fourteen additional charges of the same nature. A sixteenth count was the court's order to produce the United Copper books.[65] Otto Heinze explained the entire indictment.

"The indictment claimed F. A. was a member of Otto Heinze and Company and a member of Arthur's pool; that the loan was an overloan made on worthless collaterals; that the checks I had issued to the brokers were certified by the bank before the loan had been entered in its books and, therefore, overcertified. Not one of these charges was true or based on facts."[66]

F. Augustus's trial began in the spring of 1909. A portent of the ultimate consequence appeared when, on March 20, Justice Lacombe of the United States Court in New York ordered the shareholders for the Bank of America to discontinue their action against F. A.[67] Another favorable development was the victory of Heinze's associates in the shareholders' election of a new board of directors of the United Copper Company, on June 2, 1909.[68] The most strained court incidents concerned the missing United Copper Company books. F. Augustus, in refusing to produce the ledgers, maintained that he was

---

[63]O. C. Heinze MS., p. 64.

[64]"Comeback," *Digest*, p. 1438. Morse unsuccessfully appealed his sentence and was taken to Atlanta on January 3, 1910. After serving two years, he was pardoned by President Taft. Morse's wife was largely responsible for his release; she worked unceasingly in his behalf. By 1913 Charles Morse was again in the shipping business, with headquarters at Exchange Place, New York City.

[65]*Reveille*, May 28, 1909.

[66]O. C. Heinze MS., p. 66.

[67]*Reveille*, March 20, 1909.

[68]*Reveille*, March 20, 1909.

simply applying his constitutional rights. As he was already under one indictment, the order to produce the books could not be legally prosecuted against him. The New York *Evening World* described Heinze's conduct on May 27, 1909.

"Apparently the least concerned person in the turmoil that has grown out of the efforts of the federal authorities to investigate ... affairs of the United Copper Company is F. Augustus Heinze. Heinze has remained cool, unruffled, defiant, hedging behind 'constitutional rights.' "[69]

The story also stated that, after the hectic hours in court, F. A. returned aloofly to his headquarters at the Waldorf-Astoria, where he was host at an evening dinner party.

The case was recessed for six weeks during the summer of 1909 while District Attorney Wise traveled in Europe. Shortly after court resumed, the count against Heinze for conspiracy to obstruct the administration of justice by concealing the United Copper Company data was dismissed, as were fourteen of the fifteen counts charging misappropriation of bank funds. The single count unanswered was that Heinze had discounted one note which he knew was insufficiently secured. Later in 1909, United States Justice Hough officially and fully exonerated F. Augustus of the charges of malfeasance while in his banking position.[70]

Especially Montanans vigilantly followed Heinze's trials through 1909. A typical letter of encouragement and congratulation, from J. U. Sanders of Helena, prompted a reply from F. Augustus.

"I want to thank you most sincerely for your kindly expressions of good cheer upon my recent vindication. The efforts of the District Attorney [Wise] certainly seem to me to have been prompted by motives other than those which should have actuated them. Your letter is one of many which I have received

[69]New York *Evening World*, May 27, 1909; as quoted in the *Reveille*, May 28, 1909.
[70]O. C. Heinze MS., p. 67.

from friends all over the country, and I cherish this expression of sympathy from you more than words can convey.

"With renewed thanks, I am yours very sincerely, . . ."[71]

His name cleared and the shadow of prison removed, F. A. Heinze returned to the scene of his early triumphs. On November 7, 1909, he entered Butte; his arrival was a monumental event. Reception committees met his train at Livingston and Whitehall, Montana, and accompanied him to Butte. A lively band and an automobile procession of his followers paraded into town. Heinze himself was transported in the horse-drawn hack of Butte's reknowned liveryman, "Fat Jack" Jones—that is, until exuberant persons removed the horses and pulled the hack themselves. A large rope was attached to the wagon tongue so more men could assist in pulling their hero. All along the route, people shouted, "What's the matter with Heinze?" and answered their rhetorical cheer with yells of, "He's all right!" and "Oh, you, Heinze!"[72]

A speech at the Butte Hotel climaxed the evening. Thomas Walker, popular Butte attorney, apologized for the absence of the mayor and introduced the returned hero. F. Augustus told his listeners that he had not really sold out to the Amalgamated—for he had never stopped being an employer in Butte. He promised that the Butte properties which he still held would be developed and the number of miners working in them increased.[73]

A few days later, at the Montana Club in Helena, that city's citizens gave F. Augustus an official welcome and dinner party. The presiding officer at this affair was Edwin Norris, Governor of Montana. In his remarks, which recalled to many his stump speeches of the early

---

[71]Letter to J. U. Sanders—Sanders and Sanders, 37-38 Bailey Block, Helena, Montana—from F. Augustus Heinze—74 Broadway, New York City, New York; May 13, 1910. The original of this letter is in the Montana State Historical Society Library, Helena, Montana.

[72]*Reveille*, November 8, 1909. See also: Anaconda *Standard*, November 8, 1909.

[73]*Reveille*, November 8, 1909. See also: Anaconda *Standard*, November 8, 1909.

decade, F. A. spoke of "coming full circle" and of his plans to open new mines in the Butte district to benefit all Montana.[74]

He appeared, however, somewhat older, somewhat wiser, somewhat subdued. The fire was not being banked; it was actually dying. The confident, triumphant copper magnate who left Butte in 1906 was admittedly not the dynamo who had viciously battled Standard Oil on all fronts during the second phase of the Copper War (1896-1906). The "vindicated" ex-financier who returned to Butte in 1909, however, could successfully recreate *neither* of these popular images. In 1909 Montanans quite possibly indulged in one of the masses' prerogatives regarding a public figure; they admired and cheered *not* the F. Augustus Heinze standing before them in the Butte Hotel or the Montana Club, but the F. Augustus Heinze directing underground combat and court maneuvers with equal facility; they actually gave a testimonial dinner for the David who stood on the steps of the Silver Bow County Courthouse, convinced them of the giant's immorality, and courageously led them into battle.

Fritz remained in Montana until December 15, 1909, visiting his properties and consulting with his foremen and superintendents. During this month following his return, he took brief trips to the Ohio Company mines in Utah. When he departed Butte for the East in December, he again visited Salt Lake City to observe the Ohio's new, million-dollar mill which had recently been placed in production.[75] This activity is indicative of F. Augustus's post-Panic years.

Although the financial experiences and the concomitant court trials were the spectacular events of F. A.'s career after 1906, they did not absorb him completely. After the Panic of 1907, he entered a mining venture in Idaho and acquired the prosperous Stewart Mining Company. He returned to Canada also and, at Porcupine, British Columbia, purchased the West Dome mine which began extraction in 1911. An accident and fire postponed developments at Porcupine, but F. Augustus was planning a system to make the mine profitable in 1914,

---

[74]*Reveille*, November 19, 1909. See also: Anaconda *Standard*, November 29, 1909.
[75]*Reveille*, December 16, 1909.

when he died. He also inspected properties in Alaska and obtained some prospects in that region, although Otto Heinze does not know the extent of these acquisitions.[76]

In October, 1914, F. Augustus reappeared in New York court news. He had failed to meet his debt to Edwin Gould on the note of $650,000 for the purchase of the Mercantile National Bank which had expired in December, 1907. Otto Heinze recalls that Charles W. Morse defaulted on his note to F. A. for $500,000.[77] This failure, however, did not justify F. Augustus's own failure to fulfill his agreement with Gould.

Heinze countersued in 1914 on the contention that Charles Morse had misrepresented the bank stock to him; Morse had told him that the stock included a million dollars in hidden assets—assets not shown on the bank's books. Fritz explained that Gould had worked diligently to persuade him to buy eight thousand shares of stock in the bank and that the inducement for his purchase was the presidency of the bank, at an annual salary of $20,000. He stated further that he had delegated management of the bank to a vice-president, Miles O'Brien. O'Brien was one of Gould's executives who was retained when Heinze assumed the presidency (1907). Finally, F. A. testified that he had never taken his salary, but had left it in the bank to cover the purchased stock.[78]

Under cross-examination, F. A. said that he and Morse had controlled 14,300 shares of the bank's stock and that its deposits were $20,000,000 when he assumed the presidency (January, 1907); these deposits dropped to $7,000,000 by autumn, 1907. When asked why he had left the presidency, F. Augustus replied, "I was told by the New York Clearing House committee to get out, so I got out."[79]

---

[76]O. C. Heinze MS., pp. 67-68.

[77]Please see Section A of this chapter for a detailed presentation of this situation. Otto states (O. C. Heinze MS., p. 70) that Morse's note was collected by F. Augustus's estate lawyers after F. A.'s death in 1914. One-third of the face value of the note—or approximately $170,000—was recovered.

[78]O. C. Heinze MS., p. 69.

[79]Anaconda *Standard*, October 15, 1914.

On October 14, 1914, the court awarded Gould a judgment of $1,200,000.[80] This case was one of the most expensive which Heinze ever lost.

The Heinze brothers, whose tripartite coalition successfully weathered the second phase of the great Copper War (1896-1906) and was basic to bringing millionaire status to each, ceased to work in conjunction after 1907. This business and personal alienation is traceable to several circumstances. The dissolution was basically precipitated by the fact that F. Augustus yielded to Otto's persuasion (1905) and sold his 100,000 shares of Amalgamated stock; subsequently Amalgamated rose slightly, rather than fell, in value. This loss of potential funds determined F. Augustus to follow his own judgment and to seek no advice in future financial enterprises. Another factor contributing to fraternal dissolution was the United Copper stock pool which Arthur resolutely maintained against the wishes of the other two, with devastating results. Otto's manipulation to secure a copper corner in the autumn of 1907 was equally devastating to the brothers' relationship.

The immediate consequences of the Panic of 1907—the ruin of the Otto C. Heinze Company, the end of F. Augustus's career in banking, and the obliteration of the United Copper stock pool—brought mutual recrimination when the brothers restrospectively viewed the events of that autumn. Each blamed his two brothers: F. Augustus had persistently sought the presidency of the Mercantile National Bank; Arthur had continued the United Copper stock pool; Otto had attempted to create the corner in copper. Each brother consequently went his individual way. Given the heights to which the brothers rose while in tripartite coalition, the dissolution of the partnership is regrettable. Otto Heinze, in commenting on Fritz's secretive enterprises, inadvertently reveals that he felt some of that regret.

"He was so close-mouthed about all his property that when he died so suddenly, no one knew where much of his property was,

---

[80]Anaconda *Standard*, November 5, 1914.

except in a very general way, and I am sure much of it was lost."[81]

The term "transition" adequately characterizes the final period of F. Augustus Heinze's life (1906-1914), but perhaps the word "dissipation" is more precise. There was a dissipating action to F. A.'s movement after he left Butte. Mining ventures failed, financial endeavors proved barren, court decisions went against him, the fraternal coalition dissolved and, finally, his marriage failed. Yet Fritz remained resolute—he emerged from the Panic of 1907 still a millionaire and determinedly began to build a new copper complex. There just was not sufficient time.

---

[81]O. C. Heinze MS., p. 68.

Chapter XII

F. AUGUSTUS: A PERSONAL MOSAIC

The life of F. Augustus Heinze is a sketch of the young, energetic, daring, courageous, eager businessman typical of the turn of the century. Following his graduation from the Columbia School of Mines in 1889, F. A.'s life accelerated rapidly. It ceased that acceleration only when Fritz burned himself out in 1914; he had not reached his forty-fifth birthday. F. Augustus used—literally *used*—those twenty-five years to pursue success.

It is not difficult for one to lapse into a two-dimensional characterization of F. Augustus Heinze as "Dynamic American Capitalist, circa 1900." Involuted sequences of litigation, credit lines, political stratagems, ingenious legal devices, secretive negotiations, stock-market intricacies, mining claim boundaries, coded telegrams—all tend to flatten the personality of the protagonist. One readily accepts F. Augustus as a satanic manipulator, and studies the mechanics of his next maneuver. To inflate that two-dimensional sketch, to provide depth for the portrait, one can concentrate on the personality of the subject. This chapter provides notes for such a concentration.

XII-A. Notes:
Mode of Living

The Butte Hotel was F. Augustus Heinze's headquarters prior to 1906. After his sale to Amalgamated, the Waldorf-Astoria in New York City became his center of business and pleasure.[1] Although F. A. had stayed at the Waldorf prior to 1906, upon returning to the

---

[1] O. C. Heinze MS., p. 54.

city to embark upon a financial career, he took a double suite at the old hotel which, from 1895 to 1929, stood at the present site of the Empire State Building.

"The Waldorf was the first of the famous, fabulous, super-deluxe hotels that this country ever had. . . . It always managed to attract great and well-known people. It has entertained practically every prominent American and almost every famous foreigner to visit the United States. . . ."[2]

The Waldorf was a suitable environment for F. Augustus's eastern activities. He employed his double suite as an office during the day, and as the scene of his evening entertainment.

Rich men and lovely women gravitated to the Waldorf. In its lounges and lobbies the investments of the day, the potentialities of new inventions, and the record of past financial ventures were discussed. From its doorways, members of the Waldorf's masculine clientele emerged to participate in the buying and selling of Wall Street. Through the same doorways they returned in the afternoon to continue their discussions and, although such procedure was not recognized by Stock Exchange rules, to arrange sales and deals for the next day.[3] In its dining rooms and at the private parties hosted by its guests, the socialites of the country circulated. Good food, vintage wines, rare cordials, spirited conversation and lush, comfortable surroundings afforded pleasure.

F. Augustus Heinze moved easily in this environment. He was cultured, a good singer and skilled musician, a fine conversationalist, and a fluent linguist. His experiences in practical mining and the legal aspects of mining also provided entry into circles in which men considered mining an investment. With youth and capital to invest, F. Augustus was able to weigh the advantages and disadvantages of the various enterprises discussed, prior to deciding his next adventure.

Fritz also maintained a beautifully furnished suite on Thirty-third

[2]Rufus Jarman, "America's Grand Hotel," *Saturday Evening Post*, CCXIX (January 25, 1947), p. 21.

[3]O. C. Heinze MS., p. 54.

Street, directly opposite the Waldorf. He occupied it when he was in
New York for a lengthy visit. On these more extended residences, he
brought with him his Chinese servant, Sing. Sing had managed his
Butte apartment since early in the 1890's. This Oriental, described
by one of Heinze's former newsmen as a "quaint character of sur-
passing wisdom," was an effective organizer and could, on extremely
short notice, plan and serve a dinner for any number of Heinze's
guests.[4] In such cases Sing would secure another Chinese to cook,
while he functioned as a waiter-butler.[5]

Frequently at dinners and parties, F. A. was host to prominent persons and, thereby, he combined business with pleasure. His parties
for larger groups were given at the Waldorf.

"He entertained most lavishly—some forty or fifty men and
women at a time. The favors were frequently of gold, the
flowers profuse and beautiful, the food excellent and the cham-
pagne plentiful. At one dinner given for his Broadway friends
and actresses, there was a small envelope at each woman's place
with a hundred dollar bill enclosed. These parties usually began
late and did not end for many hours. F. A. would often play all
night and work all day."[6]

Heinze was generous, but objectively generous. A Butte acquaintance
of Fritz says that he is done an injustice by stories which relate that,
if one admired the salt shakers, the silver service, or any ornament on
the tables at his famous dinner parties, he would make it a gift to the
admirer.[7] His financial sense was too keen to permit indiscriminate
donations.

Many persons who know little of F. Augustus, nevertheless have
the impression that he was a Casanova. To some degree this characterization is correct. One can understand that women were interested

---

[4]Byron E. Cooney, "Heinze's Cabinet," Fallon County *News*, January 2, 1928.

[5]O. C. Heinze MS., p. 68.

[6]O. C. Heinze MS., p. 42.

[7]Interview with Mrs. T. J. Murray, July 21, 1943.

in Heinze: he was handsome, dominating, and wealthy. Although he could negotiate an effective business deal with almost bitter objectivity, he had a shy manner that drew the feminine spectator to him. He was practically unable to extricate himself easily or casually from a group of women.[8] Butte accepted the fact that, during his career in that city, Heinze had various mistresses. F. A., however, never flaunted them, thereby breaching Butte's social mores. Men of the town, his associates, never treated these women with disrespect, but always in the same manner that they would employ with their wives and daughters.[9]

XII-B. Notes:
Marriage

In 1909 F. Augustus met Bernice Golden Henderson, an actress who had gained minor theatrical success in New York City. A contemporary news story referred to her as, "The Titian-blonde who succeeded Kathryn Kaelread in *A Fool There Was.*"[10] Mrs. Henderson had been recently divorced from her English husband; she received custody of their young daughter, Kitty, of whom Heinze became very fond.[11] Bernice was striking in appearance: five feet, nine inches tall, slender and well-proportioned, with red hair and enormous blue eyes. She won F. Augustus's favor early in 1910.[12]

Bernice Henderson wired an acceptance of F. A.'s proposal of marriage from London and made the announcement of engagement to her friends who met her ship in New York on August 20, 1910. At this time she introduced Heinze to them, as he too was present to greet her. An account of her return to the United States placed F. A.'s name on the society page.

---

[8]Interview with Mrs. T. J. Murray, July 21, 1943.

[9]Interview with Mrs. T. J. Murray, July 21, 1943.

[10]Anaconda *Standard*, August 22, 1910.

[11]O. C. Heinze MS., p. 69.

[12]Interview with Mrs. T. J. Murray, July 21, 1943. See also: O. C. Heinze MS., p. 69.

"As soon as the customs officers had finished tossing Miss [sic] Henderson's belongings about the pier, in fruitless quest for dutiable finery, the pair were whirled away to make a brief week-end visit to the family of Otto Heinze."[13]

F. Augustus Heinze and Bernice Henderson were married on August 31, 1910, when he was forty and she was approximately ten years his junior. Sufficient interest was aroused by the affair that F. A. issued a news release.

"F. Augustus Heinze and Mrs. Bernice Golden Henderson were married this afternoon at the residence of Father H. A. Hambel (Episcopal) of 34 Jefferson Avenue, Brooklyn, who for many years has been a personal friend of Mrs. Henderson. Mrs. Golden, the bride's mother, gave her away, and Carlos Warfield of Butte officiated as best man. After the ceremony the party proceeded in automobiles to the Waldorf-Astoria where the wedding supper was served."[14]

The release also mentioned some of the guests: Mr. and Mrs. Otto Heinze, Mr. and Mrs. Arthur P. Heinze, Mrs. Stanley Gifford, and Mr. and Mrs. George Potter, among others. The account stated that only the immediate families and a few of F. Augustus's Western friends were present at the wedding dinner. It concluded by noting that the bride was "cool and smiling . . . and not at all ill at ease; she wore a becoming travel frock."[15]

Even on his wedding day, however, F. Augustus could not extricate himself from business affairs. The Anaconda *Standard*—an Amalgamated paper—carried a pertinent item immediately beneath the account of Heinze's wedding.

"Only a few hours before he was married, The [New York] *American* will say tomorrow, F. Augustus Heinze was served

---

[13]Anaconda *Standard*, August 22, 1910.

[14]Anaconda *Standard*, September 1, 1910.

[15]Anaconda *Standard*, September 1, 1910.

with a summons and complaint in a suit of Mrs. Lillian Hobart French to recover $25,000 in bonds which she says Heinze gave to her, but refused to return when she loaned them to him during the 1907 panic.

"Mrs. French has declared repeatedly that she, and not Mrs. Henderson, would be Heinze's bride."[16]

F. Augustus was apparently devoted to his wife and she seemed in love with him. Their marriage, however, was less than idyllic. Otto Heinze states that his family frequently saw F. A. and his bride in the months after the marriage, and comments regarding their relationship.

"She was nervous—in fact, neurotic. They appeared not to be getting along well. The birth of their son, F. Augustus, Jr., in December, 1911, had injurious effects upon the general health of his wife. To recuperate and rest, she went to Europe."[17]

Separation did not develop greater compatibility; Bernice sued for divorce and an interlocutory degree was issued. The final decree could legally have been entered in March, 1914, but she delayed taking it because she hoped for a reconciliation. In the spring of that year, she was stricken by spinal meningitis from which she never recovered. Her dying wish was that the divorce be expunged from the record for the sake of her son.[18] When F. Augustus learned of her grave illness, he immediately traveled to her bedside. The reconciliation was effected on April 3, 1914, just before Bernice died. Sworn affidavits of this act were taken of the nurses, and Bernice's mother and sister, so the petition for dismissal of the divorce could record the incident for the State of New York. Benjamin Spellman, Bernice Heinze's attorney, described her attitude.

"Because of her love for Heinze and her hope that something

---

[16]Anaconda *Standard*, September 1, 1910. The Murray interview indicates that Mrs. French was one of F. A.'s Butte mistresses, and that the matter was settled out of court.

[17]O. C. Heinze MS., p. 69.

[18]Anaconda *Standard*, April 4, 1914.

would bring about a reconciliation, she postponed taking the final decree which might have been entered last month. She had only until April 17 to decide whether the final decree would be taken. Again and again she told me,

" 'Wait, wait. That decree means death between me and my husband. To take it would tear my soul from my body.'

"In the last minutes of her life she repeated over and over again the request that the record be expunged."[19]

Bernice's body was taken to Toledo, Ohio, for burial in the Golden family plot on April 3, 1914.[20]

During this period, F. Augustus was closer to his sister, Lida Heinze Fleitman, who lived in Brooklyn, than to any other member of his family. To her care he entrusted his young son. While his health permitted, he went several times weekly to visit the boy.[21]

XII-C. Notes:
Of Death

Still in his early forties, F. Augustus showed the effect of his indulgent social life and of the constant strain he had experienced for years. Throughout his life he had lived well and had drunk freely—although he had never been a drunkard. Endowed with a sturdy constitution, he was able to maintain his condition by the strenuous work involved in inspecting his mines. When he was in Butte, Heinze made a practice of inspecting one property every afternoon. Promptly at two o'clock he would descend into one of his mines and would often remain below at late as ten o'clock or until hunger reminded him of the time.[22]

Nothing replaced this discipline after 1906, but F. Augustus still continued the easy life of parties, banquets, late hours, and drink. As

[19]Anaconda *Standard*, April 4, 1914.

[20]Anaconda *Standard*, April 4, 1914.

[21]O. C. Heinze MS., p. 69.

[22]Anaconda *Standard*, November 9, 1914.

he had never been a sportsman, was not a good shot or horseman, and did not care for camping or outdoor life, he received no exercise by recreation.[23] When the luxurious fare complemented the mental stress occasioned by his unsuccessful financial career, it exacted a toll from his health. Pictures of F. A. reveal the startling physical change in him. After the Panic of 1907, he was vastly older, disillusioned, almost distraught in appearance; although he was still quite young, his hair was almost white.[24]

In August, 1914, Otto Heinze for the last time saw F. Augustus alive; F. A. had come to his brother's home to see his son who was visiting "Uncle Otto." "He looked very badly, but neither complained nor said one word about his health."[25] When F. Augustus lost his suit with Edwin Gould (October, 1914), "friends said he was a very sick man and looked terrible."[26]

On November 3, 1914, F. A. went to Saratoga, New York, his official residence, to vote in the off-year election. While in Saratoga he was a guest in the home of his counsel, County Judge Nash Rockwood. That night he suffered a hemorrhage of the stomach, caused by cirrhosis of the liver; F. Augustus had suffered this ailment since June of that year.[27] A telegram was dispatched for his personal physician, Dr. Peter Irving; before he could arrive, however, F. A. died. No member of his family was with F. Augustus at the time, although his sister, Lida Heinze Fleitman, was enroute from New York City. She returned his body to her New York home. Following Episcopal funeral services on November 8, Heinze was buried at the family plot in Greenwood Cemetery (New York), beside the grave of his mother.

Butte significantly recognized the death of F. Augustus Heinze. His obituary was a main story in both the Anaconda *Standard* and the Butte *Miner* of November 5, 1914. Reviews of his life and trib-

---

[23]Interview with Mrs. T. J. Murray, July 21, 1943.
[24]Anaconda *Standard*, November 9, 1914.
[25]O. C. Heinze MS., p. 70.
[26]O. C. Heinze MS., p. 70.
[27]Butte *Miner*, November 5, 1914.

utes to him, by the men of the Anaconda Copper Mining Company and his own followers, comprised several columns. The *Miner* used again the large picture it had featured on the day that Heinze sold his holdings to the Amalgamated. On the day of his burial, a special memorial meeting conducted in the mining city coincided with the hour of the funeral in New York. There was discussion of establishing a scholarship or erecting a monument to retain his name and contribution to the city.[28] After the initial shock of his death faded, however, the talk must have ceased; no such memorial was established.

Heinze's sudden death left his personal affairs a complete mystery to his immediate family. His secretary reported that he had left an estate of one and one-half million dollars.[29] This estimate is substantiated by his brother.

"He at that time had his office downtown on Broadway just off Wall Street. He employed there a bookkeeper, a typist and a man by the name of Saake; none of them really knew anything much about his property or where he had it. After his trial in the bank case he had become exceedingly secretive, had put a lot of things in the name of friends or companies he controlled. He did have in his office and his safety deposit vault securities, which in the course of time were liquidated at considerably over a million dollars. But I am sure that the major portion of his property was lost and never found. He left no will and, as far as I know, no document stating where or what his property really consisted of. Up to the very last he seemed to have all the money he needed; sometimes he was known to carry in his wallet a large amount of cash, as much as ten thousand dollars in large bills."[30]

Insurance policies totaling $275,000 were paid to Lida Heinze Fleitman two or three days after F. Augustus's death. He had named

[28]Anaconda *Standard* and Butte *Miner*, November 5-9, 1914.
[29]Anaconda *Standard*, November 8, 1914.
[30]O. C. Heinze MS., p. 70.

her as his beneficiary and had stipulated that she was to administer the funds for his son. Lida Fleitman later adopted Fritz Augustus, Jr. She assumed a permanent residence in Paris and educated him in French and English schools.[31]

One evening at a banquet in Butte, F. Augustus passed to a friend sitting opposite him a small card which he carried in his wallet. Although the card presented singularly undistinguished verse, the lines are pertinent because F. A. found them appealing. If the verse was to gauge that which Fritz hoped would be his place in time, he asked but little.

> "When I am dead, if man can say
> 'He helped the world upon its way;
> With all his faults of word and deed
> Mankind did have some little need
> Of what he gave'—then in my grave
> No greater honor shall I crave.
>
> When I am gone, if even one
> Can weep because my life is done
> And feel the world is something bare
> Because I am no longer there;
> Call me a knave, my life misspent—
> No matter. I shall be content."[32]

---

[31]O. C. Heinze MS., p. 71.

[32]Anaconda *Standard*, November 6, 1914. This account does not identify the "friend" to whom F. Augustus showed the verse.

Chapter XIII

F. AUGUSTUS HEINZE:
AN ASSESSMENT OF THE MAN

The active career of F. Augustus Heinze extended only twenty-five years (1889-1914). In that quarter century, however, he accomplished much—because he dared much. The impressions which F. Augustus made are so varied that it is difficult for one to specify an absolute characterization. Whether they condemned or commended, those men in Butte who knew him used superlatives, for Heinze was an extraordinary young man. He was, most notably, a planner rather than a plunger. Behind every successful action of his life was a period of study and concerted preparation. F. Augustus was no gambler; the single time that he did gamble, he was virtually ruined.

During his first year in Butte (1889-1890), F. A. was apparently just another young engineer on his first job. Actually, he was a student in his new laboratory, the vein system of the Butte Hill, formalizing his blueprint for transition from worker to owner-manipulator. He learned two lessons immediately: smelting costs in Butte could be reduced if a new smelter were erected; a smelter owner, to receive a maximum return, should possess his own mine. Consequently Heinze established the Montana Ore Purchasing Company, built a smelter, and secured the Rarus mine. F. Augustus carried this type of analysis and implementation into Canada, Utah, and Idaho—where he operated both mines and smelters, as well as railroads, newspapers, and legal staffs.

"He startled the Butte community by building the most up-to-date mining plant in the country and the greatest smelter ever seen in the mining district. Not only were all known improvements embodied in these structures, but also several new inventions of Mr. Heinze himself. The practical value of these inventions was shown in the fact that his system of ore roasting was soon copied by all other concerns in Butte."[1]

Heinze was not, in the strictest sense, an inventor; rather, he was an innovator, an expert miner, and an excellent smelterman. He did not merely dictate orders to subordinates, he worked incessantly himself. Whereas the ore purchasing company yielded millions to him, it also benefited others. His smelter, for example, reduced the processing costs of the independent Butte mines by fifty percent; in effect, he placed these small operators in competition with the national organizations.[2]

An opinion prevalent in Butte during the Copper War was that "there was no accounting for the luck of Heinze." When an individual, however, consistently unearths rich lodes in prospects in which others have tried and failed, luck is not the sole explanation. F. Augustus knew his subject; legerdemain does not produce wealth in mining. Although there are, have been, and perhaps always will be "lucky" finds in this industry characterized by numerous risks, no individual could rely completely on luck to make his prospects pay. Heinze fought to control the Minnie Healy only after he was convinced by his limited experience in it that the claim was worth development—in sections not known to be rich until he uncovered them. He did not buy the Rarus until he was sure it would repay the required developmental outlay. F. Augustus did not whimsically speculate; he planted his feet firmly and utilized both his technical knowledge and common sense. A college classmate and fraternity brother of Heinze noted this characteristic.

"He first dug up the truth of the various properties and thus armed started in to buy control of such as he considered really

---

[1] Stewart, "Captains," p. 290.
[2] O. C. Heinze MS., p. 17.

good. The other side attempted to install tactics that would freeze him out and take advantage of legal force to do it. He checkmated them. Had he pursued nice, predictable, gentlemanly tactics he would have been utterly defeated—the other side 'got hoist by its own petard!' . . . The Rockefeller and Rogers interests . . . attempted to buy up the judges and civil authorities to prejudge the cases at issue, only to find Fritz had done it first! Good for Fritz! He was a fighter, not a scoundrel. A genius, not a rogue. But when his opponents were going to tamper with the law, he tampered with it first. You can say it was dishonest if you like. I say it was a stroke of unexpected genius and fully warranted in the class of warfare he had to contend with."[3]

As it became evident to Heinze that the opposition companies— first the Boston and Montana, and later the Amalgamated—would not permit a new operator in Butte, that he must either sell or fight, he was prepared to fight. If the Boston and Montana could base a suit upon the apex theory, he could derive one hundred suits from it and affect operations in many opposition mines. He used precisely this ploy for nine years, until the enemy—desperate with frustration —showed the nation that practical government is not always "of the people, by the people, and for the people."

Heinze was sufficiently sensible to delegate details to subordinates when they were more skilled than he in particular fields. Hence he and his brothers—one an expert in law, the other a master of credit, banking, and financial aid—were an unbeatable partnership. John MacGinniss, his veteran aide, managed the Butte branch of F. A.'s Montana Ore Purchasing Company. Stanley Gifford, whom Fritz recognized as a trustworthy fellow student at Columbia, remained with him throughout his career—primarily as manager of the M. O. P. C.'s New York office.

F. Augustus knew that, regrettably, the average voter was swayed

---

[3]Letter to the author from Francis D. Cleveland (Columbia, '89), Altadena, California, April 19, 1946.

less by reason than by emotion. The election campaigns that he directed were, therefore, distinguished by excitement, entertainment, and practical jokes that exhibited rudimentary humor. For instance, a favorite campaign device which he used was to send his supporters to attend the meetings of the "Standard Oil Party." As an opposition speaker approached the climax of his address, one group of Heinze's men would march en masse from the hall; as the speaker resumed his argument, another of Heinze's groups would depart. Repeated at strategic intervals, this tactic had considerable psychological value.[4]

F. A. himself used bands, catchy parodies of popular songs, talented singers, and free favors at saloons to garner good crowds. In his own speeches, he invariably attacked Standard Oil and aligned himself with the people in a mutual fight against the octopus—thereby assuring himself the votes of the working class. It is not surprising that on election day the people of Butte consistently demonstrated that they wanted the same judges, legislators and state justices as did Heinze. All these devices required planning and F. Augustus was a patient planner.

This deliberate, studied analysis prior to action always brought success to Heinze. His last notable activity—the banking sequence—appears to have been motivated by a desire to stand above the crowd, to occupy a position of social significance which would crown his victorious sale to the Amalgamated, rather than to have been the result of a sound, rational outline. Gambling, to the degree involved in the acquisition of the banking-trust chain, was alien to F. A.'s nature; he did not succeed. F. Augustus must have shared the sentiment that Charles Morse verbalized when their resignations were accepted by the Clearing House committee.

"I am mighty glad to be out of there, for there is nothing in banking for me."[5]

Significantly, the speculation in United Copper was much less F. Augustus's endeavor than it was his brother Arthur's. F. A. was

---

[4] Connolly, "Heinze and Lawson," p. 67.

[5] "Panic," *Digest*, p. 631.

culpable, however; he permitted the activity and, by holding U.C. stock in an agreement not to release it on the market during the second pool of which he disapproved, he abetted the evil.

Heinze personally testified that he had left the management of the Mercantile National Bank to a subordinate and did not inspect its books. Either banking itself did not interest him, or he had changed radically from the owner-employer who knew intimately the status of his mines and smelter in Butte. Indifference or the pressure of business, however, does not justify to the trusting depositors—who had placed twenty million dollars in the Mercantile—the terror that they experienced in 1907. F. Augustus Heinze declined as a champion of the people during his banking interlude.

F. A. was remembered for his generosity which extended throughout his life.

> "The trail of his prodigality in money, love and friendship crisscrosses the continent from the Atlantic to the Pacific and from north to south."[6]

As a small boy, he saved his weekly allowance to purchase gifts for his family, rather than to utilize for personal pleasures.[7] The Heinze family practiced exchanging gifts and marking anniversaries and other events; the custom seems to have cemented the close ties of the members. Homely references to personal elements repeatedly appear in the otherwise serious M. O. P. C. communications regarding litigation and credit. For example, in March, 1896, when F. Augustus was operating from British Columbia, he was informed by Arthur's wire of the approaching wedding of a relative.

> "Mother thinks jewelry would suit Ottilie. Wedding April 15th. Think you had better authorize purchase here, as otherwise will not arrive on time."[8]

---

[6]Anaconda *Standard*, November 5, 1914.

[7]O. C. Heinze MS., p. 7.

[8]M. O. P. C. Telegram File, March 31, 1896. Wire from Arthur Heinze at the Butte office to F. Augustus in Trail, B. C.

Although no record of Fritz's response exists, he received a similar telegram from Arthur two weeks later.

"(B. C. Code) Mama leaves for Europe on the 29th of April. Daisy likewise. Do you wish to join in the wedding present to the latter and to what amount? Are you coming East? When?"[9]

A subsequent telegram from Daisy indicates that F. Augustus did contribute to the family gift.

"Many, many thanks for the lovely present. Writing you from the steamer."[10]

A Christmas letter to F. A. from an aunt in New Jersey (December, 1899) exhibits that he had remembered her; it also provides a family perspective of his mining activities.

"My dear Fritz: I received a letter from your Mother yesterday, enclosing amongst others a check from you as a Christmas gift. I thank you most heartily, Fritz, for it was generous indeed. It was very thoughtful of you to take the time to even think of old folks when every moment must be of value to you. We often refer to the Xmas two years ago, your first at home in eight years, of the merry time we had. It was one of the evenings that, as one grows old, lingers in the memory. I hope we shall see you this year again.

"We occasionally see notices in the papers, which give us a vague idea of the magnitude of your operations. We always eagerly scan them, for it is needless to say they possess for us all the greatest interest. I heard incidentally that you had purchased a Pianola and were rivalling the club as an evening attraction for your male friends. I am sure, looking at it in that light, I should consider it a valuable investment.

---

[9]M. O. P. C. Telegram File, April 13, 1896. Wire from Arthur Heinze at the New York office to F. Augustus in Trail, B. C.

[10]M. O. P. C. Telegram File, May 2, 1896. Wire from Daisy, a Heinze relative, in the Atlantic to F. Augustus at the Butte office.

"And now with renewed thanks for your generous present, believe me, your affectionate Aunt, . . ."[11]

Men remembered Heinze's joy and pleasure in the Christmas season and its spirit.[12] A close-fisted, grasping Scrooge would take no delight in it. Apparently his enjoyment of Christmas was responsible to the true interpretation of the day—that it is "more blessed to give than to receive." Another warm note of gratitude is additional evidence of F. Augustus's generosity and family spirit.

"My Dear Old Fritz: You are, as usual, an unusual Old Santa Claus peach of a cousin and your presents to the boys and to me were very, very generous; I thank you very, very much for them —they made a very happy Xmas for all of us. It was especially kind of you to think of me in all your whirl of business and to send your present on in time for Christmas; I especially appreciated the thought (although the substantiality went to the spot) for you were the only one of my Western friends who remembered me. Not a line of greeting did I have from anyone west of the Mississippi with the exception of J. MacGinniss' telegram which I believe was instigated by you. However, it was very kind of him to send it, so please thank him very much for it and tell him it was appreciated. . . ."[13]

The judgment of the men who worked for him pertinent to his generosity might be concluded in the comment made by one of them.

"Oh, he was a good scout; he'd come along to the men working on top, throw them a dollar and tell them to get a drink. You know, we were getting but three and a half [dollars] a shift then."[14]

---

[11]Letter to F. Augustus from an undesignated aunt in New Jersey, December 27, 1899. Partial copy of the letter is included in the M. O. P. C. Telegram File.

[12]Anaconda *Standard*, November 8, 1914.

[13]Letter from an undesignated Heinze cousin, probably residing in Greater New York City, to F. Augustus at the Butte office of the M. O. P. C.; probable date, December, 1898—based on the accompanying material in the M. O. P. C. Telegram File.

[14]Interview by the author with William McNelis, June 14, 1945.

Heinze's courage was possibly the most dominant of his qualities. A quiet fearlessness certainly was apparent in his conversation with A. S. Bigelow in New York (February, 1897). In the face of Bigelow's refusal to settle the Rarus-Davitt controversy peacefully, F. Augustus confidently threatened to begin a battle that "would be heard from one end of this continent to the other."[15] To Bigelow's devastation, F. A. actuated this threat.

Whereas other men might have used an office release—since one could not trust the opposition's network of newspapers—or have sent a subordinate to answer the committee of the Butte Miners' Union during the Shutdown of 1903, Heinze chose to address the thousands of miners personally. When he began to speak, they were indifferent or hostile. By the time he had concluded, they were firmly in his corner—against Standard Oil.

No derogatory remark or insinuation aimed at F. Augustus went unchallenged. A court incident occurred during the Copper War which illustrates this point.

"There were many amusing scenes in court. . . . One of these occurred one day when F. A. was on the stand testifying. A certain lawyer from New York, Louis Marshall, was cross-examining him. He was short and fat with a round face, big dark-rimmed glasses and dark, curly, greasy hair. He suddenly raised his voice and shouted, 'Mr. Heinze, you acknowledge that you stole this ore.' F. A. turned to Clancy, requesting him to adjourn court for a few minutes; then left the witness chair, walked over to Marshall, took him roughly by the lapel of his coat and without saying a word, led the, by this time, frightened attorney out of the courtroom and said outside to him, 'Mr. Marshall, never use such an expression to me again. That sort of language may go in New York, but never here in Butte. If you should again forget yourself, I will see myself compelled to take you out of here immediately, just as today, and give you the worst thrashing

[15]Connolly, "Fight," p. 5.

that you have ever received; besides this, my advice to you is to return home; you do not belong here.'

"He turned his back and went back to the witness stand. Much shaken, fat little Mr. Marshall came back also, very much less pompous than before and requested an adjournment. . . . He left for New York shortly, said he could not stand the high altitude of Butte."[16]

Intimidation applied to F. Augustus, however, was ineffective, for it aroused his wrath. The position or prestige of the threatener did not impress him. When the litigation in Butte brought extensive suspension of operations and was a serious threat to profits, various individuals approached Heinze as intermediaries from H. H. Rogers—or pretended to be such, for the commission that they might earn. All of these individuals brought suggestions or coercions for settlement of the War. Each received the same answer: Heinze would not sell to Amalgamated.

Edward Henry Harriman, president of the Union Pacific Railroad, isolated F. Augustus at a small dinner party one evening to discuss the mining litigation which was indirectly injuring his business. Heinze's intentional lack of response and noncommital attitude annoyed and offended the railway magnate.

"Harriman said, 'Mr. Heinze, you are shipping quite some of your copper over my road; this litigation is very unpleasant to me and if it does not stop pretty soon, I shall refuse to accept your freight and I think that will stop this warfare.'

"That was a very foolish way to try to handle F. A. He turned to Mr. Harriman and said, 'Mr. Harriman, if you will consult your lawyers you will find that such action under the laws of Montana would give me the right to apply for a receiver for your road and, I do hope, you will not compel me to do that.' The party

---

[16]O. C. Heinze MS., pp. 41-42. This incident very likely occurred during a hearing of the Boston and Montana receivership case (all phases: 1898-1904), when Louis Marshall, F. J. Forbis, and William DeWitt were the lawyers for the Boston and Montana company.

broke up shortly and Harriman joined the Rogers crowd; he claimed F. A. impossible, but he never gave the order not to carry our freight."[17]

This facet of resolute solidity and asperity in business relationships was balanced in Heinze's personality by that element of tenderness and sincere regard for his mother. His devotion to her was extraordinary and impressed his associates. One of them commented that heavy responsibilities never kept F. Augustus from thinking of his mother and that, no matter how involved he was in his career, he never failed to write to her at least once each week. He also recalled that Heinze carried letters from his mother with him for days.[18]

"His devotion to his mother was of the tenderest, truest type. This was the gentlest spot in his adamantine structure. Whatever sentiment he had, centered around his mother, and her death left a wound that never healed."[19]

F. Augustus Heinze's accomplishments were extensive and substantial. These diversified achievements constitute an especially superior record when one remembers that F. A. died prior to his forty-fifth birthday and that his active career extended for only twenty-five years. For example, Heinze legislatively advanced the people's cause. The platform adopted by the Fusion Party and hawked by F. A.—particularly in the campaigns of 1900 and 1902—made Montanans more concerned and better informed regarding the direct legislative processes of initiative and referendum. When these mechanisms were adopted, on November 6, 1906, it was not because there was a specific situation for which the new weapons were needed.[20] If that were the case, there would have been initiative or referendum measures on the

---

[17]O. C. Heinze MS., p. 43.

[18]Anaconda *Standard*, November 5, 1914.

[19]Butte *Miner*, November 5, 1914. Neither the *Standard* nor the *Miner* provided the names of the men who made these observations.

[20]Raymer, *Montana*, I, p. 600.

1908 ballot; there were none.[21] The voters merely wanted a possible, democratic, and useful tool to employ if the need might arise. They learned from F. Augustus and the Fusionist campaigns that these mechanisms were progressive and beneficial.

F. Augustus Heinze and W. A. Clark, affiliates in the 1900 campaign, instituted the first eight-hour day in Montana on their mining properties. Despite Amalgamated's refusal to make the shorter working day the general policy in Butte, Heinze and Clark retained the shorter shift and raised such a popular clamor for it that the first bill passed by the 1901 legislature instituted the eight-hour shift in all Montana mining.[22] Amalgamated, faced with the inevitable, proclaimed (January 23, 1901) that the shorter shift would commence on its properties on February 1, a single day before the law was signed by the governor.[23]

F. Augustus also thundered against the D. J. Hennessy Mercantile Company of Butte which was owned by the Amalgamated. His attacks upon the organization in the 1900 campaign concentrated on presenting it as a "company store." F. A.'s charges precluded in Montana the inauguration and fixation of a true company-store system such as had plagued the Pennsylvania and Virginia coal regions for years. Senate Bill 85 in the Seventh Legislative Assembly (1901) made illegal in the state the use of script instead of money to pay employees.[24] Script was an adjunct of the company-store system, since it had purchase value only in mercantile establishments owned by the mining company.

Even the harassed legal staffs of Heinze's opponents developed, under pressure, some valuable legislation. The Fair Trials, or Change of Venue, Bill—permitting transfer of a case from the court of a district judge, believed to be prejudiced by either party, to the court of another judge—potentially benefited the average Montanan. This

[21]Anaconda *Standard* and Butte *Miner* pre-election issues, November 1-5, 1908.

[22]*Laws, Resolutions, and Memorials, 1901*, p. 62.

[23]Anaconda *Standard*, January 23-24, 1901.

[24]*Laws, Resolutions, and Memorials, 1901*, p. 147.

measure became law in 1903, in the legislature's extraordinary session.[25]

The mining and smelting industries were also developed, improved, and modernized by Heinze.

"Paradoxical as the statement may seem, Heinze's aggressive fight and his underground development finally enriched the properties of the Amalgamated. 'They say in the West that he had an enchanted pick.' In his forays into disputed territories, he uncovered vast deposits of rich ore of which the Amalgamated never dreamed, and which the timid and scholastic methods of some of its engineers would have left undiscovered for years, if not forever. To Heinze, more perhaps than to any other factor in the copper industry, are due the recent remarkable processes and discoveries outside of what was supposed to be the ore-bearing zone."[26]

Whereas the gains made for the people and the industries were permanent, that which F. Augustus accomplished for himself was somewhat transitory. American publicity spread his name internationally because of the Copper War. This publicity, however, was generally written by Heinze's opponents; it, therefore, most often presented him unfavorably. F. A. fondly quoted Shakespeare relevant to his stature in the press and in public opinion—specifically Marc Antony's terse comment: "The evil that men do lives after them, / The good is oft interred with their bones."[27] After 1906, the national press noticed Heinze little, except for its denunciatory articles concerning his relationship with the Panic of 1907.

The large personal fortune that F. Augustus possessed when he left Butte was decreased about ninety percent by the financial maelstrom of 1907. F. A. remained, however, a millionaire. The ruin of his physical assets was more serious.

---

[25]*Laws, Resolutions, and Memorials, 1903*, pp. 61-65.

[26]Connolly, "Fight," p. 228.

[27]O. C. Heinze MS., p. 38. The Shakespearian reference is to: *Julius Caesar*, III, ii, 79-80.

"The loss of his fortune in the Panic of 1907 was as nothing compared with the loss of his health. Still under forty, his genius, if capitalized, was worth more than the wolves of Wall Street took from him."[28]

After the Panic also, the comfort and pleasure that he had enjoyed in working closely with his brothers ended; the planning, the sharing, the mutual co-operation ceased, although the three were tied by prior business obligations.

F. Augustus Heinze had real ability and keen intelligence. In the realm that he chose to dominate—mining—he was an able leader. No moral scruple restrained him from employing an effective tactic or method—regardless of its ethical status—for he battled enemies who resorted to any means with which to achieve a desired end. Men in Butte found him somewhat reserved.

"A genial and, at times, a jovial and witty companion, he maintained an impenetrable dignity that was one of the signal marks of his superiority."[29]

Most men in the mining city would agree, in whole or in part, with a single assessment.

"I liked Fritz Heinze very much—and had respect for him as one who allowed no one to step on his toes."[30]

The rebellious spirit and the resentment of discipline that characterized Fritz, the boy, emerged in F. Augustus, the man, as a desire to dominate rather than to collaborate. He preferred to fight opposing copper magnates, for as long as such battle was feasible. F. A. was sufficiently self-confident to spurn the suggestions that he sell to, merge with, or assist in any manner the Amalgamated complex—as Daly and Clark respectively had done.

---

[28]Butte *Miner*, November 5, 1914.

[29]Butte *Miner*, November 5, 1914.

[30]Letter to the author from F. C. Cleveland, April 19, 1946.

"F. Augustus was self-centered to a degree, self-confident and self-contained, but not selfish in any respect."[31]

F. Augustus Heinze was a complex person. Aggressive, ruthless, unscrupulous, he was also courageous, versatile, generous, and sympathetic. Upon his death the Anaconda *Standard*, a paper controlled by his bitterest enemies, paid him eulogistic tribute.

"F. Augustus Heinze was one of the most picturesque adventurers in business and politics the West has ever known, a Monte Cristo in his sudden and upward financial experience, a creator of a new Bohemia in which he reigned and reveled, a bold operator in mining, a dashing, daring and reckless speculator in the affairs of life. He left his stamp on the affairs of Butte and Montana and, in a measure on the whole intermountain country. . . . The exciting and tense years during which he made his home in Butte and carried on his mining, worked out his personal ambitions, exercised his tastes, prosecuted his noted litigation with the Amalgamated Company are matters of keen recollection in the minds of thousands. No man ever crowded more into 45 years of life than did F. Augustus Heinze. . . . He had lived in experience and achievement many years beyond the time allotted to the average man.

"Vast and varied were the phases of life he experienced. He tasted success and he measured defeat; he enjoyed riches beyond measure and he experienced the greatest of all failures, the descent from the height of business, financial, and social success. To his friends he was loyal and many swear allegiance to him. . . . Men and women say he was a prince. Men have called him a buccaneer. He was great in many ways and a most unusual man."[32]

---

[31]Letter to the author from F. C. Cleveland, April 19, 1946.

[32]Anaconda *Standard*, November 5, 1914.

APPENDICES

Appendix I

CHRONOLOGY: F. AUGUSTUS HEINZE

1850:

May: Otto Heinze, Sr., the father of F. AUGUSTUS HEINZE (FAH), arrives in New York City from Germany.

1862:

February 12: Otto Heinze, Sr., marries Eliza Marsh Lacey in New York City.

1869:

December 5: F. Augustus Heinze (FAH) is born, the fifth child and third son of Otto and Eliza Heinze.

1874:

September: FAH enters kindergarten in New York City.

1876:

September: FAH begins Juvenile High School, Brooklyn, New York, where he studies for about two years.

1878:

June: FAH enrolls in the Nicolaey Gymnasium, a Latin high school in Leipzig, Germany, where he remains for two years.

1880:

July: FAH enters another Latin high school in Hildesheim, Germany, where he studies for two years.

1882:

September: FAH enrolls in the POLYTECHNIC INSTITUTE OF BROOKLYN, New York, where he studies for three complete terms.

1885:

June: FAH graduates from the Polytechnic Institute of Brooklyn, and passes the entrance examinations for the COLUMBIA SCHOOL OF MINES in New York City.

1886:

summer: FAH uses his summer vacation from Columbia to work in the mine fields of Upper Michigan, for the Calumet and Hecla Mining Company.

1887:

summer: FAH again applies his classroom knowledge to the practical situation; he spends the summer break from Columbia in the coal mining regions of Pennsylvania.

1888:

summer: FAH passes the Columbia interim working in the gold and silver mines of Colorado.

1889:

June 6: FAH graduates from the Columbia School of Mines, with a degree of ENGINEER OF MINES.

September: After visiting the mining regions of Pennsylvania, Colorado, and Utah, FAH arrives in BUTTE, MONTANA. He begins to work immediately as a mining engineer with the BOSTON AND MONTANA COPPER COMPANY at five dollars per day. FAH remains with the B. and M. for approximately one year, and lives in a cabin in Meaderville.

1890:

October: FAH resigns his position with the Boston and Montana and returns to New York City to secure funds for a proposed smelter in Butte. He is unable to obtain the money and remains in N. Y. C. through the winter of 1890-1891, working as a reporter for the foremost periodical in its field, the ENGINEERING AND MINING JOURNAL.

1891:

spring: FAH returns to Butte and resumes his position with the Boston and Montana. He remains approximately eight months before returning to N. Y. C. During this residence, FAH effects an informal partnership with Stanley Gifford and others; on a small scale, the partnership leases mines and concentrates some ore.

autumn: Otto Heinze, Sr., dies in N. Y. C. and the family firm—HEINZE, LOWY AND COMPANY—is reorganized. From their father's estate, each of the three brothers—Arthur, Otto, and F. A.—receives about $50,000; these shares subsequently become the basis of the Montana Ore Purchasing Company.

1892:

February: FAH again resigns his position with the Boston and Montana and returns to N. Y. C.

spring: The Heinze brothers—Arthur, Otto, and F. A.—form the MONTANA ORE PURCHASING COMPANY (M. O. P. C.) to finance FAH's smelter project in Butte.

summer: FAH journeys to Europe to secure lines of credit for the infant M. O. P. C. While on the Continent, he takes concentrated, advanced courses in geology and mining at the UNIVERSITY OF FREIBURG, Germany. FAH remains in Europe into 1893.

1893:

January 10: The ESTELLA MINE CASE is initiated in the Butte district court, with James A. Murray as the plaintiff. This suit was finally settled in FAH's favor in April, 1898.

spring and summer: FAH returns to the United States and commutes between N. Y. C. and Butte for the M. O. P. C.

March 1: The Montana Ore Purchasing Company is incorporated in Montana.

autumn: FAH, through the M. O. P. C., begins construction of a SMELTER in Butte. The first copper matte from this smelter is produced on January 3, 1894.

autumn: FAH purchases the GLENGARRY NO. 2 MINE which subsequently becomes his first mammoth producer of copper ore.

He also leases the RARUS and JOHNSTOWN properties from the Boston and Montana; he later (1895) purchases these holdings outright.

1894:

spring: FAH makes the first of his truly productive ore discoveries—within the GLEN-GARRY NO. 2 MINE. As in this initial find, much of FAH's early success in Butte is the result of his ability to uncover and exploit valuable veins in mines which other mining engineers and companies had abandoned as depleted.

summer-autumn: FAH goes to BRITISH COLUMBIA. He subsequently (1895) builds a smelter at Trail and a railroad to connect the smelter with the mines at Rossland. FAH is involved in these Canadian enterprises for four years—to 1898—but simultaneously directs the Butte mining operations of the M. O. P. C. and continuously travels between Butte and British Columbia.

November: In a state election, Montana designates Helena as the permanent CAPITAL. Helena is the preference of W. A. CLARK and is opposed by Anaconda, the choice of MARCUS DALY. The campaigns which both wage are extensive and expensive. This election especially exemplifies the tone of Clark-Daly political battles.

1895:

spring: FAH and the M. O. P. C. install a converter at the smelter site in Butte. Simultaneously FAH develops his British Columbia holdings.

summer: FAH purchases the RARUS and JOHNSTOWN properties in the name of the M. O. P. C. for $400,000. He had previously leased these properties from the Boston and Montana.

1896:

July: A financial crisis hits the Heinze firms of HEINZE, LOWY AND COMPANY, and OTTO HEINZE AND COMPANY. A director of the former organization loses approximately $500,000 of the company's securities in stock-market speculation. The Heinze brothers, however, unite and survive the experience.

late summer: FAH returns quickly to Butte to protect his properties against the Boston faction's attacks. For the following two years he spends most of his time in Butte, but travels regularly to British Columbia to manage his operations there.

late autumn: The BOSTON AND MONTANA secures an injunction which keeps FAH from mining his RARUS ore, on the contention that these ore veins apex on B. and M. property. This act marks the informal, but effective, beginning of THE SECOND PHASE OF THE WAR OF THE COPPER KINGS (1896-1906).

winter: Arthur Heinze discovers the forty-square-yard section—later the COPPER TRUST COMPANY—adjoining Marcus Daly's Anaconda, St. Lawrence, and Never Sweat claims. Arthur and FAH stake and file the small triangle which has tremendous legal potential, for it can be used to institute litigation against the three adjoining claims on the basis of the apex theory.

FAH employs the claim—as the Copper Trust Company—in this manner (spring, 1900) against the Amalgamated, which had purchased Daly's holdings in 1899. The action forces Amalgamated to close for one day, but the injunction is then rescinded. Despite FAH's failure to bind Amalgamated in this case, the minute claim retains its potential for injuring Amalgamated at any moment.

1897:

February 18: The Boston and Montana consolidates with the Butte and Boston; the two firms are initially controlled by ALBERT S. BIGELOW and have interlocking directorships.

late February: FAH confronts A. S. BIGELOW, president of the Boston and Montana Mining Company, in Boston concerning the apex theory as applied to the Rarus-Davitt ores. FAH offers Bigelow $250,000 for the B. and M.'s MICHAEL DAVITT claim. Bigelow refuses the offer as ridiculous and, upon disagreement, FAH promises Bigelow a fight "heard from one end of this continent to the other."

Bigelow retaliates with an immediate suit against the M. O. P. C. to keep it from the Davitt claim. This action *formally* initiates the second, or Heinze, phase of the War of the Copper Kings (1896-1906)—that is, FAH's mine litigation involving the Boston and Montana, the Butte and Boston, the Anaconda, and ultimately the Amalgamated.

This particular suit, THE MICHAEL DAVITT CASE, reaches a mistrial in March, 1898, and is retried in Helena early in 1900; a second mistrial forces an appeal to the San Francisco Circuit Court. Between 1900 and 1904, however, FAH employs the Johnstown Mining Company stratagem and periodically mines the Davitt. The Davitt litigation is ended only by the sale of FAH's holdings to the Amalgamated in 1906. Incidentally, Bigelow is financially ruined within three years of his confrontation with FAH.

1898:

spring: FAH sells most of his holdings in BRITISH COLUMBIA—smelter, railway, claim rights, newspaper—for an estimated $900,000. He then concentrates on the offensive and defensive actions of the Copper War.

March: The first trial of the MICHAEL DAVITT CASE begins before the pro-Boston and Montana magistrate, Judge Hiram Knowles. A mistrial of this case occurs when the jury opposes the judge's charge and finds for FAH. A retrial is set for early in 1900.

April: The ESTELLA MINE CASE, initiated by Murray in 1893, is settled in FAH's favor.

May: FAH's lawyers initiate the first in a series of suits utilizing his JOHNSTOWN MINING COMPANY. This initial action claims that the ore of the Boston and Montana's PENNSYLVANIA MINE apexes in FAH's Johnstown claim. The injunction, granted by Judge William Clancy in Butte district court, is reversed by the Montana Supreme Court on February 13, 1899. FAH commences an identical suit in 1900, with the same result (January 3, 1903). The Johnstown Mining Company is also used as a holding company against the Amalgamated in the Michael Davitt litigation (1898-1906).

June 4: JOHN MACGINNISS and JAMES FORRESTER, FAH's associates and minority stockholders in the Boston and Montana, initiate action to block a B. and M. stock transfer; they ask for a B. AND M. RECEIVERSHIP. The Montana Supreme Court upholds their contention on November 28, 1898, and designates Thomas Hinds as the receiver (December 5, 1898).

MacGinniss institutes another receivership suit against the B. and M. on July 23, 1901, and is named co-receiver in this instance. This series of litigious activity effectively postpones the purchase of the B. and M. by Amalgamated and, therefore, alters the Rogers-Standard Oil plan to form a copper trust.

summer: The AMALGAMATED COPPER MINING COMPANY is incorporated in New Jersey. This firm becomes a holding company for Standard Oil. Although it holds no significant mining properties in 1898, Amalgamated officials begin negotiations with Marcus Daly for his Butte properties. Ultimately Amalgamated holds all major mining properties in Butte, as well as other, diverse businesses throughout Montana.

November: FAH agrees, in writing, to assume MILES FINLEN'S lease of the MINNIE HEALY MINE for $54,000. Lengthy litigation ensues regarding this agreement and the Minnie Healy.

December 15: The Boston and Montana is placed in the receivership of THOMAS HINDS, but the B. and M. prevents him from assuming this position immediately. This action is an extension of the MacGinniss-Forrester suit (June 4, 1898). Hinds functions as the actual receiver only six days (April 8-13, 1899), but is not formally dismissed by the court until June, 1900, thereby preventing the B. and M. from distributing its dividends—which went primarily to Amalgamated.

December 16: HENRY H. ROGERS, effective leader of the Standard Oil plan to launch a copper trust, offers FAH the ridiculously low amount of $500,000 for his Montana properties. Although FAH refuses the offer, negotiations continue into February, 1899.

1899:

January: The Montana legislature approves HOUSE BILL 32 (Two-Thirds Act) over Governor Robert Smith's veto. This bill permits the transfer of stock without minority consent.

The same legislature elects W. A. CLARK to the United States Senate, but MARCUS DALY forces his dismissal through a Senate committee on election procedure.

February: HENRY H. ROGERS offers FAH $5,000,000 through an intermediary, Foxwell, for his Butte holdings. This amount is ten times Rogers's initial offer of December, 1898.

February 24: MILES FINLEN and his henchmen attempt to take the Minnie Healy property by force. They are physically repulsed by FAH and his armed miners.

March: H. H. ROGERS, Standard Oil magnate who had purchased the majority of Butte and Boston stock, forces A. S. BIGELOW from power in the young Boston coalition and assumes control of the interlocking directorates—although he allows Bigelow to remain as figurehead president.

April 27: The AMALGAMATED COPPER MINING COMPANY, a holding company for Standard Oil, which was incorporated in New Jersey in 1898, purchases the Montana holdings of MARCUS DALY—essentially his Anaconda property. Daly's assets become the nucleus of Standard Oil's projected copper trust and Daly is designated as Amalgamated's president.

The public announcement of this transaction is made on May 1. At this time Amalgamated also possesses control of the Boston consolidation, although it cannot hold it formally because of FAH's litigation. The Daly purchase necessitates a realignment of participants in the Copper War. Until W. A. Clark defects to Amalgamated in 1901, he and FAH oppose the trust; after 1901, FAH contests Amalgamated virtually alone.

1900:

late winter: The MICHAEL DAVITT CASE is tried for a second time, in Helena. Again the jury finds for FAH, but Amalgamated appeals the decision to the San Francisco Circuit Court on the grounds that FAH had influenced the jury by means of his anti-Amalgamated articles in some Helena newspapers. The case remains in the San Francisco court until 1906, when it is dismissed in accordance with FAH's sale to the Amalgamated.

spring: FAH uses the COPPER TRUST COMPANY to gain an injunction against Amalgamated's Anaconda, St. Lawrence, and Never Sweat claims, on the basis of the apex theory. Amalgamated closes the mines for a day, after which the injunction is rescinded by Judge Clancy. Despite this result, FAH continues possession of the Copper Trust—which has the potential of closing the same mines, almost at will.

summer: The Heinzes incorporate the DELAWARE SURETY COMPANY—also known as the Wilmington Bonding and Casualty Company—in that eastern state. This financial mechanism is useful in the Pennsylvania-Davitt-Rarus litigation of 1898-1906, which pertains to FAH's right to follow a vein, that he claims apexes on Rarus land, into the Pennsylvania claim.

autumn: Arthur Heinze suggests using THE JOHNSTOWN MINING COMPANY STRATAGEM to eliminate the court restraint on the M. O. P. C. regarding the Davitt ore. The plan is effected and results in several periods of underground warfare from 1901 to 1904.

November 5: FAH and W. A. CLARK join to push the FUSION PARTY in Silver Bow County. The Fusion ticket is elected almost exclusively in the county—including district court judges HARNEY, CLANCY, AND MCCLERNAN. The basic ploy of the Heinze-Clark campaign is the institution of an eight-hour shift on their mining properties.

November 12: MARCUS DALY dies in New York City, knowing that his bitterest enemy, W. A. Clark, has gained an undisputed seat in the Senate.

1901:

January: The Montana legislature elects W. A. CLARK to the U. S. Senate. As his seat is not contested in this instance, he finally fulfills his ambition. This election also commences his defection to Amalgamated, leaving FAH to fight the Amalgamated trust alone.

The same legislature passes two bills which were advocated by FAH in the campaign. The first makes mandatory an eight-hour shift in all mining operations; the second outlaws script as a substitute for money in paying an employee, thereby injuring any "company-store" ideas which Amalgamated might have.

February: The FAH v. Finlen-Amalgamated case, regarding Finlen's initial MINNIE HEALY deal with FAH, goes before Judge Edward Harney for the first time. Harney finds for FAH and Amalgamated appeals the decision to the State Supreme Court, which reaches a decision on July 24, 1903.

May 10: FAH submits a required bond of $350,000 to the Montana Supreme Court in the Pennsylvania-Davitt-Rarus litigation. The payment is made through the DELAWARE SURETY COMPANY.

July 23: JOHN MACGINNISS'S request is granted by Judge Harney and the Boston and Montana is restrained from paying any dividends. MacGinniss, as a minority stockholder, is named the sole receiver of the company until January, 1902, when Federal District Judge Hiram Knowles names four additional receivers.
MacGinniss's action is the third step in this series of B. and M. litigation: 1) MacGinniss-Forrester suit to halt stock transfer (June 4, 1898); 2) Hinds named as receiver (December 15, 1898); 3) MacGinniss receivership suit.

August 5/6: Representatives of Amalgamated meet with JUDGE HARNEY in the Thornton Hotel (Butte) to persuade him—with $250,000—that he had been bribed by FAH to influence his decision in the Minnie Healy case. Harney is not persuaded. On the basis of the same charges brought by Amalgamated before the Montana Supreme Court, that court (July 24, 1903) orders a retrial by Judge Clancy of the Healy case. Harney is subsequently cleared of bribery charges.

1902:

May 1: FAH merges all his properties in the UNITED COPPER COMPANY, incorporated in New Jersey, but retains the M. O. P. C. as an operating corporation.

summer: A premeditated fire destroys FAH's concentrator in Meaderville.

November 8: FAH's FUSION PARTY is highly successful in the Silver Bow County elections. Although campaigning without W. A. Clark, FAH re-elects the majority of his candidates, including Judges Harney and Clancy.

December 24: The Montana Supreme Court decides the original RARUS-PENNSYLVANIA SUIT, compromising the contentions of FAH and the Boston and Montana.

1903:

spring: JOHN MACGINNISS and DANIEL LAMM initiate a suit against the Amalgamated on the basis of the PARROT MINING COMPANY, a subsidiary of Amalgamated in which both plaintiffs are minority stockholders. Judge Clancy rules on this suit on October 22, 1903.

July 24: The Montana Supreme Court returns the MINNIE HEALY CASE to Judge Clancy's district court for retrial. Clancy finds for FAH (October 22, 1903) and again the Amalgamated appeals the decision to the Supreme Court. This court sustains Clancy's decision on April 20, 1905, thereby ending the Healy litigation.
On the same day (July 24, 1903), the Montana Supreme Court extends indefinitely the injunction which restrains the BOSTON AND MONTANA from distributing its dividends.

October 22: JUDGE CLANCY rules in favor of MacGinniss and Lamm on one count of their suit against Amalgamated's PARROT COMPANY: Amalgamated is declared an illegal trust under Montana law and its subordinate companies are enjoined from paying dividends to it.
On the same day (October 22, 1903), Judge Clancy decides the MINNIE HEALY CASE in FAH's favor—giving him title to the mine. Amalgamated subsequently appeals this decision to the State Supreme Court, which renders a decision on April 20, 1905.

October 22: In immediate reaction to the dual decisions of Judge Clancy, the trust announces THE SHUTDOWN of all its operations in Montana and, thereby affects either part or all of the income of three-fourths of the wage earners in the state.

October 26: FAH makes his famous "COURTHOUSE SPEECH" before approximately 15,000 Butte residents—many of whom were initially hostile to him.

October 31: Amalgamated dictates the terms of an EXTRA LEGISLATIVE SESSION to Governor Joseph K. Toole; given the circumstances, Toole is forced to accept the provisions.

November 10: The EXTRAORDINARY SESSION of the Eighth Legislative Assembly convenes in Helena and passes a "FAIR TRIALS BILL." Amalgamated resumes its Montana operations. This sequence of events—especially the power demonstrated by Amalgamated in forcing the change-of-venue measure—signals the eventual defeat of FAH.

mid-November: FAH leads the ANTI-TRUST PARTY'S convention in Helena, simultaneous to the meeting of the legislature in extraordinary session. This party proves ineffective opposition to Amalgamated.

1904:

January 1: Two miners, Oleson and Divel, are killed in a deliberate dynamite explosion in the MICHAEL DAVITT underground fighting.

summer: FAH purchases the LEXINGTON MINES' COMPLEX, in Walkerville, and proposes the La France Copper Company to handle the mines' activities.

autumn: Otto Heinze floats the stock for the new LA FRANCE COPPER COMPANY on the Paris market. This operating company is a subsidiary of the Heinzes' United Copper Company and is launched to organize the Lexington mine complex, purchased earlier in the year.

autumn: The Heinze brothers launch THE FIRST UNITED COPPER STOCK POOL, with Charles W. Morse, among others. At the same time they purchase a seat for the Otto Heinze and Company firm on the New York Stock Exchange, for $96,000.

November: The FAH-supported FUSION PARTY loses some strength in Silver Bow County, but still wins the majority of county posts. FAH's popular support evidently had declined little.

winter: FAH enters negotiations with Amalgamated's representatives, first in Butte and then in New York City. These talks extend for approximately fifteen months, and culminate (February 1, 1906) in FAH's sale of his Butte properties to the Amalgamated.

1905:

April 20: The Montana Supreme Court upholds Clancy's decision (1903) in the MINNIE HEALY CASE—thereby ending the litigation.

autumn: Butte has its worst town fire to this time; damage estimates are in the hundred thousands of dollars.

1906:

February 1: FAH completes NEGOTIATIONS WITH THE AMALGAMATED'S REPRESENTATIVES, John D. Ryan and Thomas F. Cole. The report of this transaction first is made public on February 14, 1906.

In the Amalgamated deal, FAH sells the majority of his Butte holdings to the trust through an intermediate holding company—the Butte Coalition Company—for approximately $12,000,000. This deal also causes the nullification of all pending legal actions; FAH held more than one hundred such suits which still required decisions.

March 3: All FAH-Amalgamated litigation is formally dismissed by mutual consent; this nullification is part of the sale deal. Approximately eighty cases are dismissed in Montana state courts and twenty-three federal suits are suspended. These aggregate claims exceed $100,000,000.

May 29: FAH launches the DAVIS-DALY ESTATES COPPER COMPANY under the auspices of the United Copper Company. The Davis-Daly concern proves, generally, to be a failure in attempting to mine ore southwest of Butte.

summer: FAH purchases control of the OHIO COPPER MINING COMPANY of the Salt Lake District, Utah. This enterprise subsequently becomes a profitable investment.

autumn: FAH oversees operations of his Lexington-complex mines in Walkerville, his Davis-Daly Estates properties outside Butte, and his Ohio Company in Utah. Late in the autumn he goes to New York City to engage in banking.

autumn: The first United Copper stock pool matures. Arthur Heinze, as legal controller of all the brothers' U. C. stock, moves into a SECOND UNITED COPPER STOCK POOL—against the advice of FAH and Otto Heinze who, however, are involved in the pool as owners of U. C. stock and as credit sources.

early winter: FAH purchases the controlling interest in THE MERCANTILE NATIONAL BANK OF NEW YORK CITY from EDWIN GOULD for $1,000,000. He becomes the president of this bank in January, 1907. FAH simultaneously becomes involved in a national banking-trust complex with CHARLES W. MORSE and E. R. Thomas.

1907:

January: FAH, as owner of the majority of stock in the firm, is elected president of the Mercantile National Bank of New York City.

October: Within a three-week period, FAH is eliminated from the New York financial scene by Standard Oil. He loses his position, prestige, and about $10,000,000 in the national financial PANIC OF 1907.

October 16: The UNITED COPPER COMPANY disintegrates as a result of the smashing of Otto Heinze's attempted copper corner. This disintegration forces the failure of the basic family firm—the OTTO HEINZE AND COMPANY—and coincides with a serious run on FAH's Mercantile National Bank.

October 17: FAH resigns as president of the MERCANTILE NATIONAL BANK. This resignation is a stipulation of the Clearing House committee, a prerequisite to any aid from this agency—manipulated by Standard Oil—to save the bank. Although FAH is forced from the presidency, he retains his majority stock in the concern until 1914.

October 24: The stock market falls completely, primarily because of the rush on the KNICKERBOCKER TRUST COMPANY, with which FAH had some indirect connections. At this point, United Copper falls sharply and never really recovers. FAH emerges from the Panic of 1907 a broken man—physically and financially. What assets he does retain—approximately $1,500,000 total value—is primarily in western mining properties.

1908:

January: FAH is first charged with sixteen counts of financial malfeasance in his position as president of the Mercantile National Bank of New York City. His trial on these charges is scheduled for March, 1909.

1909:

March: FAH is tried on charges of financial liberalities committed while president of the MERCANTILE NATIONAL BANK; he is prosecuted by New York State District Attorney Wise. After a lengthy trial, he is acquitted on all counts.

November 7: FAH triumphantly returns to Butte. Virtually all Montana receives him as a hero.

1910:

August 31: FAH marries BERNICE GOLDEN HENDERSON in New York City.

1911:

December: A son, F. AUGUSTUS HEINZE, JR., is born to FAH and Bernice Henderson Heinze.

1912:

autumn: Bernice Henderson Heinze separates from FAH and goes to Europe with her son. She files for divorce, but never completes the process.

1914:

April 3: BERNICE HENDERSON HEINZE and FAH are reconciled just before she dies of spinal meningitis. FAH places his son with his sister in Brooklyn, Lida Heinze Fleitman.

October: EDWIN GOULD files suit against FAH for nonpayment of his note for controlling stock in the Mercantile National which fell due in the autumn of 1907. FAH countersues, but his suit is denied and Gould wins the case. The judgment against FAH is $1,200,000—easily the most expensive suit that he ever lost.

November 3/4: FAH DIES in Saratoga, New York, where he had gone to vote in the off-year elections, of cirrhosis of the liver—an illness of which he was aware since the previous June.
FAH is buried in the family plot in Brooklyn, next to his mother.

Appendix II

MINING COMPANIES OF THE BUTTE DISTRICT
WHICH OPPOSED HEINZE

I. The Butte and Boston Mining Company

Organized in 1888, the Butte and Boston Mining Company suffered from poor management during its early years. Some critics believed that its financial problems were precipitated by several of its owners to force a reorganization and, thereby, to eliminate the small stockholders. The company was forced into receivership and reorganized in 1897.

E. Rollins Morse, chairman of the reorganization committee, bought its property for $3,550,000 at auction on February 1, 1897. The committee assigned Frank Klepetko, superintendent of the Boston and Montana Company, to direct the Butte and Boston. In the same month, a new company—the Butte and Boston Consolidated Mining Company, was capitalized at $2,000,000.

The board of directors of the new organization was practically the same as that of the Boston and Montana Company. On April 4, 1900, another board of directors was elected; it included so many men associated with the Amalgamated that the Butte and Boston became, for all practical purposes, an Amalgamated Company. During the second phase of the Copper War (1896-1906), therefore, the Butte and Boston functioned as an operating company for, first, the Boston and Montana, and later, Amalgamated. When Heinze opposed the Butte and Boston, in effect he opposed the Boston and Montana and Amalgamated.

II. The Boston and Montana Mining Company

The properties held by this Eastern company were reputedly the richest in the Butte district. They included the Pennsylvania, the Mountain View, the West Colusa, the East Colusa, and especially the Leonard. The B. and M. was organized in 1887 and capitalized at $3,750,000; it paid its investors well. In its first thirteen years (1887-1900), its dividends aggregated $18,725,000.

In February, 1897, the Boston and Montana consolidated with the Butte and Boston; under this mechanism A. S. Bigelow became president of both companies and the directorships of the two organizations became interlocking. In the spring of 1899, Henry H. Rogers—who, by that time, had purchased majority control in the Butte and Boston member of the young coalition—forced Bigelow from power in the Boston consolidation and assumed effective, if informal, control himself. After 1899, the Boston and Montana is, in effect, a subsidiary of Amalgamated.

The Boston consolidation—especially the B. and M.—was the projected nucleus of the copper trust planned by the Rogers-Standard Oil-Amalgamated complex. F. A. Heinze, however, by means of his litigation, was able to prevent Amalgamated from securing legal control of the B. and M. (1898-1906). For this reason, Amalgamated was forced to purchase (1899) Marcus Daly's Butte holdings to form the copper trust. From Heinze's position, after 1899 the B. and M. was an Amalgamated company, for it was effectively controlled by Rogers and used Amalgamated engineers and lawyers.

III. The Anaconda Copper Mining Company

Several years after his arrival in Butte (1876), Marcus Daly purchased what was to become the famous Anaconda mine and the properties surrounding it (1880). Although it was a silver prospect when he bought it for about $30,000 he was convinced that the property was rich in copper. Initially the Anaconda was operated as a closed corporation —George Hearst, James Haggin, and Lloyd Tevis, in addition to Daly—but in June, 1895, the company was reorganized as the Anaconda Copper Mining Company. It was capitalized at $30,000,000, divided into 1,200,000 shares at $25 each. In 1888 it earned $5,360,520 net profits and paid $4,800,000 in dividends to its stockholders. By that time the company also owned several other mining properties, three large department stores, the Butte, Anaconda and Pacific Railway, and a smelter. Marcus Daly remained the Anaconda's president throughout its existence.

In 1899 Daly entered negotiations with H. H. Rogers of Standard Oil. Rogers was interested in formulating a copper trust similar to the Standard Oil petroleum monopoly. His original scheme would have placed the Boston and Montana consolidation at the base of his trust, but Heinze had prevented the acquisition of the B. and M. through extensive litigation. Rogers, therefore, sought Daly's Butte properties as the nucleus of his proposed organization. Daly took advantage of his position: he named his price, an excessive one, and assumed the presidency of the new trust, Amalgamated. Daly remained with Amalgamated until his death in 1900. The Anaconda Copper Mining Company remained a holding and operating firm under Amalgamated until 1915, when Amalgamated dissolved and Anaconda became the dominant company in the monopolistic organization.

IV. The Amalgamated Copper Mining Company

On April 27, 1898, the Amalgamated Copper Mining Company was incorporated in Trenton, New Jersey, with a capitalization of $75,000,000. Marcus Daly, who delivered his Anaconda properties as the nucleus of the projected trust, became the firm's first president; Henry H. Rogers was the vice-president and William Rockefeller was the secretary-treasurer. Its board of directors included: F. P. Olcott, president of the Central Trust Company; Robert Bacon, of the J. P. Morgan Company; James Stillman, president of the National City Bank of New York; and R. P. Flower and A. C. Burrage, of the legal staff of the Standard Oil Company.

In addition to the Anaconda properties, the trust rapidly accumulated large interests in the Parrot Silver and Copper Company, the Washoe Copper Company, the Colorado Smelting and Mining Company, the Diamond Coal and Coke Company, the Big Blackfoot Milling Company, the Hennessy Mercantile Company, and the Boston coalition companies of the Butte and Boston, and Boston and Montana firms. The Anaconda holdings, however, remained its basis; in 1900 the Anaconda mine itself was the greatest producer of copper in the world and yielded 9.8 percent of the world's total output.

Until it purchased the Heinze interests (1906), the Amalgamated was forced to contend with F. Augustus and his companies—Montana Ore Purchasing Company and United Copper Company—on many fronts. The opposition of Amalgamated and Heinze comprised the bulk of the second phase of the Copper War (1896-1906). Although the trust did not purchase Heinze's holdings until 1906, they effectively nullified his activities after the Shutdown of 1903. Prior to the Shutdown, Heinze bound Amalgamated most proficiently in the courts. F. Augustus's lawyers and associates filed literally scores of suits against the operating companies of Amalgamated. In 1906, upon the sale of Heinze's holdings to the Amalgamated, more than 100 suits which were still pending were suspended.

In 1910, when copper was selling at the low figure of twelve cents per pound, Amalgamated commenced to coalesce its subsidiary companies under the Anaconda organization. On April 30, 1910, the Parrot Silver and Copper Mining Company's stockholders voted to sell to Anaconda for 90,000 shares of Anaconda stock. On May 27, 1910, the Alice Gold and Silver Mining Company sold to Anaconda for 30,000 shares of the latter's stock. Finally, on June 24, 1911, the Butte Coalition Mining Company—the intermediate holding company which was created in 1906 to organize Heinze's holdings within the Amalgamated—also sold to Anaconda.

Amalgamated was a diversified operation within and without Montana. At its height, it owned the vast majority of mining properties in the Butte district, copper and zinc concentrators and a sulphuric acid plant (Anaconda), a smelter refinery and zinc works (Great Falls), large lumber harvesting and milling companies (Missoula), much of the Northern Pacific Railroad and its lands (across the state), several smelters (Utah and Arizona), a lead refinery (East Chicago, Illinois), and a copper refinery (New Jersey). In 1923 the Anaconda-Amalgamated absorbed the Chile Copper Company of South America at a price reputed to have been $77,000,000. Even as early as twenty years prior to the Chilean purchase (1903), Amalgamated effectively controlled the income of three-fourths of the wage-earners in Montana.

Amalgamated was never truly a mining company; it was, rather, a large holding company for many subsidiary holding and operating companies. H. H. Rogers was its guiding force and he was its president (1900-1909) after Daly's death. In 1915 the Amalgamated dissolved itself and the Anaconda Copper Mining Company was resurrected as the parent organization of the trust. At this time John D. Ryan became its president. Shareholders of Amalgamated stock received two shares of Anaconda stock and three dollars in cash for each share of Amalgamated. The number of shares of Anaconda stock was then halved and the par value of a share raised to fifty dollars. Anaconda remains today the largest copper producer in the Butte district.

Appendix III

THE APEX THEORY

The apex theory was the subject of much controversy and the basis of many suits in equity during the second phase of the Copper War (1896-1906). It is older than the state of Montana, having been prescribed in the Federal Statutes in the 1860's. The apex theory was continually upheld by the courts because it was an effective incentive to prospectors. It gave impetus to the discovery and development of the great ore bodies of the West. The two federal statutes that are the basis of the apex theory are cited below.

I. Chapter CCLXII: An Act Granting the Right of Way to Ditch and Canal Owners Over The Public Land and For Other Purposes, 1866.

Cited in: *Statutes at Large, Treaties and Proclamations of the United States of America, from December, 1865, through March, 1867*, ed. George P. Sanger (Boston: Little, Brown; 1868), XIV, p. 252.

Section 4.

And be it further resolved, That when such entry and location of a mine shall be upon unsurveyed land, it shall and may be lawful, after the extension thereto of the public surveys, to adjust the subject to the limit of the premises according to the location and possession and plat aforesaid, and the surveyor-general may in extending the surveys vary the same from a rectangular form to suit the circumstances of the country and the local rules, laws and customs of the miners: Provided, That no location hereafter made shall exceed two hundred feet in length along the vein for each locator, *with an additional claim for discovery to the discoverer of the lode, with the right to follow such vein to any depth, with all its dips, variations and angles, together with a reasonable quantity of surface for the convenient working of the same as fixed by local rules*: And provided further, That no person may make more than one location on the same lode and not more than three thousand feet shall be taken in any one claim by any association of persons [italics mine].

II. Chapter CLII: An Act to Promote the Development of Mining Resources of the United States, May 10, 1872.

Cited in: *Statutes at Large and Proclamations of the United States of America from 1871 to March, 1873, and Treaties and Postal Conventions*, ed. George P. Sanger (Boston: Little, Brown; 1873), XVII, pp. 91-92.

Section 1.

[Declares mineral deposits in public land open to citizens].

Section 2.

The mining claims upon veins or lodes of quartz and other rock in places bearing gold, silver, cinnabar, lead, tin, copper, or other valuable deposits heretofore located, shall be governed as to length along the vein or lode by the customs, regulations and laws in force at the date of their location. A mining claim located after the passage of this act, whether by one or more persons, may equal, but shall not exceed one thousand five hundred feet in length along the vein or lode; but no location of a mining claim shall be made until the discovery of the vein or lode within the limits of the claim located. No claim shall extend more than three hundred feet on each side of the middle of the vein at the surface, nor shall any claim be limited by any mining regulation to less than twenty-five feet on each side of the middle of the vein at the surface, except where adverse rights existing at the passage of this act shall render such limitation necessary. The end-lines of each claim shall be parallel to each other.

Section 3.

That the locators of all mining locations heretofore made, or which shall hereafter be made, on any mineral vein, lode, or ledge situated on the public domain, their heirs and assigns, where no adverse claim exists at the passage of this act, so long as they comply with the laws of the United States governing their possessory title, *shall have the exclusive right of possession and enjoyment of all the surface included within the lines of their locations, and of all veins, lodes, and ledges throughout their entire depth, the top or apex of which lies inside of such surface lines extended downward vertically, although such veins, lodes or ledges may so far depart from a perpendicular in their course downward as to extend outside the vertical side lines of such surface locations: Provided their right of possession to such outside parts of said veins or ledges shall be confined to such positions thereof as lie between vertical planes drawn downward as aforesaid, through the end lines of their locations, continued in their own direction that such planes will intersect such exterior parts of said veins or ledges:* And provided further, that nothing in this section shall authorize the locator or possessor of a vein or lode which extends in its downward course beyond the vertical lines of his claim to enter upon the surface of a claim owned or possessed by another [italics mine].

BIBLIOGRAPHY

I. Unpublished Materials

II. Documents

III. Newspapers

IV. Books

V. Articles

I. *Unpublished Materials*

Beam, Paul C. Letter to E. E. Bennett, Montana State University, Missoula, Montana, July 2, 1947. Author possesses a copy.

Blaylock, S. G. Letter to the author, July 6, 1943.

Cleveland, Francis D. Letter to the author, April 19, 1946.

Gibbon, J. M. Letter to the author, July 7, 1947.

Harrington, Thomas H. Letter to the author, July 17, 1943.

Heinze, F. Augustus. Letter to his mother, Mrs. Otto Heinze, Sr. (Eliza Lacey Heinze), May 30, 1898. Original in the possession of Otto C. Heinze; author possesses a copy.

Heinze, F. Augustus. Letter to J. U. Sanders, May 13, 1910. Original is in the Montana State Historical Society Library, Helena, Montana.

Heinze, Otto C. "Otto C. Heinze Manuscript." Seventy-one single-spaced, typewritten pages of narrative written at the request of the author from 1943 to 1947, but primarily in 1943 and 1944. Original is in the possession of the author.

McNelis, William. Interview with the author, June 14, 1945.

Montana Ore Purchasing Company Telegram File. A series of telegrams, and confirmations of telegrams transmitted between the several offices of the Montana Ore Purchasing Company from March, 1896, through February, 1899. The wires are coded, but translations are attached to each and often suggestions for reply are appended. The File is in the possession of the author.

Murray, Mrs. T. J. Interview with the author, July 21, 1943.

Read, Thomas T. Letter to the author, June 21, 1943.

Scallon, William. Interview with the author, June 3, 1944.

Whitlock, Herbert F. Letter to the author, July 15, 1943.

Zinsser, F. G. Letter to the author, July 18, 1947.

218

II. Documents

Laws, Resolutions and Memorials of the State of Montana Passed at the Sixth Regular Session of the Legislative Assembly, 1899. Helena, State Publishing Company, 1899.

Laws, Resolutions and Memorials of the State of Montana Passed at the Seventh Regular Session of the Legislative Assembly, 1901. Helena, State Publishing Company, 1901.

Laws, Resolutions and Memorials of the State of Montana Passed at the Eighth Regular and Extraordinary Sessions of the Legislative Assembly, 1903. Helena, State Publishing Company, 1903.

Reports of Cases Argued in the Supreme Court of the State of Montana, Official Reports, XVII. San Francisco, Bancroft-Whitney, 1896.

Reports of Cases Argued in the Supreme Court of the State of Montana, Official Reports, XXI. San Francisco, Bancroft-Whitney, 1898.

Reports of Cases Argued in the Supreme Court of the State of Montana, Official Reports, XXVIII. San Francisco, Bancroft-Whitney, 1903.

Reports of Cases Argued in the Supreme Court of the State of Montana, Official Reports, XXXII. San Francisco, Bancroft-Whitney, 1905.

Sanger, George P., ed. *Statutes at Large, Treaties and Proclamations of the United States of America from December, 1865, to March, 1867,* XIV. Boston, Little, Brown and Company, 1868.

Sanger, George P., ed. *Statutes at Large and Proclamations of the United States of America from 1871 to March, 1873, and Treaties and Postal Conventions,* XVII. Boston, Little, Brown and Company, 1873.

III. Newspapers

Anaconda *Standard.* Selected editions from January 11, 1893, to November 9, 1914.

Butte *Miner.* Selected editions from October 23, 1903, to November 9, 1914.

(Butte) *Reveille.* Selected editions from September 1, 1900, to December 16, 1909.

Chicago *Record-Herald.* February 14, 1906.

Fallon County *News.* January 2, 1928.

Helena *Independent.* October 23, 1907.

IV. Books

Connolly, Christopher P. *The Devil Learns to Vote.* New York, Covici Friede, 1938.

Heinze, F. Augustus. *The Political Situation in Montana, 1900-1902.* Butte, no publisher, 1902.

Lawson, Thomas W. *The Crime of Amalgamated,* Vol. I of *Frenzied Finance.* New York, The Ridgeway-Thayer Company, 1905.

Murphy, Jerre C. *The Comical History of Montana, A Serious Story for Free People.* San Diego, E. L. Scofield, 1912.

Raymer, Robert G. *Montana, The Land and the People,* I. Chicago, The Lewis Publishing Company, 1930.

Stevens, Horace J., ed. *The Copper Handbook, A Manual of the Copper Industry of the World,* VI-VIII. Houghton, Michigan, Stevens Publishing Company, 1906-1908.

Walker, George L. *The Copper Mines of Butte and the Amalgamated Copper Company.* Boston, Boston Financial News, 1900.

V. *Articles*

"The Abuse of Speculation," *American Review of Reviews*, XXXVII (June, 1908).

Connolly, Christopher P. "The Fight of the Copper Kings," *McClure's*, XXIX (May, 1907).

Connolly, Christopher P. "The Fight of the Copper Kings," *McClure's*, XXIX (June, 1907).

Connolly, Christopher P. "The Fight for the Minnie Healy," *McClure's*, XXIX (July, 1907).

Connolly, Christopher P. "Heinze and Lawson, a Contrast," *Donahoe's Magazine* (January, 1905). Tear sheets of this article are bound in the Heinze file of the Montana State Historical Society Library, Helena, Montana.

"Copper Smelting in the United States," *Mineral Industry, Its Statistics, Technology, and Trade*, IV (1895).

Crozier, Alfred O. "The Recent Panic and Deadly Peril to American Prosperity," *Arena*, XXXIX (March, 1908).

"Editorial: the Panic," *American Review of Reviews*, XXXVII (June, 1908).

Flowers, B. O. "Popular Rule or Standard Oil Supremacy—Which Shall It Be?" *Arena*, XXXIX (March, 1908).

"Heinze, the Copper King," *American Review of Reviews*, XXXIII (June, 1904).

"Heinze, F. Augustus," *Who's Who in America*, ed. Albert N. Marquis, VI (Chicago: Marquis; 1910).

"Heinze, F. Augustus," *Who's Who in America*, ed. Albert N. Marquis, VII (Chicago: Marquis, 1912).

Howland, Harold J. "Standard Oil," *Outlook*, LXXXVI (September 28, 1908).

Jarman, Rufus. "America's Grand Hotel," *Saturday Evening Post*, CCXIX (January 25, 1947).

"La Follette's Theory of the Panic," *Literary Digest*, XXXVI (April 4, 1908).

Mead, F. S. "The Panic and the Banks," *Atlantic Monthly*, CI (February, 1908).

"Montana Ore Purchasing Company," *Copper Manual*, II (New York: Houston; 1899).

"Morse's Comeback," *Literary Digest*, XLVI (June 28, 1913).

"National News," *Nation*, LXXXII (February 22, 1906).

"The Panic," *Literary Digest*, XXXV (November 2, 1907).

Raine, N. McLeod. "The Fight for Copper," *Leslie's Magazine* (February, 1904). Tear sheets of this article are bound in the Heinze file of the Montana State Historical Society Library, Helena, Montana.

"Review of the World," *Current Literature*, XLIII (December, 1907).

Stewart, William R. "Captains of Industry—Part XXI: F. Augustus Heinze," *Cosmopolitan*, XXXVI (January, 1904).

"The Story of Heinze, A Tale of Copper—and Brass," *Current Literature*, XLIV (February, 1908).

"The Story of Morse," *Current Literature*, XLVIII (February, 1910).

Welby, Lord. "The American Panic," *Contemporary Review*, XCIII (January, 1908).

INDEX

A

Addison, Joseph, 6
A. J. P. mine, 140
Alaska, 173
Alice Gold and Silver Mining Company, 212
Allie Brown mine, 131
Amalgamated C o p p e r Mining Company, x, 16*n*, 32, 32*n*, 33, 51-56, 59-61, 63-66, 69, 72-90, 94, 115-117, 119-120, 122-123, 127-140, 140*n*, 142-148, 150, 155, 158-159, 161-162, 164, 166-167, 171, 174, 176, 184, 188-189, 194, 196-199, 204, *211-212*
American Consolidated Copper Company, 148
American Metals Company, 37, 40
Anaconda Copper Mining Company, x, 14, 16*n*, 53*n*, 64, *105*, 128, 140*n*, 145, 184, 211; purchased by Amalgamated: x, 63, 72-74, 129-130, *211*
Anaconda mine, 55, *105*
Anaconda *Standard*, 77*n*, 88*n*, 97-98, 115-117, 131, 133, 139, 142, 148, 180, 183, 199
Angelo mine, 131
Anti-Trust Party, 84, 207
apex theory, 29-31, 56-57, 63, 188, *213-214*
Aquila, Caspar, 2
Associated Press, 161, 165
Atlanta, Georgia, 169

B

Bache and Company, J. S., 43
Bacon, M. W., 119
Bacon, Robert, 211
Balm mine, 140
Bank of British America, 41
Bank of Montreal, 41
Bank of North America, 47, 151, 163, 169
Barney, Charles D., 156, 158, 164-165
Barron, C. W., 97*n*
Basin, Montana, 91, 147-148
Batterman, C. H., 29-30, 127
Beatty, Judge James H., 65, 88-89
Belmont mine, 53*n*, 140
Belmont Mining Company, 140
Bigelow, Albert S., 16, 16*n*, 30-32, 34, 50-51, 62-63, 122-123, 125*n*, 126-127, 193, 203-204
Bingham Central Railroad (Utah), 149
Black Diamond mine, 140
Blackfoot Milling Company, Big, 211
Black Friars Hotel (London), 3
Boston and Bay State Mining Company, 91, 148; concentrator at Basin: 91, 147-148
Boston and Montana Mining Company, ix, 16, 21, 29-32, 32*n*, 34, 41, 51-52, 55*n*, 56, 60-75, 86, 120-121, 123-125, 127-130, 145, 161, 188,

AFTERWORD

The Watchman's Daughter

by Zena Beth McGlashan

In the winter of 2018, a woman who grew up about a block from the McNelis home on the North Side, Butte, Montana, in the shadow of Big Butte and close to the towering white spire of the Immaculate Conception Church, remembered how they drove. She recalled a stop sign at the bottom of the hill. "They never stopped. I used to grab my sister and say, 'Watch out, here come the McNelises!'"

They were indeed quite a determined and confident pair, Mary and Sarah. Both were teachers dedicated to advancing in their careers. Both had to seek teaching posts in rural Montana before they were hired by Butte public schools. Both were staunch union members. Mary was the more outgoing, ever championing her sister, younger by just a year.

In a birthday message to Sarah the year she graduated from college, Mary wrote:

> Time the sure never ceasing spinner has handed you your majority. A new door opens, a new adventure begins. May a fairy lead you successfully on. In spirit, I drink to you. My glass is filled with the rich wine of love. May you live grandly! May the pattern of your life be intense, may you have a great joy, great achievement, great conflict and the crown of great success.

Sarah and Mary were the watchman's daughters, one of whom would realize a modicum of "great achievement."

233

Girls of the Hill

Typical of the Irishmen who flooded into Butte in the late 19th century, William McNelis was a miner who became a naturalized citizen in 1896. He lived in various boarding houses on the Hill, including one at 500 N. Main. Although both came from County Donegal, most likely McNelis and Anne Marie Kelly met in Butte. They married in 1910. Babies soon arrived: Mary in 1911 and Sarah in 1912. Both girls were born in April. Mary's and William's only boy was stillborn in May of 1914.

Anne steadying Sarah on a pedestal and William with Mary on his lap in this studio photograph taken fall 1912.

The family settled into a house at 126 W. LaPlatte in Centerville. Just a few blocks up steep Main Street were St. Lawrence O'Toole Church and school in Walkerville. The clapboard church, built with miners' donations in 1898, was the second parish in Butte, the first being St. Patrick's in the main part of town.

The little white church so humble on the outside had a grandeur that greeted parishioners then and still astounds visitors today. A European artist hired to come from New York City in 1906 painted 40 frescoes of Jesus, Mary, and saints and angels on the walls and ceilings. They provide a sacred setting for the intricately hand-carved main altar and two side altars, all three lacey and lovely.

The girls had plenty of company when they trudged to school. Because miners walked to work, the Hill was packed with small homes built close to mines such as the Lexington, the Buffalo, the Mountain Con, the Green Mountain, the Bell, and the Diamond.

Mary was in the third grade and Sarah in the second when their sister Helen was born in mid-October 1919. That little Helen received much love and attention seems certain. But then neither love nor prayers could banish fatal illness. Bronchial pneumonia took Helen in March of 1925. Families lost children at a tragically rapid rate in the days before antibiotics.

The girls thrived in school. Among their papers are two very large certificates proclaiming they had completed the Palmer Method of cursive writing. The spiral notebooks in the McNelises' archive, most of them from Sarah, are filled with near-perfect cursive. Sarah probably kept most of the college notebooks because she was primarily a history teacher and believed they could be useful as reference materials.

For many years Catholic kids attended the public high school. Butte Central, the high school for Catholic students, began in 1908 in a home Marcus Daly had built on the corner of Montana and Quartz streets, north of the Silver Bow County Courthouse. The building was expanded to meet the growing number of students.

In the 1920s the church began its transition away from co-education. Christian Brothers High School, commonly known as Boys Central, was built on Mercury Street just east of St. Patrick's Church. When it opened in the fall of 1924, only freshmen and sophomore boys attended; when fall term began 1926, all the boys were gone from the old Daly home. Mary was a junior and Sarah a sophomore at the now all-girls Central High School that fall.

For graduation in 1927 someone gave Mary an album with Girl's Graduate Journal emblazoned on the cover and decorated pages on the inside. She filled it with such things as an 8 x 10 photograph of her 8th grade graduating class from St. Lawrence with Father Francis X. Batens of St. Lawrence Church in the center of the group. Mary recorded the names of everyone on the back, then carefully folded it to fit within the 9 x 8 journal.

There are pages of special classmate entries along the girls' photos. A letter from her grandfather, Patrick Kelly in Ireland, written in beautiful cursive handwriting is pasted in its envelope. On the page beside it Mary wrote that she regretted never having met him.

She continued to use the journal for a few years after her graduation. On a "Snapshots" page, she pasted a photo of "Aunt Mary 1930 on her visit to see us." Centering the page is a studio portrait of young woman with the caption "Her daughter, Mary, taken in Letterkenny Ireland when Mary was attending the Loretto Academy there."

The souvenir from Sarah's senior year is a small autograph book. A little poem written by her big sister is the first entry. Full of youthful hope, it reveals just how close the girls were. The nickname "Sammy" appears in few other autograph entries and some letters from friends.

My Dearest Pal & Sister (Sammy)
Seek what is highest and best
Try hard to win success

Be loyal to Central and the old town
Even tho you win renown

Read today, the last line of Mary's doggerel seems prophetic: "Sammy" did, in fact, "win renown" in her lifetime and beyond. Sammy's classmates filled her little book with best wishes, little sketches and promises of lifelong friendship, some of them amusing, such as this from "Marge" Pullam, "Yours 'til the hearse pulls in."

Although Mary saved a letter in the journal inviting her to attend St. Mary's College in Leavenworth, Kansas, that fall she enrolled at the State Normal School (now the University of Montana Western) at Dillon to begin its two-year teaching program. Although the letter her father received from the Office of the President written Dec. 27, 1928, seems quaint today, it epitomizes the fondly patriarchal attitude toward females pursuing higher education:

> The enclosed record of Mary (obviously her report card) is very satisfactory. She has carried the full number of subjects and earned more grade points than credits. I hope that she is planning to continue with us and in due time earn our diploma.
>
> I am very sincerely, S.E. Davis, President

Since Dillon, about 50 miles south of Butte, was served both by bus and train, Mary was close to home. Not so with Sarah; she left for Kansas and a full four-year degree program at St. Mary's in the fall of 1928.

Some correspondence, largely from friends, is in the McNelis archive but the predominant record of her St. Mary's years are class notebooks, as mentioned earlier. Apparently during her junior year, Sarah made a New Year's resolution; she started a journal on January 1, 1932, entering something for each day in a spiral bound notebook.

Studying, walks and talks with classmates, even a terrific nose-bleed which took "5 hankies" to stanch and "scared me pink" are described. She enjoyed hearing one of her professors talk about the 46th annual meeting of the National Historical Association in Minneapolis, which he attended during Christmas break.

One entry begins "Jarred to consciousness by Sr. Dominica's insistent ringing of the bell for mass." Sarah was self-disciplined about her class work, but not so much when it came to chronicling her daily life. The journal ends on Jan. 20, 1932, less than three weeks after she started it.

The Watchman's Daughters

In a letter dated April 19, 1933, Mary broke the news to Sarah: "We're moving! From now on I shall visit my parents instead of living with them. This is a puzzle more advanced and more mysterious than a jigsaw." She went on, "We didn't agree to disagree. I didn't get a job. I didn't get married. I'm not moving, in fact. Mama and Papa are the deserting the camp." Continuing to tease, she wrote, "Now, Sherlock did you solve it?"

On the second page, she told Sarah the answer: the watchman at the Lexington Mine had died. Superintendent of Mines for the Anaconda Company, James Carrigan, "gave Papa the job." Since Carrigan also lived in Centerville, he probably knew McNelis as a reliable man. After all, he had been a miner on the Hill for 30 years, working at the Granite Mountain, the Bell, the Cora, the Rarus, and others.

Under company rules, Mary wrote, the man and wife must move into the watchman's house but no children were allowed. "You and I will live at 123 W. LaPlatte all summer. We will eat with the parents at the Lexington."

She also reported that she went to the "transfer business" and arranged to have stuff hauled up to the Lexington for their parents. In

The Lexington Mine in 1905. The small watchman's house is in the foreground, where laundry hangs on clotheslines. The headframe was of wood until it was replaced in 1950. The address was 1402 N. Main in Walkerville.

a more mundane entry, she said Mama "wants to know how much you'll need for the trip homeward in June."

Someone, maybe Carrigan himself, quickly realized that the "no children" rule at a mine watchman's house applied to youngsters who could get into mischief or even hurt themselves in a mine yard. The ban surely did not apply to two 20-something daughters who were school teachers.

Soon, perhaps even before Sarah returned on the train after graduating with highest honors from St. Mary's, the McNelis family was living at the Lexington's watchman's house at 1402 N. Main. William and Anne lived there for approximately six years; Sarah was with them when she was teaching at Girls Central and Mary off and on, depending on her teaching assignments.

Although he was still listed as Lexington watchman in the 1945 city directory, William bought a house on the North Side. The bungalow remained home to his wife and daughters for the rest of their lives.

Mary with the family dog in the mine yard. The McNelis collection contains several snapshots taken in the yard while the family lived there.

History at the Lex

Had Sarah not been the watchman's daughter, she might not have pursued Heinze as a thesis topic. As she related in the introduction to her 1947 thesis:

> For a time my home was at a mine residence which once had been a Heinze property. In a room no longer used was thrown hodge-podge much old paper magazines, canceled checks, personal letters. Among this debris I unearthed the telegrams damp with mold and scattered separately. Later the contents of the rooms (sic) were burned because it was a fire hazard and much that might have been added to the Heinze lore was consequently destroyed. At that time I was unaware this biography would ever engage my attention.

The Heinze materials probably were rescued soon after Sarah's return from Leavenworth. We can only speculate about their recovery. She does a leave a quote indicating that Will McNelis was fond of Heinze. We can imagine her big old Irish dad with so many years as a miner on the Hill saying Fritz was "a good scout," as she reported in her book. Was it a fondness for the youngest of the Copper Kings that made Will want to save some of the papers as souvenirs of a by-gone time? Or was it Sarah's idea because she already was an historian? Perhaps it was a combination of both.

There is a tone of regret that more wasn't salvaged. Fourteen years after the "fire hazard" was destroyed, Sarah wrote that much "Heinze lore" was lost. She also recognized that, at the time, there was no way she could foresee that her life would be so influenced by his.

The family moved to the house on the North Side probably in 1939. Will continued to be watchman at the Lexington until 1945. Years later when the McNelis home changed ownership because both Sarah and Mary died, two large and sturdy wood boxes with rope handles labeled "Aug. Heinze Butte, Mont." were in the house.

That Sarah actually lived at a mine is not mentioned at all in the book. She did say so in her thesis introduction but she does not name the Lex, describing it as "a mine property." Although she makes clear the Lexington properties were not included when Heinze sold out to Amalgamated in 1904, she does not say how Anaconda came to own the mines eventually.

Why this omission? Again we are left with speculation. She may not have identified the mine for the same reason the editors chose to leave out the detail of her living at a mine. At the time she finished her thesis as well as two decades later when it became a book, Anaconda's grip on Montana had only grown tighter. We can theorize revealing what some might consider theft from the watchman's house was best left unsaid.

Stealing from mines and mine yards was considered almost a right by the men who worked on the Hill. On the note page where

"Papa's" assessment of Heinze is typed, she recorded brief stories from other miners, such as this:

> Fellow leasing (a claim) one night expressed a wish for a (ore) car and some rails. I said, "Is that all you want?" It was a nice summer evening; I was in my shirtsleeves. Another fellow and I went over to the Cora; the men were working around. We took a car right off the sheets and ran it over the dump; then sent back and got six rails. Left it nice and handy for him. No one said a thing to us not a word.

Beginning Their Professional Lives

Both Mary and Sarah started teaching in 1933, Mary far from home and Sarah at their alma mater, Girls Central.

Mary, accustomed to city life in the leading metropolis in the state, was starting her teaching career at a school in rural western Montana. She was in Florence, south of Missoula, paying $33 per month for room and board to Mrs. John Gow. Pasted on a final page of her Girl's Graduate Journal are postcards, one labeled on the front "Mary's Mission, Founded 1841, Stevensville, Montana." Beside the card Mary wrote "Attended mass here every Sunday from September 1933 to June 1934."

The next school year, she was at the Jocko Camp school. Once again Mary's journal provides some details. Tucked in the back is a mimeographed letter dated March 15, 1935, from the superintendent of the Flathead Agency based in Dixon addressed to parents and teachers announcing the visitation of the Indian Service dentist. He would see all parents and children; dates, times and places are given. Jocko Camp is listed along with about a dozen sites.

Archival evidence indicates Mary got a camera for Christmas 1934. She took photos at Jocko and sent them home to Butte, writ-

Jocko School photo late May 1935.

Camp Jocko.

Helen McCann, who taught with Mary, holding the cradle-board with Mrs. Vanderburg's baby.

Mary and Helen McCann and a pupil at the Jocko School picnic spring 1935.

ing on the back of a few but most, including one of the four-man kitchen crew, have no information.

Back in Butte, Sarah was seeing Girls Central from a teacher's point of view; she taught there for three years, living with Mama and Papa at the Lex. In the spring of 1934 when she was finishing her first year at Central, Sarah reflected on her career as a teacher. Written on the backs of chute and level mine record forms, the outpouring reads as though it were the draft of a letter. If it was and to whom it might have been directed, we'll never know. But it reveals an analytical self-discipline (as well as a dislike of early mornings) and even includes a personal description. She was 22, "red-haired, hazel-eyed, not above average in looks, attractive size, well-proportioned, disposition of a demon and the temper of a Damascus sword."

She wrote: "Teaching is not an entirely enjoyable profession there are ups and downs and way downs and way ups. For every discouragement, I should venture there is corresponding joy which is a magic balm. Would you consider me undiplomatic if I confided that very often that joy was a particular pupil?"

She wrote of attitude: "Taking the 'wings of the morning,' the psychology of the beginning in an optimistic frame of mind is questionable.

"The average individual enjoys a display of temper. Perhaps it satisfies the same craving a Fourth of July fireworks exhibition does. Spontaneity of personal pyrotechnics should make up for the technique of the artificial variety. I have considered wearing a TNT sign but have abandoned the idea when reminded of my crowning glory red and the blazing light that can flash from two hazel eyes.

"Other days are framed in a halo of light undimmed by even a miniature thunder cloud. One task yields easily to the next and I can even love those pupils whom I know would like buy me a ticket to darkest Africa and let the lions continue work so nobly begun.

"My natural tendency is to unfold petal by petal to talk but little on first arising. I lack the buoyant effervescent that starts one off in that rare but blessed 'love the world' attitude. I am not a crank. In fact I have been charged with being a 'cheerful cherub' but the fact remains my enthusiasm is low in the pre-9 o'clock hours of the average day. To give to such disposition as the first duty of the day the task of keeping 35 freshmen girls quiet. Will the result be a gentle and sweet teacher? In nine cases out of 10 no! And I never was the exception. My poor pupils!

"I would feel sorry for them if not for my conviction concerning knowledge and a hunger to make others desire it, qualities which are neither virtues nor vices and yet partake of the character of unrelenting firmness and, you won't believe it, timidity in particular situations."

Sarah describes the difficulty of having a position on a faculty where all the other members belong to a religious order. The question "Do you like teaching here?" came inevitably a dozen times a day." She developed "stock answers some of them a trifle modified by my natural veracity. 'Oh, yes' in general. Some days I love it and other days I can't live with myself."

Forty years later in 1973 as she neared retirement, she wrote about her daily schedule at Central "that, now, I can hardly believe."

She remembered each day was divided into eight periods with an hour for lunch. Sarah taught two senior and two sophomore English classes, first- and second-year Spanish, a social studies course on career planning, and supervised a study hall. On the side, she taught journalism and worked with the newspaper and yearbook staffs.

Her salary was "unmentionably low, a pittance." Reflecting her humanitarian nature as well as her retention of facts, she added, "But I was enthusiastic and thankful to have a job when 3,300,000 (people) between the ages of 18 and 25 were out of school and out of work" because of the Depression.

Sarah was sure she could do better. She wrote to the Montana Education Association placement bureau. There was an opening that just fit her experience but it was in Turner, Montana, which to a city girl must have sounded like the end of the earth. Turner is in the eastern part of the vast state, about 12 miles from the Canadian border. It was the equivalent of Mary's going to the woodlands of western Montana but offering prairie views.

Turner High offered Sarah a far bigger salary and a more manageable teaching load than she had at Central.

But the salary was magnificent in comparison. At Central she had been making $400 a year, a little less than $7,000 in today's money. The position in Turner paid $1,300 a year, which translates to $22,500 today, and the workload was reasonable. And the tiny town boasted a real school building, not a big drafty converted home. She began in Turner the fall of 1936 and taught there for three years. The Turner experience put her on more solid ground financially as well as professionally.

The Butte School District hired Mary in the fall of 1938, Sarah in 1939.

Union Matters

Although both were dedicated members of Butte Teachers Union (BTU) Local #332, Mary was more the outspoken activist. Throughout the 1940s and 1950s they held various offices; for

Mary and a friend, left visited Sarah, right. Sarah began teaching at Turner in the fall of 1936 when construction of the dam, completed in 1940, was at its peak.

Postcard view of Turner in the '30s.

example, in 1941, Mary was elected vice president, continuing on two consecutive terms as president, 1943-1945. In the 1950s, Sarah was secretary for four years.

Mary was appointed to the Teachers Retirement Board in 1946, the same year delegates from several state locals met at the junior high school in Anaconda to discuss forming the Montana Federation of Teachers. Mary made the motion which passed unanimously. She was elected acting MFT secretary-treasurer at the Anaconda meeting, then elected secretary at the state convention. Mary was named to the Montana Board of Health in 1949.

A challenge to the BTU came in 1946; two parties fielded slates for School District #1's board: The Independent Party headed by a School of Mines professor and the People's Party. Two women remember their parents talking about this election. One, a Catholic, said, "They didn't want Catholic teachers." The other, a Protestant, said she thinks the professor's party was largely made up of anti-union Republicans reacting to Butte's being a Democrat town.

In 1959, eight Butte High teachers sued the school district and the BTU for running a "closed shop," forcing the plaintiffs to be union members. On June 29, 1959, a majority of the state Supreme Court found in favor of the plaintiffs and declared void the mandatory union membership clause in the agreement between the teachers union and the district. The furor did not soon fade away as evidenced by letters and reports in the McNelis archive which fairly sizzle with outrage, with Mary being the most vociferous, but Sarah co-authored with another teacher a strenuous objection.

It's no surprise Mary kept a union scrapbook, multiple newspaper clippings, letters, various reports, and many clips from and whole copies of the *People's Voice*, a weekly based in Helena, edited by Harry and Gretchen Billings, which was dedicated to an old-fashioned populist view: people mattered. They wrote vigorously about injustices, about the two companies ruling the state, Anaconda Copper Mining Company (ACM) and Montana Power, about politicians, about legislation, about unions, about Native American issues, about anything mainstream Montana press was not covering properly if at all.

Mary clipped some stories from the *Montana Standard* and the *Butte Daily Post* but those are few and far between and offer fact but no analysis because the papers were owned by Anaconda, as were the majority of the state's dailies. The company's unwritten policy was to largely ignore and often condemn unions as well omit any events which would reflect badly on the company, such as deaths in its mines. Any researcher interested in teachers' history in the 1940s and 1950s would be well served to turn to the McNelis archive.

Seeking to Tell Heinze's Story

The summer of 1934 after her first year of teaching at Central, Sarah began post-graduate studies in Missoula at the University of Montana, then called Montana State University, living in a women's dormitory. She attended every summer through 1937. Along with her academic courses, Sarah took the business administration department's typewriting class as a "listener" meaning she was a participant but not for credit. Being able to type was a skill she needed.

Mary started summer school in Missoula in 1938 and enrolled annually through 1948, except for 1941. She completed requirements for a bachelor's degree in English in 1948.

The women's pursuit of higher education had to do with the pay scale negotiated by the Butte Teachers Union, which took into account degree level as well as updating their credentials through continued education.

However it was more than that. Just as many mining families wanted their sons not to spend their working lives underground, they had aspirations for their daughters, too. The dangerous mines created too many widows with no safety net except charity. Even if a girl married, she should have the protection of a trade or profession.

Stories are told of young women walking from their homes on the Hill down to Butte Business College (BBC) in the center of town; many even walked home for lunch and back again for afternoon classes. BBC was on the fifth floor of a grand Victorian Owsley building which burned in the 1970s and became the site for the NorthWestern Energy building some 40 years later.

St. James Hospital had its School of Nursing, which provided income for nurses and their families as well as generations of caregivers. Some Catholic girls joined religious orders. Teaching certainly was an honorable profession.

In the spring of 1943, Sarah proposed to her thesis adviser Professor E. E. Bennett that she do a biography of F. Augustus Heinze. In June, Bennett wrote that he had taken her idea to the reference librarian "most expert in Montana and Northwestern history." He reported that Miss White said it would be "rather difficult to do much more on the Butte copper fight than has already been done."

The librarian referred to C. B. Glasscock's *War of the Copper Kings*

Anne and William McNelis, taken probably in the mid-1940s. William died in January 1948. "Mama" Anne lived with her daughters until her death in 1965.

that came out in 1935 and Christopher P. Connolly's *The Devil Learns to Vote: the Story of Montana* published in 1938. Connolly's work is his five-part 1906 series for McClure's magazine, "The Story of Montana," published posthumously in book form. (He died in 1936.)

Sarah told Bennett she had "made some investigations in the State Historical Society for materials related to Heinze." Bennett was reluctant to approve her thesis proposal but if she could find any of Heinze's papers "or any of his relatives alive who could tell about it" then perhaps she could adopt her thesis subject.

The professor did not know she was the watchman's daughter. And she would soon find a relative of Fritz.

A Brother Eager to Talk

Sarah had little trouble locating Otto, one of Heinze's older brothers. She first turned to Mrs. T.J. Murray who had been interviewed by Glasscock for his *War of the Copper Kings*. She talked with Claire Murray on July 8, 1943, at her home on the lower West Side, considered to be an upscale part of town. Claire's parents were John "Jack" and Elmira Noyes, pioneer Butte residents, and her sister, Ruth "Dollie" Noyes, married Arthur, the eldest of the Heinze brothers.

Claire told her "Fritz always had a mistress." She identified Nellie Kingsley as "his most beauteous lady of whom he may have been really fond. She later married the doctor in the retinue of the German prince traveling in Butte." Europeans of means often toured America's "Wild West" before and after the turn of the 20th century. Butte offered a civilized stop-over. "What an odd life for Butte-born girl," Claire said. "Following her marriage she lived in Germany."

Although Sarah typed her notes from the conversation, which was deliciously gossipy, details of Butte's version of the Gilded Age were not her primary goal.

The most important thing she got from Claire was Otto's address. She wrote to him the very next day, July 9, 1943.

Her inquiry about Fritz must have seemed an answer to Otto's long held hope for someone to write his younger brother's story. Ever the precise researcher, Sarah sent guidelines for what she wanted. Otto was eager to comply.

The first footnote in her book refers to Otto's letters: "The author has assembled these letters written between 1943 and 1947 into a cohesive body as, in effect, they are manuscript notes." Otto used a Dictaphone to tell his story and a secretary to type it. Sarah then retyped them into a narrative form. Certainly Sarah made a few changes, but she retained the integrity of his dialogue.

Because Otto was talking, the manuscript notes have a voice. Reading them is as though we are in the same room with Otto listening to his story of the Heinze family, the brothers, and especially of Fritz and his spectacular mining career. Otto's story is enriched because "I decided leave it (the typed copy) also to my granddaughter and am therefore making it so much more detailed."

Otto sent transcriptions two or three pages at time. She began to type them as she received them, numbering the pages. Sarah's brilliance as a researcher is evidenced by the only letter from her to Otto in the archive. As she typed the manuscript notes, she sent a copy to Otto. Which meant that she could reference page numbers in the notes when she asked specific questions, for example: "In which court trial did the incident of the lawyer Marshall (your notes Page 41) occur? Have you recalled any other amusing court scenes?" In this letter she asked other questions without reference to pages, which we can safely say she did in other letters.

In addition, Otto corresponded to Sarah on half-sheets also dictated to and typed by a secretary. For example, August 6, 1943, he wrote, " I am practically writing the history of my own early years. Fritz and I went through those years together and what happened to me also happened to him. We were so closely tied together until he went to Columbia College when our paths separated." Parted until Fritz needed his brothers to use their respective skills to aid him in his fight over the riches of the Butte Hill.

Otto did not want to slow Sarah's research. On August 12, 1943, he reports in one of his half-sheet letters that he is sending two more pages, adding "now don't bother to acknowledge the receipt of these letters. I will understand perfectly."

Predators

Sarah was approached by people hoping to profit from her work on F. A. even before she finished her thesis. The first instance was by Heinze's cousin, Louise Lacey, in 1943. She had been in contact with Otto who told Louise that he was assisting Sarah with her thesis concerning F. A.'s life. Otto wrote to Sarah telling her that Miss Lacey "was suddenly seized with a great desire to be of assistance...the trouble is that she has quite a vivid imagination and sometimes gets her statements mixed with imagination instead of reality."

Lacey contacted Montana State University in Missoula to obtain Sarah's information and then wrote to Sarah concerning a collaboration on F. A.'s life. Louise claimed to have "thrilling and interesting" facts and "dramatic details" that could add to Sarah's thesis. She wrote that she was a bridesmaid in Arthur Heinze and Dollie Noyes' wedding and "stayed six months which was when Butte was the greatest mining camp on earth...and got a great deal of information unknown to the family." Even if she was just a teenager when Arthur and Dollie wed, Louise must surely have been in her 60s by the time she came up with her scheme.

She wanted to do a movie about F. A.'s life; she said she was "in touch with the Paramount people" in New York. Lacey offered to co-write the script with Sarah "and when it is produced go 50/50 on the contract." Sarah was taken aback at this proposal considering she was writing an historical account of F. A.'s life, not a drama or dime-store novel.

Sarah contacted Prof. Bennett, asking for advice on how to handle this unwelcome advance. He, along with a dean and another senior professor, suggested Sarah write to Lacey explaining the thesis would be read by "historical scholars, and that any attempt to make it too dramatic would do Heinze more harm than good."

The second attempt to obtain Sarah's work was by Courteney Terrett in 1947. Terrett contacted Otto asking if he knew of anyone writing a book on F. A. He then wrote, "It would be kind of you if you were to suggest what I should seek, and where or from whom I might get it."

Otto wrote Sarah concerning Terrett for which she was very grateful. Sarah learned Terrett had heard of her thesis from a Butte librarian who "knew I had worked on Heinze's life story because I had done so much research in the library." Sarah wrote to Otto that she "should resent having some opportunist simply appropriate it (thesis) and with minor changes make it his own."

The third effort is attributed to T. J. Kerttula who wrote to Sarah in 1950 asking for her research on F. A. as he was planning on writing a book about him. Kerttula offered to give Sarah a percentage of profits from the book when it was finished.

In a 1951 letter, Toole, then director of the Montana Historical Society, asked her for a copy for the society saying, "I can understand your initial inclination not to permit the copying of your thesis. I have had some rather unfortunate experiences in that regard." She reluctantly sent him a copy, only after his reassurance that access would be limited.

In 1965 Dayton Lummis Jr. wrote to Sarah's mother, Anne, asking for "the present location of the letters and papers that were used" for Sarah's thesis for his own research project on Heinze's career.

She was asked by Gene Gressley of the University of Wyoming for her thesis and research on multiple occasions in 1976 and 1977 for a special Western history collection. He sent "a donor list which will bring you up to date regarding the contributors to our program." In Gressley's last letter to Sarah he starts with "at this point in time you are probably getting a little weary of seeing the name at the bottom of this page. However, as you know...we have had a very strong interest in eventually becoming the repository for your literary and historical material."

Otto and Publishers

After she finished her thesis, she sent a copy to Otto. He wrote: "from the time several years ago I received your first letter...I felt confident that you would produce a good account...and I now feel that my estimate of your ability was correct." He told her he had read "your book (thesis) several times and most carefully" and found it to be "excellent, the best description of my brother F. A.'s life I have ever seen and I want to thank you...." He praised her rigorous research, saying she had put in "a number of things I had forgotten and some I never knew...which you carefully authenticated...."

He began a search for a publisher even before she completed her thesis, talking with several people in Manhattan connected to publishing. In late May of 1948, Otto met with yet another publisher, Scribners, one of the foremost publishing houses in the nation. The people at Scribners said Sarah's work was "very carefully thought out and extremely well-written" but they did not think it had "the necessary glamour appeal and high points which would a good seller in these times."

Having been turned down by many publishers, Otto wrote that he was "down-hearted and I feel that I have reached the end of my rope." If the book was ever to be published he wrote to Sarah "it will have to be through your efforts out West." He was elderly; Otto died December 30, 1948.

Dr. H. G. Merriam, Mary's adviser as she was finishing her bachelor's degree in English, said as much when he responded on June 5, 1948, to Mary's letter asking his opinion about Sarah's thesis becoming a book. Merriam said when "one finishes reading he feels that he has facts but not that he understands the man himself." He expressed doubts about "so much reliance" upon information from Otto. If the manuscript were "popularized, made more dramatic, and interpret the man," it might be publishable, Merriam said.

Glamour and drama were never Sarah's intent. She worked hard to make her thesis accurate, well documented and thorough. It was academic, which mattered most to her. She used restraint with Otto's notes.

The people at Scribners were right about the timing for two major reasons: the first being that two books about the Copper Wars were published, Glasscock's in 1935 and Connolly's in 1938.

The second reason was after the long and costly World War II Americans were seeking a new "normal." The Heinze saga was past; the prevailing feeling at the time was "in with the new, out with the old."

On her own, even if she took the time to send her manuscript to various university presses in the Midwest and West, Sarah would have had little chance of seeing her work in print. It was, after all "just" a master's thesis, not even a doctoral dissertation. The academic pecking order, which still prevails, would have been a serious barrier. She was "just" a Montana high school teacher. And she was a woman at time when returning to normal meant women should know their proper places. Many women had left "normal" jobs to help the war effort and were now expected to find happiness in suburban kitchens or at secretaries' desks.

Symbolic of women's status at the time is a clipping found in Mary's scrapbook of news relating to education. Headlined "Miss Nutterville Receives Honor," the story from the *Montana Labor News* of February 25, 1943, reports that Catherine Nutterville had been appointed a lecturer in sociology at the University in Missoula replacing a man who had been named to the National Labor Relations Board regional office in Denver.

Nutterville joined the Butte school system in 1930 just after she received her B.A. in education from the University of Montana. A school psychologist, she also earned a doctorate in education from Columbia University in 1942. The idea that a fully qualified woman was "honored" to be a lecturer (lowest academic rank) to replace a male faculty member was not unusual at the time. In fact, the academic world only began noticing its dearth of women faculty in the 1970s when another periodic wave of feminism infused the nation.

Montana, the Magazine

In late November 1951, Sarah received a request from Toole for an article on Heinze for *Montana Magazine of History.* "I would like to balance the magazine with material subsequent to the 1880s because there is an unfortunate tendency in Montana to over emphasize the earlier period and thus far that imbalance has been reflected in the magazine."

He told her to take "any approach" and not worry about the length. Toole was familiar with the quality of her work. He cited her master's in his 1948 thesis on Marcus Daly. Toole earned his B.A. in 1947 and his M.A. both from the University of Montana. In his Mc-Nelis reference in his thesis he comments that her Heinze biography "though somewhat partisan, it gives the subject a full treatment."

Sarah said yes to his request but she wasn't snappy about it. On August 1, 1952, Toole wrote to Sarah reminding her he had yet to receive her article, setting a deadline of September 10 for publication in the October issue.

Although she makes the same point in her 1947 thesis that F. Augustus Heinze was one helluva good mining engineer (she puts it more elegantly, of course), Sarah did not just "cut and paste" her thesis to produce an article for the fledgling journal. Toole must have been pleased to receive the piece. Sarah skillfully summarizes Heinze's background so that readers are informed but not bored. Her basic premise was that Heinze, "the least well-known but most colorful of the key figures" in the 1896-1905 Copper War, was an innovator. His "scientific and engineering training were doubtless responsible for his being the pioneer in advanced methods of mining and smelting."

The Heinze article in her copy of *Montana Magazine* in the McNelis collection has a few lightly penciled-in editing marks correcting errors, probably placed there by the author herself.

A Real Book, At Last!

In February 1968, Sarah was both "surprised and pleased" to get the request from Toole to publish her work on Heinze. She told Toole "it is a satisfaction to know that you, who have had so varied and distinguished career in the field of history, regard my thesis as worthwhile." Being singled out by Toole truly was a big deal. Toole earned his doctorate at U.C.L.A., headed the Historical Society in Helena, directed the Museum of the City of New York, then was director of the Museum of New Mexico before returning to his beloved Montana.

When Toole chose to publish her work, Sarah was 56. Taking advantage of summer breaks she had done extensive post-graduate work attending the University of Wyoming, Stanford University, the University of Chicago, and a special course in reading technique at the University of Pennsylvania. Sarah enjoyed being a scholar. For over 30 years, she had been teaching a range of courses, largely history, her specialty, but also journalism, among other subjects.

Toole assigned a professor and a graduate student to edit her manuscript. Ready to be a cooperative author, she must have gritted her teeth over some of their changes which she did not see until

Toole sent her the pages proofs, the final step for a manuscript before going to the printer.

October 22, 1968, she wrote to Toole about the page proofs:

> I suppose that editors and authors do not always see eye to eye. I am reminded of a story Mr. Pat Burke, a Butte newsman, once told a journalism class of mine. He said that when he first began as a reporter, he had an editor who never let anything stand as it was written; when he was once challenged, the editor's defense of his close supervision was, 'Listen, if you brought the 'Lord's Prayer' to me, I would change it.' I concede that there is that quality in all successful editors.

A woman involved in this re-publication project suggested it would be interesting to compare Sarah's thesis with the book to determine the changes. "But, I guess that would be just too much," she said with a laugh. Indeed "too much" in this case but a couple of examples indicate just how much Sarah's original work may have suffered under these academic editors. In the first page of the introduction, she wrote Heinze's actions in Butte "spread" Montana's name throughout the United States. Her editors changed "spread" to "promulgated" an example of using twelve dollar word where a three dollar one will do. In this example, "spread" is what she meant about the press coverage nationally. "Promulgate" means pushing an idea; it's even the wrong word.

Sarah McNelis was an exceptionally good writer as her book, written over 70 years ago, proves to the contemporary reader. She was well acquainted with the do's and don'ts of journalism one of which is never change a quote.

On page 209 of her thesis, Sarah cites her father:

"Oh, he was a good scout; he'd come along to men working on top and throw them a dollar and tell them to get a drink."

Sarah followed that quote with the statement:

At this time the daily wage for miners was three dollars and a half.

Her editors probably were good historians. Editing was quite another thing. They combined the quote with Sarah's statement of fact about pay which she inserted to show Heinze's generosity. And, the editing gods forbid, they invented the rest of sentence.

Oh, he was a good scout; he'd come along to men working on top and throw them a dollar and tell them to get a drink. You know, we were getting but three and a half (dollars) a shift then.

In her letter to Toole, she also explains a serious error in a clever way:

Some changes I don't like. One occurs on page 15 is in the information that Meaderville is north of Butte; it is, in fact, southeast. To old timers and others here this would be like telling the Sons of Liberty that the Boston Tea Party was in Philadelphia.

She told Toole, "Many of the changes are improvements. A number of my editorializing comments are better omitted." She liked the chronology.

Jack Ryan, former newspaperman who had become the university's information officer, issued a press release on October 28, 1968, announcing 1,000 copies of "Copper King at War" would go on sale Nov. 15.

On Thursday, November 14, 1968, Hennessy's department store advertised that Sarah would be "autographing" her Heinze biography Friday evening from 7 to 9 in the book department on the mezzanine in the massive building that also housed the Anaconda Company's Butte headquarters.

The book soon sold out.

Sarah at her book signing in 1968 with Mary standing by her.

Reaction and a Reprint

In the late 1960s, the concept of "new journalism" had not been widely adopted by Montana newspapers. Straight news, considered objective, prevailed. Newspapers did announce Sarah's book had been published but most used the press release sent by the University. Only one story in the McNelis archive gives details of Sarah's background and indicates that the reviewer actually read the book.

Heinze's story is presented "with interest, color, drama and insight," the reviewer wrote, referring to him as "a many-sided genius."

Sometime after she read that her book was being reprinted, Sarah wrote Toole asking if there was a possibility of a royalty. His response, written February 6, 1969, was, bottom line, "As for royalties, there are none."

He said that the story about reprinting her book shouldn't have been released when it was. True, 1,500 reprints had been ordered, 1,000 to be bound and 500 unbound. But, in a lengthy paragraph describing all the costs of publishing a book, the underlying tone of which can be described as "it seemed like a good idea at the time," he ended on a disheartened note:

> I doubt that the University of Montana Press will survive beyond another volume perhaps two. It was a worthy endeavor and an interesting experiment and I suppose all of us involved from the beginning that the odds were very much against are staying alive very long.

In 1969, UM Press did publish another in the hoped-for series, "The Frightful Punishment," the story of Con Orem by Warren Brier, dean of the School of Journalism. Orem was a famous boxer in the 1860s who fought in Virginia City and Helena. The dust jacket of this book were in the same style as Sarah's: white with red slab-serif frontier type. Instead of the stylized red headframes on her book, the Brier's title began with an abstract red fist.

Always a Historian

Sarah's love for learning was not diminished by her brief moment of fame. In 1966 she applied for and received a National Defense Education Act grant to attend a historiography institute at the University of Chicago. Between then and her retirement in the late

1970s, she traveled to or took correspondence from six different universities in courses ranging from directed readings in Spanish to counseling and guidance. Some of her post graduate study in the summers may have been inspired by the universities' locations.

She and Mary also traveled when they could. One of Prof. Bennett's letters when she was doing her master's expresses the hope that she had a good time on her trip to California. The McNelises went to New York City at least twice while Otto was alive but didn't meet him. In letters, he said he was disappointed that he was not in the city when they visited. They went to education and labor conferences both in Montana and at cities around the nation.

Of course, they attended church regularly. They read constantly. And as their archive attests, collected brochures from places they had either been or hoped to go. One archival file is labeled "brochures found in books."

World Museum of Mining photo archives volunteers circa 1980s from left, Camille Maffei, Al Hooper, Elizabeth Morissett, unidentified, and Sarah McNelis.

An activity after her retirement was especially appealing: Sarah was a volunteer at the photo archives of the World Museum of Mining.

Built around the towering headframe of what was once an operating mine, the Orphan Girl, just west of the campus of Montana Technological University "Tech" (originally the Montana School of Mines), the museum was opened in 1965 by local volunteers dedicated to preserving Butte's mining heritage. The museum also features a prototype frontier village, each structure filled with period artifacts.

From the museum's inception, people have donated thousands upon thousands of items, from heavy equipment and ore wagons to Victorian hatpins and photographs. Lots of photographs, all of which require identification and cataloging, a process which is still on going.

Because most of the effort has gone to buildings to contain exhibits of interest to visitors, behind the scenes workplaces were (and still are) primitive. Photo archivists are still working in the same cramped area where Sarah did. With a major improvement: the wood stove which used to burn brightly to heat the room has been replaced by something more efficient and much safer.

The Expert Speaks

The September 24-26, 1982, symposium, "Butte: The Urban Frontier," was sponsored by the Butte Historical Society and billed as a public conference to examine the history of Butte mining, radical labor and politics, and cultural life. Sarah was invited to be on the politics panel; although her response was positive she made sure that the organizers knew that McNelis was spelled with only one L.

Her paper was titled "Apolitical F. Augustus Heinze." She was an accomplished, confident historian who used words with wit, as in this passage about William A. Clark and his bid to become a senator: "From 1893 to 1901 this curmudgeon's tenacious pursuit of his goal corroded and polluted the politics of the state and the nation." Setting the tone for her opinions about F. A. she wrote: "...despite his participation and interest in many local elections, politics was not his motivation...." His "activities in American and Canadian politics grew out of his specific need to make a gain for his economic enterprises."

Sarah's last known public presentation about Heinze was on October 14, 1997, when she was invited to speak at the Butte Archives by the Butte Historical Society. She was 85. James D. "Curly" Harrington, longtime Butte High teacher, was a Butte and Montana historian, teaching courses at Western and Tech. When he introduced her, Jim joked about her having taught at Turner, a reference indicating that she had told her colleagues about that long ago experience in the tiny town.

Her talk was tape-recorded. On the first part of the tape she can be heard talking about Heinze and the fact that his family called him Fritz. Then she says, "I think I'll put my coat right here." Alas, evidently she put it in front of the tape recorder. Even with intervention from audio experts, the tape remains unintelligible.

Those few audible words on the tape do settle one thing which might have faded from historic memory. The family name is indeed pronounced as two syllables, "Hine-zee," not "Heinz" as in the well-known company that produces ketchup. Some people do pronounce the surname that way, but not the Heinze family of Brooklyn Heights, New York.

Sarah would know. She was the watchman's daughter.

Editor's note: Lindsay Lambrecht Mulcahy was research assistant for the McNelis project and wrote the Predators section of the Afterword.

Postscripts

Like His Sisters

Sarah kept control of her papers which were safe as long as she and Mary were alive and functioning. What would have become of all the boxes of research and memorabilia had they not met Harold Walker is painful to imagine.

After Walker retired as precipitation plant manger after years of working for the Anaconda Co., he had time for projects helping friends and neighbors. "We lived across the street from Mary Louise Carlson, who was a teacher. They were looking for a handyman. She recommended Dad to them," according to his son "Buddy" Walker.

"He loved them like they were his sisters."

As the years passed, Harold became their caretaker, driving them to doctors' appointments and visiting the rest home where Mary was. Both died in 2003, Sarah in July and Mary in December. Harold delivered the boxes containing the McNelis papers to the Archives.

Otto's Manuscript Notes

Historical eras' names are an artifice created by people who write about and study them. And they tend to overlap no matter the time periods that bracket them. The Heinze story is one of the Gilded Age, 1870-1910, which doesn't mean the excesses of the wealthy ended, kerplunk!, in 1910. The Progressive Era began before the Gilded Age faded away. Ironically, as this is printed, we are in the midst of a second Gilded Age when the very few own most of America's wealth.

Otto Heinze's manuscript notes garnered from letters he sent between between 1943 and 1947 are about not only the battles on the Butte Hill and in the courts but also the lifestyles of the rich. When Otto says the Waldorf-Astoria Hotel, Fritz's favorite in New York, compared favorably to some of the most elegant hotels in Europe, that means Otto experienced them.

The 73-page single-spaced document refers to Fritz's first love, Otto Sr.'s Masonic membership unknown to his family until some of his lodge brothers marched into Greenwood Cemetery to conduct graveside rituals, suicides, death threats, the cost of Fritz's excessive gambling during the latter part of his years in Butte, Otto's observation that some Westerners had negative attitudes toward men from the East. So many things that Sarah chose not to use. She kept on task.

However if Sarah had been more generous with her research after her book was published, perhaps Montana's history would be better for it. A good example is how Judge William Clancy, who has gotten such a bad rap from subsequent historians. Even Toole believed that Clancy was a pawn of Heinze. In Sarah's book, the studio photograph of Heinze standing behind the seated judge suggests subservience. In reality, Clancy answered to no one but the law as he read it and his own principles.

One historian who did not buy Connolly's and the *Anaconda*

Standard's version of Clancy was Sarah's teaching colleague, Jim "Curly" Harrington (1937-2013). Apparently Harrington didn't have access to Otto's manuscript notes in which he states emphatically the Heinze brothers did not bribe judges.

Jim told his Butte history classes that Clancy was a populist "who hated monopolistic companies." Clancy is depicted as an uneducated ignoramus by Connolly in his 1906 series for McClure's magazine, which became the 1938 book, *The Devil Learns to Vote: the Story of Montana,* as mentioned earlier.

In fact, Clancy served in the Union Army in the Civil War, became a lawyer, co-owned, wrote for, and edited a Democrat newspaper, and was elected mayor of Edina, Missouri. As Harrington told a few folks after one of his college classes, he knew Clancy wasn't a crook because his housekeeper was Father Phelan's sister and the priest wouldn't let his sister work for anyone who wasn't on the up and up. Then Jim smiled and chuckled.

A copy of Otto's manuscript notes is in the Archives' library.

What Happened to Junior?

Frederick Augustus Heinze Jr. was born December 6, 1911. His mother, Bernice Golden Henderson Heinze, died of spinal meningitis on April 3, 1914; his father died 10 months later, on November 3, 1914. Not quite three, little Fritz was an orphan but one from a family that could well afford nursemaids and nannies.

When Sarah McNelis interviewed Claire Noyes Murray in 1943 she asked about the young Fritz. Claire said he was "practically adopted" by his Aunt Lida and her husband. Lida married well; her husband, William "Willie" Fleitmann owned a dry goods importing firm in New York City. Willie and Lida invested in F. A.'s Trail, British Columbia, enterprises (McNelis, p. 23).

When he was 12, Lida took Fritz to the Fleitmanns' home in Bremen, Germany. He no doubt experienced the same multi-lingual upbringing and possibly similar rigors of German schools as had his father and Uncle Otto.

Fritz was with his Uncle Willie when he died "unexpectedly" in Paris in March 1929. Fleitmann was described as "cosmopolitan" in his obituary in a Brooklyn newspaper "having been educated in France and Germany and spent a great deal of time and travel abroad."

Perhaps it was to escape the strict system and pursue his own dreams that inspired Fritz in the spring of 1932 when he was 21 to stowaway on a ship sailing from Le Havre, France, to New York City. An immigration officer met the ship and took him to Ellis Island. He probably wasn't too worried because he had relatives in New York. This relates to what Claire Murray told Sarah:

> As a young man he came to America and is said to have tried to qualify for the movies in Hollywood. His enormous blue eyes inherited from his mother were probably his most distinguishing feature. Seems not to have succeeded in cinema-land for the very good reason that he constantly informed directors that "General _____ would never do it that way." General _____ was a friend he had known earlier; may have been his teacher. (Sarah probably used underscoring because Claire did not remember the General's name.)

Fritz and Louise Kendell were married in New York in 1936. According to information Fritz gave to U. S. immigration officers at Rouses Point, New York, in 1942 when he walked over the border from Canada, Louise was still his wife. He told them he had lived in Germany, that he was in Great Britain in 1932, and listed his occupation as truck driver. Apparently he had delivered a truck and its cargo into Canada.

His next marriage was to publicist Helen C. Mauer of Long Island, New York, in 1956. She was 33, he 44. On the register in Alexandria, Virginia, he lied, listing "first marriage." Transportation was his occupation. They were living in Miami-Dade County, Florida, when she died of natural causes on 1961.

His third wife, Dorothy Clark Flint, was a 64-year-old widow from Menlo Park, California. This time Fritz, who was then 58, was honest about his status, putting down widower, residing in the Shelton Hotel in New York City. The couple wed in Arlington, Virginia, in 1968.

Fritz and Dorothy resided at the Grand Hotel in Cannes on the French Riviera, when Fritz lost his wife, again of natural causes. Dorothy died in January 1970. She was cremated in Marseille; the form reads: "the urn is in the possession of the widower" whose address was listed as Villa Elizabeth in LaNapoule, a town next to Cannes.

No entries for children nor a final resting place were found in the genealogical search.

Thanks to . . .

Lindsay Lambrecht Mulcahy for being an interested and engaging research assistant for the McNelis project and for researching and writing the Predators section of the Afterword.

The Butte-Silver Bow Public Archives staff: Ellen Crain, director; Nikole Evankovich, assistant director; Aubrey Jaap, administrative assistant; Irene Scheidecker, senior technical archivist; Harriet Schultz, archivist; Kim Murphy-Kohn, scheduler and archivist, for their friendly and expert help.

Ashby Kinch and the Board of the University of Montana Press for granting the Friends of the Butte Archives use of copyright to republish McNelis' Heinze biography.

Mary Lou Fitzpatrick, Archives volunteer, for her recollection of how they drove, winter 2018.

Wilma Blewett Puich, "Where We Went to School 1876-2015: A History of the Buildings of Our Schools," published 2015. Available at the Archives.

John Astle, "A Brief History of The Butte Teachers Union Local #332," 1985. Unpublished article; a copy is at the Archives.

Dennis Swibold, 'The Education of a Muckraker: The Journalism of Christopher P. Connolly," *Montana: The Magazine of Western History*," Vol. 53, No. 2, Summer 2003, pp. 2-19.

Mindi Nash Stevens, of Salt Lake City, Utah, for using her extensive skills as a genealogist to "find" Fritz Jr.

David Ferrig, Federal Reserve Bank of Minneapolis newsletter, "F. Augustus Heinze and the Panic of 1907," Aug, 1, 1989.

Carmen Winslow, Shirley Kernick, Meg Guenin for editing; Judy Cyr, for "translating" letters to Fritz written in cursive; Carolyn "Carrie" Johnson (1941-2018), for suggesting a comparison between Sarah's thesis and her edited book; Jim Killoy, World Museum of Mining photo archives volunteer for his knowledge; Mark

Berg, BTU, for obtaining a copy of Astle's 1985 article; photographer Norma J. Duffy for assistance.

Clark Grant, general manager, KBMF, Butte, and the staff at Eugene, Oregon, Audio Services, for doing their best to enhance and restore the tape of the final talk by Sarah. The Archives does have an audible tape of Sarah speaking at the Sept. 24-26, 1982, symposium: "Butte: The Urban Frontier."

The Montana Historical Society Press for permission to use material that first appeared as an article in *The Montana Magazine of History* (Sarah McNelis, "F. Augustus Heinze: An Early Chapter in the Life of a Copper King," *The Montana Magazine of History*, vol. 2, No. 4 (Oct. 1952), 24-32).

Zena Beth McGlashan
November 2018